William Phillimore Watts Phillimore, Frederic Johnson

Norfolk Parish Registers - Marriages

Vol. IV

William Phillimore Watts Phillimore, Frederic Johnson

Norfolk Parish Registers - Marriages
Vol. IV

ISBN/EAN:

Printed in Europe, USA, Canada, Australia, Japan

Cover: Foto ©Suzi / pixelio.de

More available books at **www.hansebooks.com**

NORFOLK

PARISH REGISTERS.

—

Marriages.

IV.

PHILLIMORE'S
PARISH REGISTER SERIES.
VOL. XCV. (NORFOLK, VOL. IV.)

One hundred and fifty printed.

W. P. W. Ph.

Norfolk
Parish Registers.

Marriages.

EDITED BY

W. P. W. PHILLIMORE, M.A., B.C.L.,

AND

FREDERIC JOHNSON.

VOL. IV.

London :

ISSUED TO THE SUBSCRIBERS BY PHILLIMORE & CO.,
124, CHANCERY LANE.
1909.

PREFACE.

The fourth volume of the Marriage Registers of Norfolk is now placed in the hands of the subscribers.

Of the nine Registers included, six date from the sixteenth century, the remaining three belong to the succeeding century.

As before, entries are reduced to a common form, and the following contractions have been freely used :—

w.=widower, *or* widow.	p.=of the parish of.
s.=spinster, single woman.	co.=in the county of.
b.=bachelor, *or* single man.	dioc.=in the diocese of.
d.=daughter of.	*lic.*=marriage licence.

For the transcription of the Registers, the Editors have to acknowledge the valuable assistance of Dr. W. T. Bensley, the Rev. E. Kinaston, the Rev. R. A. Oram, the Rev. J. G. Poole, and the Rev. R. Fetzer Taylor and Miss Fetzer Taylor, who contributed two Registers. Hickling was transcribed by Mr. Johnson.

Thanks are due to the clergy who have given permission for these records to be printed. Their names are mentioned under the respective parishes. 1379191

It is of the highest importance that we should not delay in printing the Registers as rapidly as possibly, as this is the only way in which their contents can be effectively preserved. Greater care undoubtedly is taken of these invaluable personal records than was formerly the case, but loss of Registers still goes on, and it may be mentioned that in more than one instance Registers have been lost, or their condition has seriously deteriorated, since they were transcribed, although it is but ten years since this series of printed Parish Registers was commenced.

It may be well to remind the reader that these printed abstracts of the Registers are not legal "evidence". For certificates, application must be made to the local clergy.

The Editors will gladly welcome help in the work of transcribing the Registers of Norfolk. It is only by volunteer assistance that it becomes feasible to issue this series of Parish Registers. And subscribers will greatly aid if they will take every opportunity of making known the existence of this series, for with sufficient support it should be possible, as in other counties, to issue two volumes yearly. With so large a county as Norfolk, it is obvious that adequate progress in printing the Registers can be made so long only as that rate, at the least, is steadily maintained.

W. P. W. P.
F. J.

124, *Chancery Lane, London,*
June, 1909.

Contents.

Marriages at Barton Turf,

1558 to 1837.

NOTE.—Barton Turf is an ancient parish, and the Parish Church is at
least five hundred years old, and there are evidences of earlier
buildings on the same site.

Volume I. This consists of 92 parchment leaves, the leaves are
numbered and have two pages to each leaf. Leaves 1 to 40
contain Baptisms from 1560 to 1770; 41 to 52, Marriages from
1558 to 1753; 53 to 60, Baptisms from 1770 to 1790; 61 to 86,
Burials from 1558 to 1790. The rest of the book is blank, except
the last page, which contains an account of the Church Rate for
1671. At the end of this there is a statement of the clerk's fees,
amongst which are : "For buryall with a coffin, 2s. 6d.; without
a coffin, 1s. 6d. The condition of this volume is generally good;
size, 12 in. by 5 in.; binding, stiff cardboards covered with parchment. Of the part relating to Marriages, the latter part of leaf 45
is blank, date 1645-66, in which period there is only one entry.
There are blank spaces also on leaf 47. Where the name of the
parish is not given, Barton Turf is to be understood.

The Register begins with the words:—"Register Bocke for the
Towne of Barton then made and [———] according to the
Cannons and ecclesiasticall constitutions published and set forth
by the Archbishop, Bishops, and the rest of the clergie of the
province of Canterberye in the Sinnod begune at London the
20 daye of the munth of October in the yeare of our Lord God
1597 and in the Rayne of our most Cristiane Princis Ladye
Elizabeth by the grace of God of England, France, and Ierland,
Defendris of the fayth, &c., the thirtyenynth." It is signed :
"Per me E. Greene."

"Note that everye yeare begines the 25 daye of Marche." The name
of Esdras Greene occurs in the Marriage Register, June 26, 1597.

From 1610 to 1730 the handwriting varies a great deal and in places
it is bad and difficult to read.

Probably only the first four leaves of this book were written by E.
Greene. They contain the copy of the original Baptismal
Registers, 1558 to 1594. The copying of the Registers of
Marriages and Burials, and all the other entries up to 1610 are by
another hand, presumably that of Edmund Cooke, the Vicar, who
was buried May 30th, 1610.

Volume II contains Marriages from 1754 to 1812. Only about the first quarter of the book, to p. 52, is used for Marriages. The greater part is blank, and the rest contains Banns, 1754 to 1884. The handwriting is generally good. The covers are bound in leather, but much worn; size, 10½ in. by 8 in. Volume III contains Marriages from 1812 to 1837. Only the first 25 pages of this book are used, the remainder are blank. It has a parchment cover, size 15½ in. by 10 in. These extracts have been made by the Rev. J. G. Poole, of Barton Turf, and are now printed under his supervision after collation with the Register.

VOLUME I.

"The names of all them which were Married from the yeer of our Lord God 1558."

John Bowman & Cecilie Gylbert	15 May	1558
John Palmer & Jone Derslye	27 Apr.	1559
Adam Jaye & Christian Howard	25 Sept.	„
Nicholas Wright & Ellenn Gylbert	18 Feb.	„
John Rogers & Ellenn Postell	24 Mar.	„
John Raspoole & Margerie Alysander	4 July	1560
William Corpe & Agnes Browne	17 Feb.	„
Roberte Trett & Elyzabeth Corpe	7 May	1561
John Bekker & Jone Turke	12 Nov.	1564
Roberte Emmonds & Agnes Kirstedd	6 July	1567
William Steward, of Slolye, singleman, & Brigett Becker	10 July	1569
George Ives, w., & Elizabeth Tret, w.	6 July	1570
John Emson & Ursulye Hall [*or* Riall]	12 Nov.	1571
Roberte Becker & Margaret Bott	20 Dec.	„
Henry Morton & Fayth Kyrsted	4 Nov.	1574
Roberte Joye & Elizabeth Galt	4 Nov.	„
Gregorie Goodale & Margarett Joye	19 June	1575
John Bagaley & Alce Owbred	29 Nov.	„
John Bayspoole, of Beaston, & Mrs. Cicelye Rybonds	17 Dec.	1576
George Ives & Katherine Read, of Ranworth	17 Dec.	„
John Grosse, of Norwich, & Cicelye Acocke	24 June	1577
Roberte Shirlocke, clerke, & Anne Amys	9 July	1578
Nicholas Hart & Agnes Corppe	24 Nov.	„
William Sadler & Margaret Emson	1 Oct.	1579
Roberte Kirsted & Anne Potter	10 Jan.	„

Anthonie Lyster & Elyzabeth Beane	.. 18 Feb. 1580
Barnard Steward & Brigett Backester	.. 5 Feb. 1581
Daniell Warren, of B., & Alice Hall, of Neatishard	.. .. .. 18 June 1582
Nicholas Wright & Margaret Jeffers, of Neatisherd	.. .. 15 Nov. ,,
George Raspoole & Millesent Broweinge	.. 12 July 1584
William Wright & Elizabeth Jefferes	.. 8 Nov. ,,
Clement Corpe & Margaret Hudson	.. 18 July 1585
Christopher Ellis, w., & Barbara Chaplen	.. 3 Dec. 1587
Roberte Joye, w., & Elizabeth Lingwood	.. 14 July 1588
Thomas Cooke, w., & Cecilie Howsego	.. 9 Feb. ,,
James Turner, w., & Dorathie Slappe	.. 20 Apr. 1589
John Rayspoole & Margaret Alyns	14 July ,,
Nicholas Jefferes & Fayth Rust	.. .. 26 Oct. ,,
Nicholas Wright, w., & Margarie Raspoole ..	25 Jan. ,,
Edmunde Cocke, w., & Agnes Life	.. 30 Nov. 1590
Roberte Raspoole & Marie Aliard ..	.. 25 July 1591
John Lancaster & Agnes Raspoole	.. 3 Oct. ,,
John Browne & Marie Poyt	.. .. 28 May 1592
Roberte Walton & Grace Bootes ..	.. 7 Jan. ,,
Robert Turner & Anne Key	.. .. 28 Oct. 1593
Henry Jlbird & Alice Kinge	.. 30 Apr. 1595
John Dawson & Jone Aliard	.. 8 Jan. ,,
John Chernely & Margerie Maninge	.. 11 July 1596
Esdras Greene & Anne Norgate	.. .. 26 June 1597
Thomas Mortimer & Brigett Bayspoole, w.	10 Sept. 1599
Peter Norton & Dorathe Turner, w.	7 Oct. ,,
Richard Thurston & Margerie Norton	.. 28 Oct. ,,
Roberte Larwood & Marie Lancaster	.. 25 Nov. ,,
Henry Leche & Dorathie Cherneley	.. 12 May 1600
William Whittred & Elizabeth Elvie	.. 10 Dec. ,,
William England, w., & Dyonis Watsonn, w.	26 June 1601
Thomas Giles & Ele Tayliar	.. 11 Oct. ,,
Thomas Norton & Dyonis Beane ..	17 July 1603
Richard Snelling & Frannces Cherneley	.. 28 Sept. ,,
John Joye & Alice Pearson	.. .. 7 Oct. ,,
Thomas Browne & Elizabeth Tompson	.. 27 Sept. 1604
Thomas Chaplen & Margerie Corpe	.. 16 Nov. ,,
John Muse, of Catfield, & Anne Myhill	.. 23 Apr. 1605

Clement Faultricke & Katherinn Anger	..	14 July 1605
James Raynold, w., & Anphelis Anger	..	15 July „
Luke Haugh, *alias* Elizabethson, & Dorathe		
Leggate		27 Jan. „
John Hamlin & Jone Ansell	..	27 May 1606
Nycholas Joye & Cecilie Amys	..	20 June „
William Selfe & Anne Tracey	..	28 Jan. „
Roberte Gallt & Elizabeth Joye	..	15 June 1607
John Cursted & Grace Ward	..	5 July „
John Larwood & Alice Appelbie	..	18 July 1608
Roberte Cursted & Margaret Elie	..	31 July „
John Gower & Freeswid Bryant	..	12 Jan. „
John Wegg & Elizabeth Fox	..	22 Jan. 1609
John Chapman, of Burston, neere Disse, &		
Ann Turner, d. of James Turner, of B.		11 Apr. 1611
France Besson & Ellin Snelling	..	— June „
Ambros Tegall, of Somerley, & Annes Gower,		
of Barton		31 Jan. 1613
John Kirsted, w., & Annes Jordan, of Catfield		17 June 1614
Peter Carles & Ales Cates	..	21 Aug. „
Robert Trett & Marie Bugden	..	25 Sept. 1616
Phillip Suffield & [———] Kyde	..	1 Feb. 1617
Stephen Larwood & Anys Snell	..	24 Apr. 1618
John Tret & Margaret Wright [?] ..	..	24 June „
Thomas Buterfield & Elizabeth [———]	..	— Nov. „
John Kinge & Margarett Browne ..	..	18 Apr. 1619
Robert Kirsted & [———] Ames [? *or* Emes]		31 May „
Francis Parr & Dorothie Church [?]	..	18 Oct. 1620
Ciprian Ret[?]ham & Ursula Gray [? *or* Crow]		20 Oct. 1622
Robert Cley & Kathrine Balls	..	20 Oct. 1623
Thomas Dawsonne & Christian Bridge	..	22 Oct. „
Thomas Starkie & Sara Pulley [?] ..	..	26 Apr. 1624
Thomas Dawsonn & Amphilis [———]	..	24 May „
John Larwoode & Elizabeth Amis ..	..	6 Nov. 1626
Daniell Greene & Annis Larwoode	..	18 Oct. 1627
Esdras Amis & Annis Emmes	..	26 Oct. 1628
John Chanlor & Cathrine Trace	..	25 Nov. „
Thomas Norton & Blith Calowas [?], of		
Smalborowe		20 July 1629
John Carman & Blith Norton	..	29 Sept. 1631

John Roger [?] & Annis Vinyard ..	..	1 Feb. 1631
Edward Chanlor & Christian Walsham [?] ..		28 May 1632
Robert Warnes & Mary Gower ..	..	7 July 1634
Thomas Battcle & Anne Nicholes ..	..	13 July ,,
Thomas Watts & Anne Drake ..	..	29 July ,,
William King & Mary Herde ..	..	2 Nov. ,,
John Goodman & Anne Starkey ..	..	10 Mar. ,,
Edwar Veawe [?] & Mary Corpe, w.	..	8 Sept. 1636
Nicholas Crowe & Catherine Dawson	..	10 Oct. ,,
Thomas Pirkstone & Susan Alldredg	..	2 Oct. 1637
John Balls & Margaret Chapman ..	..	2 June 1640
Thomas Chaplaine & Faith Batteley	..	8 July ,,
John Bevis & Mary Chandler ..	..	12 Aug. ,,
Geiorg Kerstead & Sicily Duffcild ..	..	31 Jan. ,,
William Goffin & Grace Stubine	..	3 Nov. 1643
William Coop & Elizabeth Rising ..	..	18 July ,,
Thomas Lacy & Elizabeth Lockward		15 Apr. 1645
Thomas Galt & Elizabeth Gedny ..		17 Nov. ,,
John Massey & Alice [?] Gid ..	..	15 June 1656
Thomas Watterson, p. Edingthorpe, &		
Susanna Punge	..	10 Jan. 1666
Mathew Joy & Mary Cauc ..	..	14 Feb. ,,
John Chandler & Lydia Watson ..		14 Feb. ,,
John Turner & Sarah Balls, w. ..	..	20 July 1668
Thomas Carr & Dorithie Fitt ..	..	3 Dec. ,,
Francis Turner & Christian Trett ..	..	10 Dec. ,,
Stephen Yaxly & Elizabeth Bussy ..	..	2 Dec. 1672
John Chapman & Ann Roll, of Neatisheard ..		30 Sept. ,,
William Watson & Deborah Watts	..	25 Dec. 1674
Stephen Yaxly & Martha Sammon ..	..	24 Jan. 1686
Adam Scot & Elizabeth Auger ..	..	7 Sept. 1688
John Massy & Mary Harris ..	..	1 Oct. ,,
Thomas Amis & Ann Pollard ..	..	10 Aug. 1691
Joseph Theobald, of Beeston, & Marthe		
Emeris	..	20 July 1692
Thomas Fish & Frances Messenger	..	10 Jan. 169⅔
Richard Ellis, gent., & Susan Ward, w.	..	6 Mar. 169⅔
Christopher Amis & Ann Clarke, both of		
Tunstead	..	2 Oct. 1694
Thomas Dye & Mary Robinson ..	..	22 Oct. 1695

William Turner & Sarah Wats	29 June	1697
Stephen Yaxly & Bridget King	16 Nov.	1699
Gabriel Baldwin, of Neatishead, yeoman, & Elizabeth Willis	28 Oct.	1700
John Emms, b., & Alce Joy, s., of Irstead ..	12 June	1702
Michael Stretch, of St. Peter's Mancroft, Norwich, & Jane Fisher, of Smalburg, *lic.*	4 June	1703
Robert Ward, of Walcot, Norf., gent., & Margaret Holt	31 Aug.	„
John Witchingham, b., of Horning, & Susan Margetson, s., of Hofton St. John ..	5 Jan.	170$\frac{3}{4}$
Thomas Kemp, of [———], & Bridget Amis	8 Oct.	1704
John Pinkny, of St. August., Norwich, & Jane Lusky, of No Walstra [North Walsham]	2 Jan.	1705
John Chandler & Mary Suggate	25 June	1706
Thomas Brady, b., of St. Mary, Norwich, & Mary Beechino, s. [*this name is some- times spelt "Beechineau"*]	20 Mar.	17$\frac{10}{11}$
Luke Whittleton, of Neatishead, w., & Bridget Yaxly, w.	15 Apr.	1711
Robert Jeffreys, of Neatishead, & Sarah Emms	23 July	„
Mathew Neeve & Mary Trory, of Beeston	5 Aug.	„
John Neeve & Elizabeth Starr	13 Aug.	„
Thomas Mordew & Elizabeth Ems ..	25 Sept.	1712
Joseph Purdy & Elizas Wright, w. ..	8 Dec.	„
Robert Joy, of Irstead, & Mary Paul, of Roughton, Norfolk	26 May	„
Thomas Barber & Mary Bidwel [?] ..	28 Sept.	1713
Nathaniel Wright & Sarah Burrows ..	29 Mar.	1714
Mr. Mathias Earbury, w., & Mrs. Mary Preston, w.	27 Sept.	1715
Francis Turner, w., & Elizabeth Wall, s. ..	31 Oct.	„
Joseph Lines [?] & Hannah Johnson ..	25 Dec.	„
William Cubit & Elizabeth Beecheno ..	1 Oct.	1717
Joseph Purdy & Ann Ames, w.	31 Dec.	„
John Eagurm & Sarah Cutting	10 Nov.	1718
Edmund Lovick & Susan England	4 Jan.	„
John Brown & Mary Wickham	3 Apr.	1719

John Starling, b., of Worstead, & Susan Powell	25 June 1719
William Ryall & Elizabeth Haiam, living in Yarmouth	14 Sept. „
John Gallant, gent., & Penelope Munfor	15 Oct. „
Benjamin Peed, of Neasted, b., & Elizabeth Dyball, w., of Cattfield	17 Oct. „
William Addams & Judah Neave	21 July 1720
John Dason & Sarcy Holl	6 Oct. „
John Trorey & Mary Crane	9 Oct. 1722
Daniel Shakill & Mary Piggon, both of Scottow	29 Jan. „
Robert Mace & Mary House, both of Scottow	17 Dec. „
John Beechino, b., & Martha Hurt, s., of Beeston St. Lawrence	8 Nov. 1723
Thomas Plaifur, b., & Ann Salay, s., both of Scottow	3 Aug. 1724
James Gunton, b., & Susanna Harrison, s., both of Scottow	1 Sept. „
Joseph Dyball, b., & Elizabeth Pycroft, s., both of Scottow	9 Nov. „
Joseph Boyse [?], b., & Elizabeth Harrison, s., both of Scottow	29 Nov. „
William Chapman, b., & Mary Shakill, w., both of Scottow	13 Jan. „
John Hastings, b., & Elisabeth Tracey, s.	30 Sept. 1725
William Cutten, b., & Elizabeth Calaby, s.	24 Dec. „
Stephen Man & Anne Willby, both of Hofton	10 May 1726
Thomas George & Margarett Ivory	16 May „
William Rice & Mary Batch, both of Scottow	3 Oct. „
Martin Wheeler & Elisabeth Piggon, both of Scottow	18 Jan. „
John Nuell, b., & Sarach Ampelford, s.	27 Dec. 1727
James Fot, b., & Elizabeth Stewerd, w.	7 Feb. „
Valentine Rook & Mary Eastgate, both of Scottow, *lic.*	30 Sept. 1728
Thomas Holl & Judith Brown	22 Oct. „
Richard Baker & Sarah Bush	14 Apr. 1729
Robert Worstead & Elizabeth Baker	25 May 1730
John Curteis, w., & Sarah Fysh, both of Hoveton St. John	5 Oct. „

Barzillai Elden & Hannah Balls, both of
    Hoveton St. John ..   ..   ..   8 Oct.   1730
Andrew Doughty, b., & Elizabeth Bullyn, s.,
    both of Stalham   ..   ..   ..   26 Aug. 1731
Joseph Neve, b., & Elizabeth Siser, s., *lic.* ..   4 July 1734
Nathaniel Bloome, b., & Susan Hickling, s.,
    both of Ludham, *lic.*   ..   ..   29 Apr. 1735
Robert Barber, b., & Elizabeth Wacey, s.,
    both of Horning   ..   ..   ..   6 May „
William Gay, b., & Alice Nockolds, s., both
    of Horning   ..   ..   ..   13 May „
Robert Nursey, of Poswick, w., & Mary Ann
    Hovill, s., of Horning   ..   ..   26 June „
John Thirtle, b., & Mary Barber, s., both of
    Ashmanhaugh   ..   ..   ..   11 Nov. „
John Gotts, b., & Mary Smith, s., *lic.*   ..   5 Dec. „
Mr. Robert Scott, b., of St. Clement, Norwich,
    & Elizabeth Bernard, s., of Sprowston,
    lic.   ..   ..   12 Feb. 173$\frac{5}{6}$
Ambrose Mayes, b., & Mary Riches, s., both
    of Hoveton St. John, *lic.*   .   ..   6 Sept. 1736
Jacob Steward, b., & Susan Witchingham, s.,
    both of Horning   ..   ..   ..   6 Sept. „
Matthew Neve, b., & Ann King, s., both of
    Horning ..   ..   ..   6 Oct. „
George Wheeler, b., & Sarah Hurt, s., *lic.* ..   24 Jan. 1737
Edmund Cubitt, b., & Hannah Amis, s., *lic.*   12 Feb. „
William Smith, w., & Elizabeth Cock, s.,
    both of Norwich Thorpe, *lic.* ..   ..   10 June 1738
Robert Barleyclow, b., & Alice Panke, s.   ..   22 Oct. 1739
Richard Baker & Judah Holl, *lic.*   ..   ..   21 Nov. „
Robert Haylett, b., & Hannah Cubitt, w.   ..   17 June 1742
Robert Burton, b., & Sarah Dawson, w.   ..   29 June „
William Watson, b., & Mary Rose, s.   ..   1 Oct. „
John Mortar & Elizabeth Moll, w., of Smal-
    burgh   ..   ..   6 May 1743
John Brett & Mary Ickills, both of Neatishead,
    lic.   ..   ..   21 Aug. „
John Gillham, of Hoveton St. Peter, & Eliza-
    beth Roll ..   ..   31 July 1744

John Webster, b., of North Walsham, & Mary
   Lockett, *lic.* .. . .. 26 Mar. 1745
John Green, b., & Elizabeth Smith, s. .. 1 Oct. ,,
Thomas Rudderham, b., & Mary Palmer, s. 20 May 1746
Thomas Howse Roll, b., & Jane Porter, s. .. 13 Oct. ,,
Robert Adams, w., of Smalburgh, & Mary
   Grise, w. .. .. 9 Feb. 1747
John Pickrill, b., & Ann Benns, s. .. 27 June 1748
William Ford & Rose Borows, both of Irstead 30 June 1750
Samuell Amis, b., & Elizabeth Annyson, s. 26 Dec. ,,
Thomas Doe, b., of Westwick, & Elizabeth
   Clipperton, s., *lic.* .. .. .. 12 Oct. 1753
Robert Woolterton, b., & Martha Clipperton,
   s., *lic.* .. .. 12 Oct. ,,

VOLUME II.

James Fitt, w., & Elizabeth Gryse, w. .. 17 July* 1754
Daniel Dawson & Jane Hunter, p. Neatishead 1 July ,,
Robert Bloome & Sarah Dawson .. .. 22 July ,,
Thomas Wittacre & Martha Miller .. 22 Oct. ,,
Robert Neeve & Mary Ann Worstead .. 28 Oct. ,,
William Hobart, p. North Walsham, w., &
   Ann Field, *lic.* .. .. .. 18 Nov. ,,
Philip Sadler & Susanna Wilkins .. .. 14 Apr. 1755
John Annison & Mary Amiss .. .. 11 May 1757
John Doyley & Elizabeth Ward .. 23 May ,,
James Nobbs & Mary Steward, w., *lic.* 10 Oct. ,,
William Kirk & Elizabeth Wright .. .. 6 Feb 1758
John Wright & Lucretia Hunt, *lic.* .. .. 26 Apr. ,,
John Barker & Mary Barnard [*signs* Bernard],
   lic. .. .. 1 June ,,
Daniel Livick, w., & Mary Ann Neve, w. .. 20 June ,,
Thomas Amys & Elizabeth Nobbin .. 5 Dec. ,,
John Jones & Sarah Barnard, w., *lic.* .. 23 Feb. 1759
Henry Mace & Mary Potter, p. Lessingham 11 July ,,
Daniel Livick & Hannah Woolterton .. 10 Sept. ,,

* From this date, unless otherwise stated, the parties are invariably of
Barton Turf, and respectively bachelor and spinster.

Edward Atthill, p. Cawston, & Jane Clipperton,
  lic.   ..   ..   19 Sept. 1759
Thomas Mendham & Sarah Neale ..   ..   17 Dec.   „
John Sidal & Mary Woolterton   ..   ..   15 Apr. 1760
John Snelling, w., & Elizabeth Warnes, w. ..   18 May   „
Thomas Cooper, esq., p. North Walsham, &
  Mary Hammont, *lic.*   ..   .   30 July 1761
Samuel Jones & Mary Cook   ..   13 Oct.   „
William Watts & Sarah House   ..   ..   4 Nov. 1762
Robert Beckett, p. Neatshead, w., & Mary
  Steward, *lic.*   ..   ..   ..   5 Jan. 1763
Robert Steward & Ann Bell   ..   ..   10 July „
Henry Roll, p. St. Andrew's, Norwich, w., &
  Martha Woolterton, w., *lic.* ..   ..   24 Oct.   „
Benjamin Munfer, w., & Sarah Clark, w.   ..   22 Nov.   „
John Snelling & Elizabeth Watts ..   ..   9 Dec.   „
Thomas Goodens & Alice Bradley ..   ..   4 Jan. 1764
Thomas Dyball, p. Scottow, & Elizabeth
  Ayers, *lic.*   ..   ..   ..   18 Nov.   „
John Norgitt & Phillis Burton   ..   ..   5 Aug. 1765
John Thirtle, p. Horning, & Elizabeth Ellison 11 Oct.   „
John Scrape & Ann Jee ..   ..   ..   24 Oct.   „
Joseph Amess [*signs* Aymes], this p., & Martha
  Puley, p. Hoveton St. John ..   ..   10 Feb. 1766
John Skipp, p. Neatishead, & Elizabeth
  Bernard ..   ..   22 July „
Robert Gay & Ann Watts   ..   ..   12 Oct.   „
Robert Bensley & Sarah Press, *lic.*   ..   8 Nov. 1767
John Goodson & Sarah Wittrick ..   ..   26 Jan. 1768
Thomas Macgoon, this p., & Sarah Bradfield,
  p. Neatishead, *lic.* ..   ..   ..   1 July   „
John Steward, p. Ashmelaugh, & Sarah
  Sydel ..   ..   4 Aug.   „
Stephen Bruster & Elizabeth Rudherham ..   6 Nov. 1769
Thomas Parmer, p. Bafield, co. Norf., &
  Martha Jones, *lic.* ..   ..   ..   26 Jan. 1770
Thomas Mason, p. Irstead, & Mary Myall ..   30 Jan.   „
Henry Shreeve & Mary Watts, *lic.*   ..   3 July   „
William Hewett & Elizabeth Goodens, w. ..   6 Aug.   „
John Bennett & Bridgett Chandler   ..   10 Oct.   „

Edmund Liveuck, p. Irstead, & Sarah
  Steward, w.   ..   ..   ..   20 Apr. 1771
John Smith, p. Neatshead, & Ann Codling .. 24 Oct.   „
William Long & Mary Cooper   ..   ..   9 June 1772
Thomas Durrant, esq., p. Scottow, & Susanna
  Custance ..   ..   28 Oct.   „
James Blyth, p. Tunstead,& Mary Pickerell,*lic.*   1 July 1773
Robert King, p. Hainford, & Lucy Chandler,
  w., *lic.*   ..   ..   4 July 1774
Robert Frances, this p., & Martha Nockels, p.
  Smallburgh   ..   ..   ..   18 July „
John Barker, p. Hickling, w., & Phillis Burton,
  lic.   ..   ..   11 Sept. „
Daniel Gunnel, p. Hoveton St. John, & Williby
  Cooper   ..   ..   25 Dec. 1775
John Howse & Elizabeth Woolston, *lic.*   ..   14 Jan. 1777
Joseph Flexman, p. Neatishead, & Margaret
  Hastings ..   ..   15 Jan.   „
James Manning, p. Hasbro', & Elizabeth
  Picknell, *lic.*   ..   ..   ..   26 Mar.   „
John Rudderham & Elizabeth Bansley   ..   24 Nov.   „
Francis Griffin, p. Waxham, co. Norf., &
  Frances Francis, *lic.*   ..   ..   29 Dec.   „
Edmund Clipperton & Sarah Jones   ..   26 July 1779
Samuel Bulman & Elizabeth Dugdale   ..   25 Nov.   „
William Coal & Mary Woodrow   .   ..   20 Feb. 1780
William Starling & Sarah Frosdick   ..   19 Mar.   „
Samuel Manning, p. Irstead, & Charlotte
  Dawson   ..   ..   12 Oct.   „
James Watts & Hannah Annison ..   ..   18 Oct.   „
John Annison, w., & Sarah Goodson, w.   ..   6 Dec.   „
John Shackle, this p., & Elizabeth Dady, p.
  Smallburgh   ..   ..   ..   23 Jan. 1781
John Cooper, this p., & Elizabeth Watson, p.
  Beeston   ..   ..   23 Apr.   „
Richard Barber, p. Honing,& Phyllis Kidd, *lic.* 25 Sept. „
John Annison, w., & Sarah Riches, w., *lic.* .. 18 Mar. 1782
Edmund Lubbock [*signs* Liveuck], w., & Sarah
  Annison, w., *lic.*   ..   ..   ..   4 Aug. 1783
Samuel Dugdil, w., & Alice Annison   ..   29 Sept. „

John Rose & Sarah Goodens	10 Oct.	1783
Isaac Watts & Elizabeth Doyley	30 Oct.	,,
Matthew Dugdil & Elizabeth Annison ..	12 Apr.	1784
Samuel Strikes & Elizabeth Bush	30 Sept.	,,
Thomas Rudd & Ann Yallop . ..	5 Oct.	,,
William Pike & Hannah Shackle	24 Dec.	,,
William Capon, p. Neatishead, & Elizabeth Clipperton, *lic.*	13 Jan.	1785
Augustine King & Sarah Pell	31 Jan.	,,
Joseph Cubitt, p. Dilham, & Hannah Lubbock	18 July	,,
James Hunter & Mary Livock ..	6 Nov.	1786
James Gilden & Elizabeth Amos	13 Nov.	,,
John Snelling & Maria Preston	15 Apr.	1787
William Umphrey, p. Belaugh, & Elizabeth Claxton	16 Apr.	,,
William Barns & Jane Dutchess	9 Oct.	,,
Martin Robertson & Hannah Watson ..	12 Nov.	,,
John Blundell & Martha Dugdale	24 Dec.	,,
Christopher Knights & Mary Gee	26 May	1788
James Tate, w., & Ann Long, *lic.*	23 Sept.	,,
Mark Mornement, p. Neatishead, & Mary Mack, *lic.*	23 Sept.	,,
James Dugdale & Hannah Ames	19 Jan.	1789
Samuel Appleton & Hannah Annison ..	6 Apr.	1790
Robert Hewit & Alice Gay	10 Aug.	,,
James Fisher & Sarah Barnard	25 Oct.	1791
George Baker & Mary Lodes	19 Dec.	,,
William Dawson & Mary Ann Steward ..	17 Jan.	1792
Edmund Brown, p. Ingham, & Elizabeth Hewit	6 Feb.	,,
Samuel Gladden, p. Marsham, & Mary Barnard, *lic.*	25 Oct.	,,
John Williams & Mary Watson, w.	29 Oct.	,,
Robert Shackle, w., & Sarah Mack, w., *lic.*	3 Dec.	1793
John Jones, w., & Elizabeth Dawson, w. ..	30 June	1794
John Chandler & Lydia Doyley	13 Oct.	,,
William Pike, w., & Mary Pickerel ..	23 Mar.	1795
John Cook & Francis Willimite	26 Oct.	,,
John Collins, p. Shotley, & Martha Hopwood	10 Nov.	,,
James Gildon, w., & Lydia Amis	21 Feb.	1797
John Amos & Rosamond [*signs* Rosement] Gee	13 Aug.	,,

Henry Slaughter & Mary Bullemer	.. 22 Oct.	1798
William Hewit, this p., & Elizabeth Warner,		
p. Erpingham	.. 26 Nov.	,,
John Nobbin & Ann Arpingham ..	.. 10 June	1799
James Collins & Willoughby Watts	.. 5 July	1800
Joseph Amos & Ann Gay ..	.. 19 Jan.	1801
John Hannant & Elizabeth Long ..	.. 25 May	,,
Thomas Watts & Elizabeth French	.. 3 Aug.	,,
Richard Hazel & Lydia Amis	.. 12 Nov.	,,
Edward Lubbock & Sarah Cobb ..	.. 16 Aug.	1802
Robert Gay, w., & Elizabeth Snelling, w.	.. 20 Sept.	,,
William Finch, p. Ashmanhaugh, & Elizabeth		
Bryanton	.. 12 Oct.	,,
John Cook & Sarah Annison ..	.. 1 Nov.	,,
John Ling, w., & Rose Steward ..	.. 7 Dec.	,,
Isaac Watts & Hannah Jones ..	.. 27 June	1803
Manning Hunter & Sarah Jones, *lic.*	.. 18 July	,,
Thomas Howard & Ann Starling ..	.. 21 Nov.	,,
Richard Walpole & Hester Cole ..	21 Dec.	,,
Benjamin Harmer, w., & Sarah Baker	.. 31 Jan.	1805
Samuel Grimbel, p. Happisburgh, & Mary		
Watts	.. 26 Feb.	,,
James Amis & Pamela Bullimore [*signs*		
Pamala Bullamine]	.. 19 Nov.	,,
Joseph Palmer & Eleanor Bullemer	.. 24 Mar.	1806
David Moulton, w., & Elizabeth Bullemer, w.	7 Aug.	,,
Joseph Amis, w., & Martha King, w.	.. 25 Aug.	,,
Jonathan Cully & Mary Gunner [*signs* Gunnell		
or Gunnett]	.. 27 Oct.	,,
John Chandler, w., & Sophia Russels	3 Nov.	,,
John Bullemer & Sarah Cooper, w.	.. 1 June	1807
John Doyley, w., & Margaret Howard	.. 31 Oct.	1808
Simon Long & Mary Tate ..	.. 15 May	1809
George Moy, p. Cottishall, & Sarah King, *lic.*	28 Sept.	,,
Henry Slaughter, w., & Sarah Suckling	.. 3 Oct.	,,
Richard Hazell, w., & Elizabeth Amis	.. 23 Jan.	1810
George Tate & Mary Edrich ..	.. 10 Sept.	,,
Abraham Turner & Elizabeth Harmer	.. 20 Nov.	,,
Matthew Baldwin, p. Smallburgh, & Elizabeth		
Bullemer	.. 21 Nov.	,,

Samuel Cocks & Ann Watts *or* Worts	..	25 Mar. 1811
Thomas Hedge & Sarah Robertson	..	7 Apr. „
John Gibson & Barbara Hare	..	17 Oct. „
James Neave & Christmess Milem ..	..	12 Feb. 1812
Benjamin Cully & Hannah Watts ..	..	11 Aug. „
Simon Gidney & Elizabeth Hedge ..	..	16 Nov. „

Volume III.

James Cox & Maria Kerrison	.. ..	1 Feb. 1813
Henry Watts & Eliza Cox	.. ..	15 Mar. „
William Nockolds, w., & Elizabeth Gibbs, w.		21 July „
John Clark, w., p. Ickborough, Norfolk, &		
Mary Jones	.. .. ..	14 Sept. „
John Francis & Ann Browne	.. ..	12 Oct. „
Timothy Smith, p. East Carlton, Norfolk, &		
Sarah Francis	.. .. ..	1 Nov. „
Robert Lubbock & Margaret Annison	..	31 Oct. 1814
Henry Nockolds & Elizabeth Watts	..	1 Dec. „
James Harvey, p. Neatishead, & Jemima Long		22 Dec. „
John Batt Roll, p. Ludham, & Elizabeth		
Clipperton, *lic.*	.. .. ..	26 Apr. 1815
Charles Buxton & Elizabeth Pointer, w.	..	7 July „
John Hewit & Elizabeth Hunn	.. ..	23 Jan. 1817
James Watts & Mary Nockolds	.. ..	17 Mar. „
Daniel Cooper & Hannah Sandle, p. Small-		
burgh	.. ..	2 May „
William Platford, *als.* Playford, p. Neatishead,		
& Elizabeth Starling	.. ..	23 June „
Thomas Gibson & Ann Knights	.. ..	11 Nov. „
William Bullemer & Hannah Starman	.	29 Dec. „
James Hewitt & Susanna Whittleton [*signs*		
Suan Wittleton]	.. ..	3 Mar. 1818
Daniel Cole & Ann Cox ..	.. ..	1 June „
Thomas Pratt, p. Smallburgh, & Elizabeth		
Francis ..	.. .. ..	17 Nov. „
John Mack, p. Tunstead, & Mary Anne Harris,		
lic. ..	.. .. ..	22 Dec. „
Robert Grimmer, p. Neatishead, & Elizabeth		
Watts ..	.. .. ..	1 Feb. 1819

John Ling, w., & Christiana Lyndo	19 July	1819
James Cotton, p. Suffield, & Ann Cooper	14 Oct.	„
John Gales & Maria Tate	27 Oct.	1820
James Buttivant, *als.* Amis, p. St. Margaret's, Lynn, & Lydia Watts, *lic.*	15 May	1821
John Harmer & Eleanor Cutting	31 Dec.	„
Abraham Beales & Maria Watts	9 June	1822
George Alcock, p. Neatishead, & Ann Francis	22 Oct.	„
Henry Edrich & Juliet Remmends, p. Neatishead, *lic.*	13 July	1823
John Haylett & Mary Hewitt	28 Sept.	„
John Sendall, p. Ingham, & Elizabeth Dugdell	13 Nov.	„
John Wilkins, p. Hickling, & Eleanor Manthorpe	18 Oct.	1824
Robert Curtise, p. Smallburgh, & Elizabeth Baldwin, w., *lic.*	8 Dec.	„
Isaac Watts, w., & Sarah Clipperton, w.	9 Dec.	„
Benjamin Myhill & Frances Hewitt	14 Mar.	1825
William Hazel & Ann Norgate	13 June	„
James Howes, w., p. St. Clement Danes, Middlesex, & Mary Bacon, *lic.*	30 Mar.	1826
Thomas Hewitt & Elizabeth Myhill	19 Oct.	„
James Ames & Susanah Duck	18 July	1827
James Gay, w., & Elizabeth Gildon	5 Sept.	„
Benjamin Gildon & Mary Hewett	5 Dec.	„
Robert Mileham, p. Smallburgh, & Elizabeth Bullemer	4 Mar.	1828
Samuel Dugdale & Kezia Thornton	15 Mar.	„
Edward Smith & Lydia Gilden	31 Mar.	„
John Cork & Mary Whitaker	14 Apr.	„
Joseph Palmer & Marianne Rudd	28 Apr.	„
John Yaxley & Hannah Watts	23 Dec.	„
William Lines & Maria Cox	15 Jan.	1829
Christopher Mileham & Pamela Palmer	23 Mar.	„
John Curtis & Frances Walpole	10 Dec.	„
John Pike & Hannah Myhill, p. Neatishead	15 July	1830
Thomas Walpole & Susan Howard	15 Sept.	„
Samuel Felstead & Elizabeth Hewett	17 Sept.	„
James Neave & Margaret Attew, *lic.*	24 Nov.	„
Richard Starling & Jemima Wears	2 Jan.	1831

John Goose, p. Worstead, & Sarah Jones
  Clipperton, *lic.* .. .. .. 17 Feb. 1831
James Nockall, p. St. Benedict, Norwich, &
  Mary Ann Dobson, *lic.* .. .. 24 Jan. 1832
John Whittleton, w., & Sarah Smith .. 10 Feb. ,,
Robert Cox & Eleanor Palmer .. .. 7 Aug. ,,
John Gilden & Marianne Starling .. .. 22 Sept. ,,
George Hewitt & Maria Trory .. .. 6 Dec. ,,
Henry Hazel & Maria Whitaker .. .. 13 Dec. ,,
Samuel Pollard & Myra Ransom .. .. 31 Jan. 1833
William Paine & Marian Norgit .. .. 29 May ,,
George Baldwin & Clarissa Amis .. 3 Sept. ,,
Charles Lines & Mary Ann Cox .. .. 29 Sept. 1834
James Gibson & Elizabeth Ashby .. .. 16 Oct. ,,
John Walpole & Willoughby Neave .. 24 Nov. ,,
Robert Cooke, p. Stalham, & Elizabeth Wells,
  lic. .. .. 20 Oct. 1835
Richard Hazell, w., & Elizabeth Smith 29 Oct. ,,
Benjamin Culley & Salome Dobson .. 24 Nov. 1836
Robert [*signs* Robber] Bloom, Irstead, &
  Maria Postle .. .. .. 25 Nov. ,,
Edward Gilden & Hannah Saul .. .. 5 Dec. ,,

Marriages at Hedenham,

1559 to 1812.

NOTE.—The Marriage Register of Hedenham Church, Norfolk, begins in the year 1559, and until recent years is contained in the same volumes as the Baptisms and Burials. The Volume extending from 1559 to 1711 is of vellum, in shape a kind of small narrow folio, without any title, measuring 10¾ inches by 4¼ inches ; the first entries being simply headed "Maryages, 1559". It is in very fair condition.

Volume II contains the Marriages from 1711 to 1754, with, of course, Christenings and Burials as well. It is also of parchment, but bound in rough leather, a good deal worn. It measures 15¼ inches by 7⅜ inches. The handwriting is generally very good. On the inside of the cover at the beginning of this Volume is as follows :—"Hedenham Register : John Bedingfeld, LL.D., Rector; William Baker, Curate, 1722 ; William Baker, M.A., Rector, 1729. Nascimur morituri, W. Baker." At the end of the Volume is a list of the Rectors of Hedenham, with the dates of institution, etc., from A.D. 1306, and also several interesting parochial notes, largely in Mr. Baker's handwriting.

Volume III contains the Marriages from 1754 to 1812. It is of paper, bound in rough leather, in very good condition. The latter part of this Volume contains the entries for publication of Banns down to the present time, except between the years 1868 and 1901. Size 10⅝ inches by 8¾ inches.

These Marriages have been extracted by the Rev. R. Fetzer Taylor, of Hedenham Rectory, and are now printed under his supervision.

VOLUME I.

John Kempe & Johane Steele	..	..	2 Sept. 1559
Phillip Tynke & Margarett Bucke	..	..	15 Oct. „
Robert Smythe & Agnes Cobell	..	..	3 July 1560
Robert House & Elizabeth Morris	..	..	27 Nov. „

"Noe Mariages 1561, 1562."

Edmond Alborowe & Christian Skeete	..	24 Aug. 1563
Robert Geldenstow & Barbery Fayrchild	..	13 Aug. 1564
Michell Church & Johane Wych	..	..	22 Oct. „
Robert Laund & Katheren Bemunt	..	28 Jan. „

"Noe Mariages 1565, 1566."

John Gowinge & Agnes Bryggs	.. ..	25 Nov. 1567
William Jolye & Katherina Richman	..	2 Sept. 1568
Edward Tynke & Brigitta Buck	.. ..	2 Oct. 1569
William Bunnett & Elizabeth Vale	..	15 July 1571 ·
John More, of Hoxne, & Margareta Wolnall, of Fresingfeld	.. .. ..	9 Aug. 1570
John Bardwell & Prisca Base	.. ..	21 Apr. 1572
Galfridius Smyth, of Bungay, & Elizabeth Lawne	.. ..	25 Aug. „
Robert Clarke & Agnes Sones, of Worlingham Magna	.. ..	24 May 1573
Christopher Fayrchild & Susana Playford	..	5 July „
Henry Clarke & Agnes Fayerchild	..	26 Jan. 1574
Christopher Smyth & Maria Dera ..	..	1 Oct. 1575
Henry Freman & Elenora Bunninge	..	17 Oct. „
Randolph Sylles, of Yarmoth Magna, & Alicia Richman ..	.. .. ..	11 Mar. 1576
William Fiske & Elizabeth Tynke ..	..	21 Jan. 1577
John Cromb & Anna Clarke	.. ..	12 Oct. 1578
Robert Durrant & Alicia Taylor	.. ..	2 Aug. 1579
"Noe Mariages 1580."		
Robert Manne & Agnes Playford ..	..	20 June 1581
Lancellot Belward & Margeria Fiske	..	16 Sept. 1582
John Kettle & Margaret Sindall	.. ..	4 Oct. „
Henry Smyth & Matilda Andrewes	..	14 Oct. „
John Bardwell & Elizabeth Sparrain	..	3 May 1583
John Kempe & Katherina Callowe ..	..	28 Oct. „
Richard Thacker & Ellena Tynke ..	..	2 Mar. „
Robert Fiske & Alice Burrowe	..	1 Feb. 1584
Jerimye Hayle & Elizabeth Figg ..	..	24 Aug. 1585
Richard Benstone & Margaret Callowe	..	9 May 1586
Robert Serman & Elizabeth Wysman	..	15 Sept. „
Robert Spyllinge, of Bungay, & Anna Smeth, of Aylesham	.. .. ..	21 Nov. 1587
Thomas Caley & Lettice Shene	.. ..	24 Jan. „
Philip Lawne & Margaret Buck	.. ..	25 July 1588
William Harrison & Johane Shene..	..	6 Oct. „
James Stalworthye & Agnes Lawne	..	14 Oct. „
John Pitt & Agnes Smyth	.. ..	28 Oct. „
William Smyth & Agnes Spillinge	..	19 May 1589

Henry Wright & Maria Nele	3 Oct.	1589
Francis Andrewes & Agnes Kellett	6 Oct.	„
William Vesye, gent., & Maria Bedingfeld	13 Sept.	1590
William Page & Agnes Durrant	29 June	1591
Philip Jarman & Sisely Turner	4 Nov.	„
Hamond Elsinge & Maria Collins	31 Jan.	„
Robert Durrant & Margaret Ellis	15 May	1592
Egidius Roke & Jane Turner	9 July	„
Roger Turner & Elizabeth Thurton	12 Oct.	„
John Tynke & Dorathya Selbye	6 Feb.	„
Richard Fyske & Agnes Smyth	25 July	1593
Edward Norton & Maria Reighnould	12 Aug.	„
Thomas Nitingall & Elizabeth Marett	7 Feb.	„
John Cooper & Margaret Pryor	8 July	1594
Henry Chenye & Agnes Turner	16 Sept.	„
Gregory Browninge & Johana Buninge	9 Feb.	„
John Folser & Emma Andrewes	24 Sept.	1595
Robert Cobbell & Dorathia Bunfellowe	14 Oct.	„
William Turrell & Margery Wyman	16 Sept.	1596
Richard Smyth & Maria Kybert	20 Sept.	„
Philip Tynke & Katherina Bryerton	4 Oct.	„
Edward Fale & Susana Manninge	4 Oct.	„
Richard Scarlett & Ellena Tynke	11 Oct.	„
William Callowe & Agnes Cooke	24 June	1597
Antony Moses & Susana Parchmore	18 Sept.	„
Mathy Sotherton & Katherine Richman	20 Feb.	1598
Thomas Seele & Elizabeth Wisman	1 May	1599
John Farrow & Ruth Bates	29 Jan.	„
Richard Calver & Margery Kingsles	25 May	1600
Robert Hagasse & Helena Fiske	21 Oct.	„
Philip Tincke & Agnes Goslinge	4 Oct.	1601
Thomas Lawne & Agnes Newbrig	24 May	1602
William Fiske & Maria Kelliat	28 Aug.	1605
Thomas Spillinge & Margaret Fiske	23 Sept.	„
Peter Downinge & Elizabeth Yallopp	7 Oct.	„
Thomas Bond & Frances Man	20 Jan.	„
Richard Chettleborow & Sisly Estone	15 June	1606
Randolph Smith & Maria Mason	12 Oct.	„
Robert Browne & Marye Pretyman	6 Oct.	1608
Randolph Edwardes & Alice Fairchilde	15 May	1609

John Dicham & Elizabeth Barber ..	..	17 Sept. 1609
Laurence Potter & Elizabeth Freman	..	20 Sept. „
Robert Carsye & Mariana Belwarde	..	30 Sept. 1610
Thomas Earle & Marrian Easy ..	..	27 May 1611
John Marshall & Elizabeth Smyth ..	..	30 Sept. „
Richard Smith & Dorathie Stannard	..	2 July 1613
Michaell Hussye & Margaret Crooke	..	4 Oct. „
Richard White & Ann Miles ..	..	2 May 1614
Jhon Randall & Elizabeth Crofoot ..	..	11 Aug. 1615
Jhon Richman, of Yarmouth, & Agnes Smith, of Heddenham	..	14 Sept. „
Thomas Newman & Elizabeth Drane	..	12 Oct. „
Christopher Fairechild & Ann Stowe	..	27 Nov. „
Robert Smith & Prudence Woodward	..	2 Sept. 1616
Francis Bun & Ann Woocock ..	..	3 Oct. „
James Owers & Elizabeth Bunnet ..	..	17 Feb. 1617
Richard Sparrham & Agnes Selbye	..	4 May 1618
Robert Hussye & Francis Outlawe	..	11 Oct. „
Mathew Chur[——] & Margaret Goodwine ..		6 Apr. 1619
Robert Blundevill & Elizabeth Bardwell	..	19 May „
Arthure Langerwood & Margaret Owerds	..	20 June „
Christopher Fayrechilde & Catherine Edwards		4 Oct. „
Jhon Smith & Elizabeth Andrewes ..	..	1 Sept. „
George Manning & Mary Fiske ..	..	5 Nov. 1622
Robert [——] & Margaret Calver	..	10 Oct. „
Jhon Killiat & Elizabeth Andrewes	..	21 Feb. „
Miles Edgar, gent., & Dorothie Richman	..	22 Feb. „
Ralph Pell, parson of Ditchingham, & Ann Braband, of Thwate	..	2 Jan. 1623
Richard Smith & Joane Mingay ..	..	18 Oct. 1624
James Jeninges & Jane Terrill ..	..	10 Jan. „
Thomas Fincham, gent., & Frances Richman		31 Jan. 1625
Thomas Harrise & Margaret Cooper	..	3 Feb. 1626
John Tynke & Honor Staffe ..	..	10 May 1627
William Bodham & Marie Fouldsher	..	17 July 1628
John Gower, of St. John's, & Minna Adamson, of this p.	..	28 July „
Thomas Browne & Agnes Andrewes	..	29 Sept. „
Thomas Boller & Susan Palmer ..	..	14 Oct. „
Francis Andrewes & Thomasin Turrell	..	26 Dec. „

Richard Smith & Anne Thrower ..	.. 27 Oct.	1628
John Lawrence & Rose Meeke ..	.. 4 Nov.	,,
Edmund Gooch & Mary Stanton ..	.. 2 Aug.	1629
Arthur Edmunds & Martha London	.. 28 Oct.	,,
John Fouldsher & Marie Tower ..	.. 29 Oct.	,,
Jeffrie Dawes & Alice Seweall ..	.. 1 Apr.	1630
Francis Andrews & Sibill Pickston	.. 21 Dec.	,,
William Smith & Jane Francis ..	.. 4 Oct.	1631
Thomas Granger & An Palmer ..	.. 3 May	1632
John King, of Diching, & Martha Crooke	.. 20 Nov.	,,
John Harrison & Collet Havers, widow	.. 17 Dec.	,,
William Pulchard & Lydia Tower ..	.. 20 Jan.	,,
John Pescod & Sara Mansur ..	3 Oct.	1633
Thomas Sergeant & Alice Thurston	.. 15 Oct.	,,
Francis Cooke & Jane Whall ..	.. 14 July	1634
William Stanhawe, gent., & Mary Richman ..	9 Mar.	,,
John Raven & An Harlin	.. 14 Apr.	1635
Richard Bode & Alice Pilkinton ..	29 Sept.	,,
Francis Stamford & Hellen Bunnet ..	20 Oct.	,,
Thomas Stone & Elizabeth Cofer ..	25 July	1637
Robert Baker & Anne Thickpennie ..	9 Oct.	,,
Robert Fernie & Elizabeth Penning ..	27 Dec.	,,
Thomas Browne & Anne Todd ..	.. 3 Dec.	1638
John Preston & Prudence Coppin ..	.. 1 Apr.	1640
Ralfe Grint & Mary Chettleburgh ..	.. 3 Nov.	,,
James Ewers & Prudence Saccar ..	.. 13 May	1642
William Crickmer & Judith Fenne ..	.. 14 June	,,
Edward Randoll & Elizabeth Livicke ..	17 Nov.	,,
Owen Church & Susan Jennings ..	.. 9 Feb.	,,
Philip Launde & Ellen Goate ..	.. 8 Aug.	1649
William Moyse & Mary Bucke ..	.. 12 Mar.	,,
George Watts, gent., & Catherine Richman ..	28 Apr.	1650
Thomas Browne & Anne Cobbe ..	.. — —	1651
Matthew Cobbe & Anne Nuttall ..	.. 11 Apr.	,,
Thomas Fen & Bridgett Carrier ..	9 Jan.	1661
John Fiske & Mary Thurketle ..	2 Dec.	1662
Joseph Barber & Margerie Rose ..	.. 2 Mar.	,,
Thomas Palmer & Mary Ray ..	.. 17 Sept.	1663
John Harris & Ann Edwards ..	.. 8 Oct.	,,
Daniel Sewell & Elizabeth Bowler ..	6 Oct.	1664

Robert Corbold & Barbarie Ellenor	..	30 Mar. 1665
Edward Randall & Frances Starke	..	27 Sept. 1666
William Raven & Sarah Bunnett ..	..	4 Oct. „
William Whitcloaf & Margarett Jermy	..	29 Oct. „
Robert Spink & Elizabeth Gibson, of Shipdham		18 Sept. 1667
Thomas Thing & Grace Clarke, of Stoake	..	4 Oct. „
John Rand, clerk, of Peasenhall, Suffolk, &		
An Ketle, of Norwich	..	24 Oct. „
John Calloe & An Hayward	..	5 Oct. 1669
William Hartly & Lidia Punchard	..	23 Dec. „
Philip Jay & Martha Jay, of Earsham	..	5 Oct. 1671
William Hulluck, of Brome, & Mary Benton,		
of Earsham	.. ..	15 Oct. 1672
John Andrews & Mary Smyth	.. ..	18 Oct. „
Edward Hanworth & Mary Agass ..	..	7 Nov. „
Samuel Gurney & Susan Sergeant	..	11 May 1673
Thomas Harcock, of Woodton, & Elizabeth		
Gostling, of Hedenham	.. ..	14 July „
Robert Dixon, of Norwich, & Sarah Jones, of		
Broome	..	7 Oct. „
William Garold & Lydia Gower, of Redenhall		7 Oct. „
Robert Flatman, of Earsham, & Margarett		
Tuck, of Hedenham	.. ..	20 Apr. 1674
Thomas Clark & Elizabeth Baldry ..	..	30 Sept. „
Samuel Lucas, of Norwich, & Susan Wake, of		
Burgh-Apton	.. ..	30 Sept. „
George Smyth & An Smyth	.. ..	5 Oct. „
William Mousier, of Ditchingham, & Mary		
Sayer, of this p.	..	9 Oct. 1677
Robert Jermin & Mary Goodwin, of Topcroft		20 May 1678
Thomas Whiteing & Mary Punchard, w.	..	21 Oct. „
William Clarke & Elizabeth Smyth	..	19 May 1679
James Skelton & Mary Calloe	..	23 June „
Richard Briggs & Mary Knights ..	..	24 Sept. 1680
"No Mariages 1681, 1682."		
John Field, of Rickingale Superior, & An		
Child, of Broadwash	.. ..	15 June 1683
William Raven, widower, & Catherine Ed-		
monds, w.	..	1 Apr. 1684
Robert Adams & Sarah Spinke, of Starston ..		30 June „

Richard Hott, of Ditchingham, & Mary Fisk	1 July	1684
Nicholas Raven & Dorothy James	9 Sept.	„
Samuel Lucey, of Fritton, & Margarett Peirson,		
of Bunwell	20 Jan.	„
Robert Hobman & Sarah Swigate, w. ..	26 Apr.	1685
John Punchard & An Spinke ..	13 Jan.	1686
William Davy & Elizabeth Bunnet ..	21 Jan.	„
Richard Wright & Mary Bardwell ..	3 July	1688
Francis Hill & Mary Wright ..	10 Oct.	1689
Thomas Fairchild & An Buck ..	3 Oct.	1690
John Ellis & Elizabeth Sewell ..	12 Nov.	„
John Baldry & Mary Sparrow ..	6 Oct.	1691
Robert Legate & Anne Smyth, Rumborow,		
Suffolk	13 May	1692
Richard Wily & Frances Smyth ..	23 Feb.	„
Thomas Morphew & Elizabeth Plumstead ..	16 Mar.	„
William Sadler & Elizabeth Tye ..	28 June	1693
Edward Deny & Elizabeth Foulsham ..	28 June	„
Thomas Baldry & Catherine Can ..	22 Jan.	1694
Edmond Symons, of Woodton, & Hellen		
Bunnett, of this p.	14 May	1695
Thomas Nudds & Mary Andrews ..	17 Oct.	„
Francis Fisk & Susan Nubrig ..	10 Feb.	„
Robert Baldry & Elizabeth Wiely ..	30 June	1696
Jeremiah Stone & Elizabeth Fulsher ..	11 Jan.	1698
Thomas Springall, clerk, w., & Mary Atwood, w.	9 July	1700
Edward Basenthawite & Anna Smyth ..	2 Sept.	1701
John Raven & Mary Baker ..	1 Oct.	1703
Samuel Thrower & Mary Hane ..	25 Oct.	„
George Mayhew & Mary Burlingham ..	2 Oct.	1704
"Noe Marriages 1705-07."		
Robert Davy, esqr., & Elizabeth Bedingfeld,		
both of Ditchingham	24 May	1708
William Hall & Elizabeth Fen ..	3 Oct.	„
John Holmes, of Bergh-Apton, & Katherine		
Shreeve, of Heddenham ..	6 Feb.	1709
Edward Becket & Esther Legate ..	24 Apr.	1710
Charles Love, gent., & Frances Jacob ..	16 Oct. .	„
Jonathan Turner & Mary Marjoram ..	15 Dec.	„
John Lockwood, w., & Frances Callow, w. ..	12 Feb.	„

VOLUME II.

Anthony Freestone & Elizabeth Turner	..	1 Oct. 1711
William Brewerton & Elizabeth Smith	..	7 June 1712

"No Mariages 1713-15."

John Magub & Mary Smith ..	..	30 Sept. 1716
Thomas Bowman, of Brisley, & Elizabeth Shreeve, of Heddenham, *lic.*	..	30 June 1717
John Buck & Dorothy Edwards ..	..	14 July „
Timothy Cleybourne & Elizabeth Deal	..	1 Oct. 1718
Francis Wright & Mary Sewel, w. ..	..	14 June 1719
John Bedingfeld, clerk, & Catherine Garneys		1 July „
William Soan & Jane Keddey were married at Ditchingham	..	7 June 1720
Edward Wotten & Elizabeth Wright	..	12 June „
William Coppin, of Saxlingham, & Mary Shreeve, of Heddenham, *lic.* ..	..	25 July 1721
John Raven, w., & Mary Nud, w. ..	..	23 Feb. 1722
John Youngs & Elizabeth Plumb ..	..	17 Feb. 1723

"No Marriages 1724."

John Raven & Sarah Marcon	..	2 Nov. 1725

"No Marriages 1726."

John Sallows, of Carlton, & Susan Callow, of H.		4 Sept. 1727
John Callow & Barbara Fen, of Heddenham		4 Nov. „
Edmond Whithopole, of Topcroft, & Elizabeth Stowers, of Heddenham ..	..	10 Dec. „
Richard Alcock, of Earsham, & Sarah Mayhew, of Heddenham	..	6 Oct. 1729
John Smith, of Caston, co. Norfolk, & Mary Lamb, of St. Andrew's, co. Suffolk, *lic.*		25 Oct. „
Robert Woodcraft & Mary Offord ..	..	19 Jan. „
Wm. Price & Ann Betts, both of Bungay, w., *lic.*		12 May 1730
Joseph Carr & Elizabeth Rudram ..	..	16 May „
Robert Balliston, of Earsham, & Elizabeth Webster, of Hedenham	..	15 June „
Thomas Smith & Sarah Jaye, of Earsham ..		12 Oct. „
Thomas Fiske, of Bungay St. Mary's, & Elizabeth Smith, of Earsham ..	..	23 Oct. „
Thomas Wade & Martha Foulger, both of Ditchingham	..	25 Nov. „

David Baldry & Mary Mallctt, both of Earsham   10 Dec. 1730
John Buxton & Ann Mussell, both of Lowes-
 toffe   ..   ..   8 Mar. „
James Hemblin, of Bungay, & Ann Grimston   20 Apr. 1731
William Searle, of Bungay, w., & Barbara
 Spilling, of Earsham   ..   ..   18 May „
Charles Smith, of Sprouston, & Elizabeth
 Knights   ..   ..   6 June „
Isaac Piper & Bridget Mills, both of Earsham   2 Oct. „
Noah Aggas & Ann Jerviss, both of Earsham   17 Oct. „
Robert Morris, of Bungay St. Mary, & Ann
 Youngs, of Bedingham   ..   ..   7 Dec. „
John Austin, w., & Rebecca Gower, w., both
 of Earsham   ..   ..   3 July 1732
John Ellis & Alice Caley ..   ..   ..   6 Aug. „
Robert Derby, of Bungay, w., & Ann Matthews,
 of Earsham   ..   ..   ..   13 Aug. „
Robert Chasen, of Woodton, & Mary Gousty,
 of this p.   ..   ..   30 Sept. „
William Stevenson, of Pakenham, co. Suffolk,
 & Ann Allen, of Earsham, co. Norfolk   10 Oct. „
Edmund Browne & Esther Mills, both of
 Ubbeston, co. Suffolk   ..   ..   16 Oct. „
Robert Johnson & Elizabeth Mills, both of
 Earsham ..   ..   10 Apr. 1733
John Mallett, w., & Mary Browne, both of
 Bungay   ..   ..   30 May „
Henry Sarsnet, of Bungay, & Sarah Cremer,
 of Palgrave, w.   ..   ..   ..   3 June „
Job Robinson & Ann Girling, both of Bungay   14 June „
John Whitwood & Elizabeth Fairhead   ..   30 June „
John Pope & Susanna Lenton, both of Bungay   24 Aug. „
John Alburgh, w., & Elizabeth Skerry, both
 of Bungay   ..   ..   ..   9 Sept. „
John Rawling & Sarah Tyrrill, both of
 Bungay   ..   ..   30 Sept. „
John Wink & Ann Cunningham, both of
 Bungay   ..   ..   28 Oct. „
William Paxman, of Bungay, & Margaret
 Latten, of South Cove, co. Suffolk   ..   30 Oct. „

Richard Bloy & Catherine Potter, both of
    Mourning Thorpe ..   ..   ..   13 Dec.   1733
John Crotch, of Ellingham, & Mary Hill, of
    Bungay ..   ..   1 Jan.   „
John Gurling & Elizabeth Holdrich, w., both
    of Bungay   ..   ..   ..   11 Jan.   „
John Irish, of Wessett, co. Suffolk, w., & Ann
    Marly, of Bungay, co. Suffolk   ..   7 Feb.   „
John Baldwin, of St. Giles, & Ann Baxter, p.
    St. Gregory, Norwich   ..   ..   9 July   1734
Nicholas Bacon, p. St. Gregory, Norwich,
    w., & Mary Dalling, of Bungay   ..   16 July   „
John Martin, w., & Susan Rayner, both of
    Bungay ..   ..   21 July   „
Stephen Webster, w., & Mary Botwright, both
    of Bungay   ..   ..   ..   29 Oct.   „
William Turner, of Diss, & Catherine Alcock,
    of Bungay   ..   ..   ..   28 Sept.   1735
Henry Jaye, of Earsham, w., & Ann Ayres, of
    Bungay ..   ..   12 Oct.   „
Francis Cutts & Susan Gray, both of Woodton   18 Nov.   „
Henry Baker & Eliz. Malum, both of Bungay   18 Jan.   „
John Jefferies & Sarah Cook, both of Bungay   23 Mar.   „
Robert Scott, w., & Mary Pitchers, both of
    Bungay ..   ..   24 May   1736
Robert Clarke, w., & Elizabeth Cullingford, w.,
    both of Bungay   ..   ..   ..   1 July   „
Robert Mills & Susan Parcely, both of Bungay   1 Oct.   „
William Burton & Amy Hugman, both of
    Bungay ..   ..   1 Oct.   „
Robert Grimston & Mary Pope, both of this p.   23 Oct.   „
Thomas Gilney, of Chedgrave, & Sarah
    Higgins, of Loddon   ..   ..   11 July   1737
George Albrow, of Bungay, & Elizabeth Cut-
    ler, of Wheatacre Borough ..   ..   18 July   „
Thomas Martin & Elizabeth Cooper, of Bungay   24 July   „
John Leman & Mary Gowing   ..   ..   20 Oct.   „
Edmund Wade, of St. Margaret's, & Mary
    Kemp, p. St. Matthew's, Ipswich, co.
    Suffolk   ..   ..   7 Mar.   „

James Folkerd & Elizabeth Barkway, both of
Scole .. .. 26 June 1738
John Ward & Mary Holdridge, both p. Trinity,
Bungay .. .. 7 Aug. „
Robert Beales, of St. Marie's, & Sarah Gissing,
p. Trinity, Bungay, w. .. .. 25 Sept. „
George Hammond & Elizabeth Andrews, both
p. St. Mary's, Bungay .. .. 4 Oct. „
John Noble, p. St. Margaret, Ipswich, w., &
Elizabeth Balls, p. St. Mary, Bungay 19 Nov. „
Timothy Bennet, doctor of physick, p. St.
Andrew, Norwich, & Miss Margaret
Mounseir, of this p. .. .. 22 Jan. „
Jeremiah Carpenter, of the city of Norwich, &
Ann Crancher, of St. Peter's, Mancroft,
in the said city .. .. .. 11 Mar. „
Thoms Smales, w., & Mary Knighten, w., both
of Bungay .. .. .. 24 Apr. 1739
John Wallage, w., & Elizabeth Rowe, w.,
both of Bungay .. .. .. 5 May „
Thomas Browne, w., & Ann Vincent, w., both
of Bungay .. .. .. 21 May „
William Lamb, of Bungay, w., & Elizabeth
Morse, of Beccles .. .. .. 11 July „
Michael Alborow & Mary Doughton, both of
Bungay .. .. 17 July „
Robert Girling, of Framlingham, & Ann Smith,
of Leyston, co. Suffolk .. .. 5 Aug. „
Benjamin Frost, of Wacton, co. Norfolk, &
Hannah Stanton, of Waybred, co. Suff. 27 Sept. „
John Randall & Ann Burgess, both of Ditch-
ingham .. .. 27 Sept. „
Samuel Johnson, of St. Giles, Westminster, &
Frances George, of Bungay .. .. 4 Nov. „
William Whiting, of Alburgh, & Sarah Robin-
son, of Bungay .. .. .. 21 Nov. „
James Milligan, of Stoke Ferry, & Jane Fenne,
of Bungay .. .. .. 7 Apr. 1740
John Cook & Mary Robinson, w., both of
Bungay .. .. 26 June „

Edward Baldrey & Margaret Dunt, both
    this p. .. .. 27 Sept. 1740
Edward Chapman & Elizabeth Doughton, both
    of Bungay .. .. .. 18 Oct. „
William Aldhouse & Temperance Palmer,
    both of Woodton .. .. .. 9 Dec. „
Thomas Reeve & Mary Browes, both of
    Bungay .. .. 16 Feb. „
Samuel Forder & Mary Shiman, both of
    Gillingham .. .. .. 14 Mar. „
Henry Spragge & Mary Briggs, w., both of
    Bungay .. .. 24 Mar. „
William West & Mary Larter, both of Bungay 13 July 1741
Charles Ducke, clerk, A.M., & Miss Mary
    Mounseir .. .. 13 Aug. „
William Pells & Ann Browne, both of Bungay 25 Sept. „
Michael Rose & Edetha Lindow, both of
    Bungay .. .. 29 Sept. „
Thomas Dade & Hannah Hayward, both
    this p. .. .. 27 Oct. „
Andrew Spratt & Elizabeth Bruerton, both
    this p. .. .. 29 Oct. „
John Diggens & Bridget Flowers, both of
    Bungay .. .. 27 Jan. „
Samuel Wright & Jane Browes, both of
    Bungay .. .. 31 Jan. „
William Barber & Elizabeth Alcock, w., both
    of Bungay .. .. .. 18 Mar. „
Robert Mosely, p. St. Peter, Mountegate, Nor-
    wich, & Anna Orger, of Bungay .. 4 Apr. 1742
Henry Nash & Ann Martin, w., both of Bungay 6 June „
Richard Mapes, of Surlingham, w., & Ann
    Driver, of Bungay, w. .. .. 25 June „
Samuel Holman & Emma Taylor, both of
    Bungay .. .. 22 Aug. „
John Sherwood, of Shottesham, & Mary Bald-
    rey, of this p. .. .. .. 18 Nov. „
John Smith & Sarah Lord, both of Bungay .. 27 Nov. „
Philip Kerrich, of Ditchingham, & Annabastel
    Easter, of Bungay .. .. .. 26 Jan. „

John Thurston, w., & Ann Reeve, both of Bungay	7 Apr.	1743
Philip Butterton & Finite Butcher, both of Bungay	10 Apr.	„
Thomas Garner, p. St. Augustin's, Norwich, & Mary Smith, of this p.	3 May	„
Philip King & Mary De Gray, both of Bungay	4 May	„
John Mayes & Frances Drane	4 May	„
Edward Gaskin & Mary Fransham, both of Yelverton	19 June	„
Robert Fenne & Ann Hall, both of Bungay	28 Aug.	„
James Taylor & Sarah Browne, both of Bungay	18 Sept.	„
Samuel Easto, of Halesworth, co. Suffolk, & Mary Freeman, of this p.	25 Sept.	„
Jacob Pitchers & Susanna Ebbage, both of Bungay	1 Nov.	„
Jonas Gosling & Eunice Brock, both of St. Cross, co. Suffolk	14 Nov.	„
James Wills, of Bungay, & Mary Jermy, of Ditchingham	5 Feb.	„
John Honeywood & Elizabeth Foulger, both of Bungay	18 June	1744
Edward Pooley, of Cratfield, & Susanna Moon, p. St. Margaret, South Elmam, Suffolk	19 June	„
Stephen Webster, w., & Susan Saltonstall, w., both of Bungay	22 June	„
Henry Rodes, of Mettingham, & Joyce Hammond, of this p.	1 July	„
Daniel Hudson, of Ufford, co. Suffolk, w., & Sarah Miller, of this p.	8 July	„
Thomas Delf, of Denton, w., & Mary Packwood, of Bungay	21 Aug.	„
William Baker, clerk, M.A., Rector of this parish, w., & Matilda Tanner, relict of William Tanner, clerk, late Rector of Topcroft and Redenhall, w., married at Worlingham, co. Suffolk, by Mr. Commissary Tanner	24 Sept.	„
James Cunningham & Susan King, both of Bungay	4 Oct.	„

Francis Hill, w., & Elizabeth Ward, both of Bungay	6 Oct.	1744
Samuel Godbold & Mary George, both of Bungay	22 Oct.	„
John Wallage, w., & Mary Holman, both of Bungay	5 Nov.	„
Charles Cocking & Mary King, w., both of Bungay	26 Nov.	„
James Arnold & Jane Dring, both of Woodton	1 Jan.	„
Benjamin Margerom, of Beccles, & Mary Turner, of this p.	21 Feb.	„
Walter Calver, w., & Martha King, w., both of Bungay	26 Feb.	„
William Carpenter, of Aldeby, & Margaret Browne, of Toft Monks, w.	17 June	1745
John Richmond & Elizabeth Hunt	12 Sept.	„
John Archer & Martha Mapes, both of Bungay	24 Sept.	1746
Robert Grimston, w., & Ann Carver, both of this p.	2 Oct.	„
John Dady, of Redenhall cum Harleston, w., & Elizabeth Seales, of Topcroft	9 Oct.	„
John Read & Honor Staff	26 Oct.	„
Matthew Spilling & Rhoda Cushing, both of Bungay	3 Feb.	„
Joseph Burcham & Jane Steygold	15 Feb.	„
John Rope, of Aye, co. Suffolk, & Elizabeth Alp, of Metfield, w.	28 Feb.	„
James Barber, of Mutford, & Mary Dalby, of Bungay	19 May	1747
Robert Carsey & Elizabeth Edwards, both of Loddon	27 July	„
James Barnham, gent., & Miss Mary Gamble, both of Bungay	28 Sept.	„
Isaac Rumsby & Elizabeth Edge, both p. St. Andrew's, Ilketshall, co. Suffolk	31 Jan.	„
William Wilby & Elizabeth Shaften, both of Bungay	9 Feb.	„
Thomas Browne & Mary Butterton, both of Bungay	17 Feb.	„
John Folkard, w., & Mary Church, of Bungay	24 Apr.	1748

Lawrence Newson, of Pistrey, & Rebeccah
  Spence, of Bungay .. .. .. 19 May 1748
Ellis Buxton, w., & Elizabeth Wilby, w., both
  of Bungay .. .. .. 3 July ,,
Francis Gibson & Sarah Berry, both of
  Bungay .. .. 22 Sept. ,,
John Honeywood, w., & Ann Goodwin, w.,
  both of Bungay .. .. .. 26 Sept. ,,
John Skelton, of Saxlingham, & Susanna
  Horn, of this p. .. .. .. 12 Oct. ,,
William Honeywood & Ann Boast, both of
  Bungay .. .. 23 Oct. ,,
William Cooper & Ann Alger, both of Kessing-
  land, co. Suffolk .. .. .. 20 Dec. ,,
Samuel Lane & Ann Smith, both of Bungay 29 Jan. ,,
Thomas Hammond, of Fressingfield, co.
  Suffolk, & Elizabeth Oretts, of this p. 3 Apr. 1749
Joseph Hannent, of Covehithe, & Susan
  Shimman, of Benacre .. .. 5 Sept. ,,
Samuel Girling & Mary Mason, both of
  Bungay .. .. 1 Oct. ,,
James Snelling & Susan Hatcher, w., both of
  Huntingfield, co. Suffolk .. .. 1 Oct. ,,
Jonathan Sewel, p. St. Margaret's, Ilketshall,
  & Susan Barber, of Bungay .. .. 2 Oct. ,,
Nicholas Foreman & Mary Pretty .. .. 23 Oct. ,,
Bartholomew Leavould, of Brampton, & Mary
  Dimar, of Henstead, co. Suffolk .. 19 Nov. ,,
John Scott & Frances Delf, both of Bungay 4 Dec. ,,
Thomas Harvey, of St. Edmund's Bury, &
  Margaret Manthorpe, of Bungay, w. .. 30 Jan. ,,
Edward Cooper & Mary Gilman, w., both of
  Bungay .. .. 5 June 1750
Joseph Beets & Susan Groom, both of Bungay 30 July ,,
Dunham Gaines, of Stalham, clerk, & Miss
  Deborah Pake, of this p. .. .. 3 Sept. ,,
Francis Tovell, of Sisland, & Elizabeth Smith,
  of Claxton .. .. .. 30 Sept. ,,
Samuel Sheperd & Susan Kent .. .. 3 Oct. ,,
Stephen Tufts & Elizabeth Kersey, w. .. 26 Oct. ,,

James Russels & Mary Burridge, both p. St.
  Margaret's, Ilketshall   ..   ..   2 Oct.   1750
Robert Solomon & Mary Margerom, both of
  Bungay   ..   ..   25 Dec.   „
Samuel Larter & Susan Barber, both of Bungay   15 Mar.   „
Henry Smith, of Ellingham, & Sarah Kett, of
  Bungay   ..   ..   21 Dec.   1751
John Johnson & Elizabeth Smith, of Bungay   7 Apr.   1752
John Minns, of Loddon, & Susan Manclarke,
  of Bungay   ..   ..   ..   31 Aug.   „
Edward Reynolds & Ann Atkinson, both of
  Bungay   ..   ..   25 Sept.   „
Jonathan Hunter & Elizabeth Cullingham   ..   6 Jan.   „
Mr. John Wink, w., & Hannah Manclarke,
  w., both of Bungay   ..   ..   13 Feb.   „
Daniel Cullington & Elizabeth Fickling   ..   5 Mar.   „
John Underwood & Mary Kent   ..   ..   23 Apr.   1753
Thomas Cocker, late of Backwell, co. Derby,
  now a soldier in Lord Ancram's regiment
  and a sojourner at Bungay, & Susan
  Catchpole, of Bungay   ..   ..   21 Aug.   „
James Browne & Mary Dunt, both of Bungay   10 Oct.   „
George Harden, of Ditchingham, & Susan
  Cook, of Bungay, w.   ..   ..   21 Oct.   „
Mr. Stanton Penny, of Beccles, & Miss Mary
  Matthew, of Bungay   ..   ..   24 Oct.   „
Mr. Jonah Cullingham & Miss Sarah Lagden,
  both of Bungay   ..   ..   ..   20 Nov.   „

VOLUME III.

John Chilver, of Thelveton, & Mary Sewel,
  of Bungay   ..   ..   ..   *2 Feb.   1754
William Hawke & Susanna Simmonds, both
  of Beccles ..   ..   28 Feb.   „
Samuel Boycatt, of St. Edmunds, City of Norwich, clerk, M.A., & Miss Mary Baker,
  dau. of W. Baker, Rector of this p.   ..   1 May   „

---

* After this date, unless otherwise stated, the parties are invariably
of Hedenham, and respectively bachelor and spinster.

John Raven & Hannah Cleybourne	..	23 Sept. 1754
William Howlett, w., & Mary Howles, of Raydon, co. Suffolk	.. ..	30 Apr. 1755
Edward Crisp & Mary Bensley	.. ..	4 Feb. 1757
Hamlet Millatt & Rebeckah Crickmore	..	8 Aug. „
Timothy Gowing & Martha Johnson	..	10 Oct. „
Nath. Harvey, of Gillingham, & Mary Kersey		12 Oct. 1758
John Rackham & Ann Ludbrook	.. ..	31 Oct. „
William Jasper & Amy Kersey	.. ..	11 Oct. 1759
Joseph Philips, w., & Jane Staff	.. ..	2 Feb. 1760
William Leach & Elizabeth Dawson	..	13 Oct. 1761
John Manclarke & Mary Carring	.. ..	24 Nov. „
John Sewell, of Gillingham, & Hannah Clarke		10 Jan. 1763
John Grimmer, of Herringfleet, co. Suffolk, & Hannah Dade	.. .. ..	6 Aug. 1765
Francis Crickmore, of Mendham, co. Suffolk, w., & Jane Phillips, w.	.. ..	29 Aug. „
Robert Lazar & Susannah Fairhead	..	1 Oct. „
John Spilling, of Earsham, & Mary Fickling		8 Nov. „
William Stygale & Ann Jasper	.. ..	19 Jan. 1766
John Howlett & Ann Smith	.. .	13 Oct. „
Thomas Mendham & Mary Chamberlain	..	6 Oct. 1767
Samuel Hipperson & Sarah Moffet	..	29 Oct. „
John Scratton & Margaret Jex, of Reddisham, co. Suffolk	.. .. ..	17 Dec. „
William Abbet, of Needham, co. Norfolk, w., & Ann Hemblen	.. .. ..	9 Oct. 1768
Israel Dunnett, of the parish of St. Mary at Coslany, in the City of Norwich, & Elizabeth Woodyard	.. ..	25 Dec. 1769
Robert Beckct, w., & Frances Waters, w.	..	17 Apr. 1770
James Flowardew & Sarah Carter, of Earsham		27 May „
James Boatwright, of Ellingham, & Mary Woodyard	.. .. ..	20 May 1771
William Thompson, of the parish of St. George at Colgate, in the City of Norwich, & Ann Gooch	.. ..	17 Oct. „
Henry Gooch, w., & Elizabeth Beaumont, w., of the parish of St. Peter per Mountegate, in Norwich	.. .. ..	21 Nov. „

Stephen Rayner, of Woodton, & Susannah
    Woodyard   ..   ..   ..   16 Jan.   1772
Edward Howes & Sarah Spink, of the parish
    of the Holy Trinity, in Bungey   ..   14 Apr.   „
John Trower, of Bedingham, & Ann Marshall,
    w.   ..   ..   21 Apr.   „
Isaac Smith, w., & Elizabeth Peed, w.   ..   10 Aug.   „
William Howard, of Bedingham, & Sarah
    Lines   ..   ..   8 Jan.   1773
James Johnson & Sarah Todd, of the parish
    of the Holy Trinity, in Bungey   ..   19 Jan.   „
Michael Baldrey & Mary Burcham   ..   22 Feb.   „
Robert Becket, w., & Hannah Palmer   ..   5 Sept.   „
William Edwards, of Ditchingham, w., &
    Susanna Bun   ..   ..   ..   16 Oct.   „
John Roe & Elizabeth Goldsmith   ..   ..   5 Nov.   „
Thomas Feltom, of the parish of Shottisham
    All Saints', & Mary Hemblen   ..   1 Mar.   1774
Thomas Smith, of the parish of Bungay St.
    Mary, & Ann Woodyard ..   ..   26 July   „
Isaac Barmby, of the parish of St. Peter, at
    Mancroft, in Norwich, & Sarah Wood-
    yard, of this parish   ..   ..   14 Sept.   „
Thomas Eastick & Elizabeth Loveday   ..   8 Oct.   1775
Michael Playfoot & Susanna Holmes   ..   21 Oct.   1777
James Riches & Mary Taylor   ..   ..   14 July   1778
David Dickerson, of Berghapton, w., & Sarah
    Blackcloth, *als.* Barleyclove ..   ..   19 Oct.   „
Joseph Bircham, of Ditchingham, & Mary
    Hammond   ..   ..   ..   25 Dec.   „
Thomas Clarke & Frances Kibert   ..   ..   14 July   1779
William Shorten & Mary Minns   ..   ..   21 Dec.   „
Thomas Roberts & Ann Thurston ..   ..   30 Mar.   1780
Thomas Hammond & Abigail Roe   ..   28 May   „
Brampton Gurdon Dillingham, of Grundis-
    burgh, co. Suffolk, w., & Mary Howard   26 July   „
William Browne, of Scottow, & Martha Roe   18 Oct.   „
Thomas Smith & Elizabeth Petty ..   ..   11 Oct.   1781
William Serjant, of Thelveton, & Abigail Minns   20 Dec.   „
Samuel Folkard & Mary Palmer, of Ditchingham   4 Apr.   1782

1379191

Samuel Barker & Ann Hanworth	7 Nov.	1782
Joseph Thompson, of Norton, & Elizabeth Sewell	11 Mar.	1783
Thomas Wright & Martha Holmes ..	9 June	„
John Raven & Elizabeth Snelling	23 Feb.	1784
Moses More & Sarah Roberts	21 June	„
James Neale & Elizabeth Holmes	15 Nov.	1785
William Cullingford & Elizabeth Hanworth ..	29 Dec.	„
Henry Knights & Frances Mendom	10 Oct.	1786
James Varble & Ann Hanworth	20 Nov.	„
Van Millatt & Honour Staff	11 Dec.	1787
Robert Alcock, of Bungay St. Mary, w., & Sarah Sparrow	19 Jan.	1789
James Cushing, of Newton, & Mary Belt ..	19 Jan.	„
Thomas Smith & Sarah Palmer	27 Jan.	„
Thomas Olyett, w., & Margaret Scratton, w.	11 Mar.	„
Moses Fulcher, p. St. Mary, Bungay, & Elizabeth Folkard	27 Mar.	„
Robert Mudd & Frances Brown	12 Oct.	„
Joseph Rings & Jane Clark, w.	1 Dec.	„
Charles Palmer & Jane Peckard	2 Nov.	1790
Edward Forster, Esq., of Baliol College, Oxford, & Elizabeth Ann Addison, w. ..	27 Dec.	„
Benjamin Hayward, of Ditchingham, & Hannah Palmer	28 June	1791
William Marler, of Bungay St. Mary, & Alice Potter	23 May	1792
Samuel Skinner & Sarah Goldspink ..	12 Nov.	„
Charles Smonten, of Bedingham, & Martha Mendham	17 Apr.	1793
Thomas Crompton, clerk, of Belton, co. Suffolk, & Elizabeth Forster	21 June	„
Charles Jacobs, of Gillingham, & Mary Raven, w.	14 Apr.	1794
Amos Becket & Elizabeth Gates	27 Nov.	„
John Marshall & Eunice Holmes, of Thurton	16 June	1795
Robert Abraham & Elizabeth Puncherd, of Earsham	13 Oct.	„
Jonathan Mallet & Mary Hipperson ..	24 Nov.	„
William Flood & Maria Procter	18 Aug.	1796

Emanuel Leach & Martha Smith	6 Oct.	1796
Isaac Folkard & Honour Lord .. .	13 Oct.	,,
Robert Cairn, of Lakenham, & Lucy Tyler ..	14 Oct.	,,
John Burton of Seething, & Elizabeth Roe ..	28 Nov.	,,
John Flood & Elizabeth Pierce	11 July	1797
William Abraham & Susanna Jermy ..	25 Sept.	,,
Robert Lawrence & Sarah Flood	15 Nov.	,,
Samuel Purse, of Metfield, co. Suffolk, & Elizabeth Balls	6 Apr.	1798
William Westgate, of Hardwick, & Sarah Spratt	16 Oct.	,,
James Barnaby & Elizabeth Manclark ..	8 Apr.	1799
Thomas Minns & Mary Gowing, p. St. Mary, Bungay	1 Oct.	,,
Henry Gooch, w., & Elizabeth Hirst, w., p. Holy Trinity, Bungay ..	13 Oct.	1800
Enock Wallage & Mary Kersey	8 Feb.	1802
Jarvis Bultitude & Phebe Hanworth ..	11 Oct.	,,
John Hood & Susanna Baker ..	20 Dec.	,,
James Sparke & Ann Roberts	10 Oct.	1803
Roger Fosdick, of Topcroft, & Mary Middleton	6 Dec.	,,
Robert Quadlin, of Ditchingham, & Sarah Folkard	14 May	1804
Enoch Alden, of Alburgh, & Hannah Spratt	27 Sept.	,,
John Brown & Catherine Tibenham ..	19 Nov.	,,
Robert Smyth, w., & Mary Ringer ..	4 June	1805
Jonathan Baker & Sarah Barker	15 Dec.	1806
David Norton & Mary Shibden	11 July	1807
John Jordan & Mary Barker	2 Nov.	,,
Thomas Brown & Judith Hawks	3 Nov.	,,
Charles Bell & Sarah Hipperson	27 Nov.	,,
John Tompson & Abigail Hammond ..	8 Dec.	,,
Richard Shepperd & Anne Baley	26 Sept.	1808
John Eastaugh & Esther Harvey	19 Sept.	1809
Thomas Folkard & Anne Piggin	18 Nov.	,,
Robert Lawrence, w., & Mary Fleg ..	22 May	1810
Charles Flood, w., & Sarah Hollin ..	11 June	,,
Osmund Clarke, of Sisland, & Susan Spratt	26 Sept.	,,
John Barker & Sarah Jermyn	29 Oct.	,,
Michael Reeve & Charlotte Raven	11 Jan.	1811

William Fodder & Jane Houlders ..	25 Mar.	1811
Joseph Churlish & Elizabeth Jasper	..	3 Mar. 1812
John Felton & Sarah Hammond ..	..	25 Mar. ,,
William Masterson, of Sandcroft, Suffolk, &		
Hannah Chittleburgh ..	..	8 Apr. ,,
Robert Juby & Elizabeth Cook ..	..	2 Nov. ,,

Marriages at Weeting.

St. Mary's Parish,

1558 to 1746.

NOTE.—There were originally two parishes in Weeting, St. Mary's and All Saints'. They were united in 1651. The church of the latter was dilapidated by the fall of the tower some 200 years ago.

Volume I, consisting of parchment leaves, well preserved, and bound in parchment, records the Marriages in St. Mary's parish from 1558 to 7 November 1746, except those in Volume III below. Up to 1650 they are in Latin. In the first 40 years they are not original.

Volume II, also in bound parchment, contains the Marriages in All Saints' parish from 1561 to 2 October 1748, except those in Volume III below. They are entered along with Christenings and Burials. Some of the leaves, particularly those of the years 1631, 2, 3, 9, are much faded.

Volume III is a parchment register, unbound, and contains the Commonwealth Marriages by a "sworne Register" [*sic*] from both parishes, and many in which both parties came from other parishes, from 3 January 1653-4 to 16 January 1659-60.

Volume IV, in parchment, contains the Marriages in the united parishes from 1749 to 1755, and also from 1778 to 1786. These latter ones are also entered in Volume V.

Volume V contains the Marriages solemnized in the parish church of St. Mary from 19 October 1754 to 29 December 1812, from the united parishes. These are on printed paper forms.

These Marriages have been transcribed by the Rev. R. A. Oram, the present Rector, and are printed here with his permission.

VOLUME I.

WETINGE, BEATE MARIE.

"A Register of all the Christenings, Weddings, and Burials happened there since the 22nd day of November, Anno D'ni 1558, and in the first year of her ma^{t's} most gracious reign, made the 20th day of Sept., in the fortieth year of her said ma^{th's} reign, as followeth."

Johannes Master & Johanna Blowden	..	12 July 1558
Thomas Cooke & Agnes Cadge	..	14 Sept. 1559
Galfridus Gaye & Alicia Elson		16 May 1560

Jacobus Shaftinge & Margeria [?] Wade .. 6 July 1561
[1562-3, *no entry.*]
Willelmus Lyncolne & Margareta Restor .. 26 Oct. 1564
Thomas Mychell & Anna Leader .. .. 5 Nov. „
[1565-6, *no entry.*]
Swithune Goondaye & Anne Patterson 13 Oct. 1567
Thomas Browne & Jhoane Wade .. .. 26 Sept. 1568
John Cole & Jhoane Master .. .. 11 Oct. „
[1569, *no entry.*]
James Shaflyn & Jhoane May .. .. 30 Nov. 1570
Georgius Bennet & Dorothea Porter .. 21 Oct. 1571
Richardus White & Christiana Crane .. 28 Nov. „
Johannes Hartnes & Anna Porter .. .. 28 July 1572
Thymas Wade & Awdria Bishop .. .. 10 Oct. 1573
[1574, *no entry.*]
Thymas Cragge & Collet Mower .. .. 2 Oct. 1575
Georgius Gibbans & Helena Sego [?] 13 May 1576
Andreas Rom[w]tlicee & Alicia Watts 6 Sept. 1577
[1578-9, *no entry.*]
Abell Browne & Katharine Gathercole 14 May 1580
[1581, *no entry.*]
Edmundus Rushbroke & Constans Wright .. 17 Apr. 1582
Nicholaus Palmer & Johanna Gunthorpe .. -- — „
[1583, *no entry.*]
Thomas Wade & Anna Mayis .. .. 6 Sept. 1584
Richard Munke [?] & Katharina Grene .. 18 Oct. „
Thomas Denton & Margareta Ailmer .. 25 Jan. 1585
Robertus Mandall & Vidna Miller .. .. 10 Oct. 1586
[1587, *no entry.*]
Johannes Butler & Dorothea Bennett, w. 17 Oct. 1588
Robertus Fabyan & Elizabetha Stevenson .. 26 Oct. 1589
Thomas Mynnes & Margareta Myrhell .. 10 Dec. 1590
[1591, *no entry.*]
Willelmus Poterell & Cecilia Heygrene .. 28 June 1592
Robertus Racke & Alicia Wright .. .. 29 June „
Johannes Gooddaye & Elizabetha Bullinge .. 15 Oct. „
Petrus Tayler & Margareta Sayer .. .. 4 Nov. 1593
Richardus Cappe & Agnes Myrhell .. 7 Feb. „
Swithunus Gooddaye & Margeria Johnson .. 29 Apr. 1594
Jacobus Myller & Margareta Aylemer .. 4 Aug. „

Johannes Brocke & Emma Newell ..	..	6 Oct. 1594
Anthonius Drewry & Alicia Chapman	..	13 Oct. ,,
Georgius Rogers & Anna Burgesse		21 Sept. 1595
Edwardus Bullymer & Johanna Angnishe		25 Nov. 1596
Thomas Butter & Brigitta Myrhell ..		9 Oct. 1597
Robertus Downynge & Susanna Cappe	..	11 June 1598
Johannes Vyncent & Dorothea Brooks	..	12 Nov. ,,
Thymas Bemrose & Katharina Walmar	..	17 June 1599
Richardus Gunthorpe & Margeria Rackham		27 Mar. 1600

[1601, *no entry.*]

Robertus Barker & Margareta Mandall, w.	..	7 Mar. 1602

[1603, *no entry.*]

Richardus Grenling & Maria Wright		6 Dec. 1604
Robertus Jhonson & Maria Chapman	..	26 Jan. ,,
Johannes Bennet & Brigitta Walman	..	14 May 1605
Georgius Caverley & Alicia Oxborowe	..	28 July ,,
Henricus Lawse & Elizabeth Myller	..	13 Oct. ,,

[1606, *no entry.*]

Johannes White & Anna Bennet	..	20 Oct. 1607
Henricus Palmer & Katharina Browne	..	25 Apr. 1608
Thomas Kydde & Agnes Drewry ..	..	12 May ,,
Johannes Shawe & Margeria Gunthorpe	..	23 June ,,
Edwardus Hewar & Mariona Mandall	..	11 Oct. ,,
Henricus Palmer & Maria Burton ..	..	13 July 1609
Thomas Walman, w., & Margareta Meade	..	5 Oct. ,,
Willelmus Galle & Agnes Baldwyne		26 Oct. ,,

[1610, *no entry.*]

Willelmus Sillet & Agnes Myller ..		23 May 1611
Thomas Steede & Agnes Aylemer ..	..	28 May ,,
Johannes Rande [*or* Rands] & Martha Palmer		15 Sept. ,,

[1612, *no entry.*]

Robertus Fabian & Brigitta Bennit	..	8 Apr. 1613
Gulielmus English & Johanna Woode	..	4 May ,,
Johannes Rumbold & Agnes Cappe	..	10 Oct. ,,
Henricus Bennet & Alicia Adkinson	..	10 Oct. ,,
Robertus Kinge & Ellen Bullimer ..		9 Nov. ,,
Thomas English & Brigida Palmer	..	9 Oct. 1614
Richardus Aylmer & Sara Seily ..	..	30 Apr. 1615
Willelmus Bemrose & Johanna Andrews		29 May ,,
Johannes Mandal & Agnes Sillet ..	..	2 Aug. ,,

Robertus Olive, b., & Susanna Downing, w.   15 July 1616
Thomas Barker & Maria Bigges, s.   ..   9 June 1617
[1618, *no entry.*]
Robertus Harrison & Johanna Browne, s.   ..   21 Oct. 1619
Edmundus Newell, b., & Maria Lincolne, w.   14 June 1620
Thomas Bateman, b., & Johanna Bemrose, s.   15 Oct.   „
Richardus Garnon & Etheldreda Fisher, s.   ..   2 Oct. 1621
Georgius Clerke & Alicia Russell, s.   ..   6 Oct. 1622
Edmundus Newale, w., & Anna Harre, s.   ..   25 July 1623
Gregorius Peny, b., & Agnes Kidde, w.   ..   1 Feb.   „
Henricus Bennet, w., & Anna Sherman, s.   ..   23 Mar.   „
Adam Bennet & Elizabetha Walby, w.   ..   4 Nov. 1624
[1625, *no entry.*]
Roger Bemrose & Dorothy Atmeare   ..   10 Apr. 1626
Symon Wing & Francisca Jubie   ..   ..   1 Oct.   „
George Harvey & Brigetta Williams   ..   9 Nov.   „
Johannes Shaften & Johanna Saltmarsh   ..   2 Dec. 1627
Gulielmus Lea & Margareta Wayman   ..   3 Dec.   „
Willelmus Shaften & Johanna Bateman, w.   ..   14 Apr. 1628
Johannes Shaw & Elizabetha Paine   ..   23 July 1629
Gulielmus Miller & Millecent Seman   ..   30 June 1630
Gulielmus Ashfield & Alicia Skeete   ..   26 Aug.   „
Henricus Jackler & Sarah Fisher   ..   .   29 Sept. 1631
Jacobus Russel & Barbaria Younges   ..   19 July 1632
Robertus Cullen & Catharina Davy, w.   ..   10 Oct.   „
Jacobus Russel & Thomasina Palmer   ..   11 July 1633
Christoferus Newton & Agneta Jubye   ..   22 July   „
Richardus Isaac & Elizabetha Harvey   ..   12 Aug. 1634
Johannes Cap & Margareta Miles   ..   ..   16 Oct.   „
Robertus Wats & Alicia Ferrier, w.   ..   5 Feb.   „
Robertus Fisher & Maria Baker, s.   ..   11 Feb. 1635
Henricus Waker & Grace Spenser, s.   ..   27 Apr. 1637
Thomas Lea & Amy Bemrose, s.   ..   ..   3 May   „
Thomas Sexton & Ursula Wright, s.   ..   24 Aug.   „
Richardus Keny & Elizabeth Hamlen, s.   ..   21 Sept.   „
Johannes Cleark & Elizabetha Baker, s.   ..   15 Jan.   „
Gulielmus Blown & Elizabetha Vincent, s.   ..   22 July 1638
Gulielmus Peck & Dorothea Feria [Ferrier], w.   13 Dec.   „
Robertus   Brundish,   cler.,   &   Francisca
Cunstable, w.   ..   ..   ..   17 Dec.   „

Thomas Tailer & Amica Keny, s.	2 Feb. 1638
Robertus Brame & Jana Fowler, s. ..	8 Mar. 1640
Franciscus Conier & Florentia Rumbal, s. ..	17 Oct. 1641
Thomas Vincent & Dorothea Wats, s. ..	1 Nov. „
Johannes Starling, b., & Agneta Harrison, s.	7 July 1642
Thomas Tassel, b., & Maria Witeman, s. ..	24 Apr. 1643
[1644, *no entry.*]	
Henricus Palmer & Alicia Clerke, w.	23 Oct. 1645
Henricus Waker, w., & Margeria Story, s. ..	25 June 1646
Jacobus Steward & Elizabetha Walgrave ..	— Sept. „
Thomas Butter & Elizabetha Butcher ..	28 Jan. „
John Mandall & Ellen Barow	29 Sept. 1647
Thomas Vincent, w., & Tryphena Stevenson, s.	2 Dec. „
Richardus Scripwith & Mercia Hall, w. ..	13 Jan. „
Gulielmus Sell, b., & Elizabetha Machin, w. ..	2 Oct. 1648
Thomas Elmer & Susanna Baily	2 Nov. 1649
Thomas Stephens & Agnes Clerk ..	23 Apr. 1650
William Sutton & Tryphena Vincent, w.	5 Aug. „
Franciscus Harrison & Elizabetha Browne ..	6 Jan. „
[1651, *no entry.*]	
Thomas Bell & Anna Raines	30 Sept. 1652
William Fenne & Mary Rust	26 May 1653
Thomas Pooley & Anne Armiger	31 May „

[*Commonwealth marriages*, 3 *Jan.* 1653-4 *to* 16 *Jan.* 1659-60, *are contained for both parishes in another Register, and are transcribed on pages* 54-56 *post.*]

Robert Cooke, of Mildenhall, & Mary Mason, of W.	10 Jan. 1659
William Bennet & Elizabeth Ransom, both of Downham, co. Suffolk	30 Jan. „
John Watson, w., & Jane Mountaine, both of Methwold	9 Feb. „
Henery Barfoote, w., & Anna Ward, both of Feltwell	14 Feb. „
Robert Palmer & Anna Pooley, w.	14 Feb. „
[1660, *no entry.*]	
John Mole, w., & Susan Caney, w.	25 June 1661
John Jacob, w., & Alice Cataway, w. ..	13 Jan. „
[1662, *no entry.*]	
Henery Miller & Elizabeth Jud	28 May 1663

Robert Manning & Elizabeth Caney	..	6 Oct. 1663
Thomas Armiger & Elisabeth Jacob	..	10 Oct. 1664
Thomas Rumball & Mary Fokes ..	..	27 July 1665
Thomas Boyton & Margaret Maivo [?]		5 Nov. „
Edmund Thurrold & Mary Armiger		27 Sept. 1666
Samuel Clough & Prudence Bennet		16 Oct. „
[1667, *no entry.*]		
John Baily & Anna Heycock	..	16 June 1668
Dr. Thomas Craske & Mrs. Judith Wright	..	30 Sept. 1669
Richard Caney & Elizabeth Manning, servants		
to Mr. Holman, the former Incumbent		26 Dec. „
Osborn Stallon, p. Hockold, & Elizabeth		
Wright	..	19 May 1670
John Knights & Margaret Eldred ..	..	25 Apr. 1671
[1672, *no entry.*]		
Henry Plumbe & Alice Saull	..	26 June 1673
Robert Knapton, p. W. Dereham, & Mary		
Eaton, p. Brandon, by Mr. Camborn ..		22 Jan. „
Richard Newell & Elizabeth Heath		6 Oct. 1674
Lawrence Cadge & Mary Watts ..	..	26 Oct. „
Edward Edwards & Frances Conyard	..	25 May 1675
William James and Elizabeth Burges		29 June „
[1676-7, *no entry.*]		
Robert Holland & Hannah Traise ..	..	16 Jan. 1678
George Garner & Mary Thurston ..	..	21 Oct. 1679
[1680, *no entry.*]		
Robert Cheston & Elizabeth Wright	..	3 Apr. 1681
Sylvester Spinks & Mary Funnell ..	..	6 Oct. „
Richard Wellman, b., & Catharine Wright, w.		10 July 1682
[1683-4, *no entry.*]		
Samuel Clough & Ann Hodson, p. Wilton	..	9 June 1685
Osbert Denton & Abigail Mead ..	..	6 Apr. 1686
Francis Hunns & Mary Johnson, w.	..	23 Jan. „
Thomas Dunnit & Elizabeth James, w.	..	3 Apr. „
John Baly & Mary Woods	..	18 Jan. 1687
George Dawkin & Margaret Cock ..	..	22 Nov. 1688
[1689, *no entry.*]		
Thomas Butter & Elizabeth Cany ..	..	18 Jan. 1690
[1691, *no entry.*]		
William Starling & Elizabeth Beeton	— —	1692

James Wiffin & Elizabeth James	19 Oct.	1693
William Beeton & Ann Armiger ..	25 July	,,
Thomas Crane & Elizabeth Horlett	27 Nov.	1694
Anthony Durrant & Bridget Miller	3 8ber.	1695
Nicholas Tilbrook & Ellen Wright ..	14 Jan.	,,
[1696, *no entry.*]		
Thomas Hooker & Bridget Cranner ..	30 Sept.	1697
John Cock, junr., & Ann Jordan	13 June	1698
Mr. Thomas Haslewood & Mrs. Jane Pepys ..	31 8ber.	,,
William Beeton & Philometty Farrow ..	13 9ber.	,,
[1699, 1700, 1701, *no entry.*]		
James Cock & Amy Butter	— —	1702
Stephen Fowler, p. Holborough, & Susan Beeton, w.	14 1ober	,,
John Docking & Mary Johnson	22 Dec.	,,
Wortley Reyner & Mary Guttridge ..	14 Feb.	,,
[1703, *no entry.*]		
Samuel Clough & Placence Bird	18 May	1704
William Sutton & Mary Baley	23 May	,,
John Jacob & Susan Piper ..	26 Sept.	,,
Philip Sharp & Ann Chapman ..	2 June	1705
Silvester Spinks & Mary King	24 Sept.	,,
[1706-8, *no entry.*]		
Richard Caney & Elizabeth Starnell ..	24 July	1709
Robert Parsons & Elizabeth Howlett	2 Nov.	1710
Thomas Cany & Jane Docking ..	2 Oct.	1711
John Townshend & Elizabeth Carey	28 Apr.	1712
William King & Mary Brett ..	31 July	,,
John Bacon & Mary Mead ..	1 Oct.	,,
John Mandall & Mary Jordan ..	15 Oct.	,,
[1713, *no entry.*]		
Charles Wellham, b., & Mary Whitley, s. ..	30 June	1714
Edmond Carey, b., & Mary Walker, s. ..	27 Jan.	,,
William Sutton, w., & Hannah Robinson, s.	4 Mar.	,,
[1716, *no entry.*]		
Philip Spalding, b., p. Brandon, & Dinah Heminger, s., of W.	24 Apr.	1717
William Pearse, w., p. Porringland, & Mary Harris, w., of W., *lic.*	10 May	,,
Edward Franks & Anne Sallows, s. ..	2 Oct.	,,

Robert Jewell & Anne Quentral, s.	..	11 Nov. 1718
John Willett, p. Brandon, & Mary Jeny, s.	..	24 Nov. „
Richard Butter & Anne Walker	..	22 Oct. 1719
Jo. Bacon & Mary Dow	..	30 Sept. 1720
William Hardy & Ellen Sconge	..	3 Oct. 1721
John Ayres & Sarah Wright, p. Feltwell	..	16 Jan. „
William Sturgess & Elizabeth Bullock	..	12 June 1722
John Arminger & Sarah Bennett	..	23 July „
Matthias Ash & Elizabeth Arminger	..	20 May 1723
William Croner & Mary Spinks, w.	..	3 June „
Robert Gore & Susan Larner	..	28 Aug. 1724
Thomas Spinks, junr., p. Feltwell, & Mary		
Verdon, p. Methwold	..	22 Mar. „
William Jempson & Rebecca Curvice	..	28 Sept. 1725
Thomas Rudland & Amy Carey, p. Felt-		
well	..	21 Nov. „
John Knights, b., p. Watlington, & Ann Green-		
acre, s., of Tottenhill-row	..	2 May 1726
John Coats, w., p. Barton, co. Suffolk, &		
Frances Jeneper [?]	..	18 Aug. „
John Allen, b., p. Stoke, & Mary Thorn, s.	..	3 Aug. „
Edward Payn, w., & Elizabeth Starling, w.	..	9 Apr. 1727
John Cadney, b., p. Hockwold, & Anne Mesh,		
s., p. Brandon	..	7 Apr. „
William Otley, b., & Anne Bullbrook, s.	..	29 Sept. 1728
Richard Clarke, w., p. Methwold, & Margaret		
Gore, w., of W.	..	21 Oct. „
Robert Fuller, b., & Mary Field, s.	..	12 Oct. 1729
Peter Dent, b., p. Duddington, & Dorothy		
Crask, s.	..	28 Oct. „
William Sparks, b., p. Brandon, & Anne		
Coppinger, s.	..	30 Oct. „
Mr. Daniel Greenaway & Mrs. Jane Cayton	..	31 Mar. 1730
William Denton, b., & Mary Starling, s.	..	14 June „
William Laws, w., & Margaret Parish, s.	..	29 Sept. „
John Peck, b., & Catharine Isgate, s.	..	9 Oct. „

[1731, *no entry.*]

John Harding, b., & Elizabeth Miller, s.	..	2 Feb. 1732
John Fawkes, junr., b., & Mary Jacob, s.	..	1 Nov. 1733

[1734, *no entry.*]

Mr. Robert Miller, b., & Mrs. [*sic*] Sarah
    Carter, s., *lic.* .. .. .. 7 Dec. 1735
        [1736, *no entry.*]
John Miller, b., & Ann White, s. .. .. 2 Jan. 1737
William Francis & Mary Ward, s., p. Cres-
    singham .. .. 12 June „
John Malin [?], b., & Mary Smyth, s., p.
    Hockwold .. .. .. 20 Sept. „
Robert Jewell, w., & Mary Cooke, w. .. 2 Oct. „
John Addison, b., p. Stradset [?], & Margaret
    Wilson, s., p. Fincham .. .. 3 Oct. „
William Cron[*or* u]k, w., & Elizabeth Frost, s. 5 Nov. 1738
Benjamin Turner, b., & Sarah Roddall, w. .. 2 Jan. „
John King, b., p. Brandon Ferry, & Tabathy
    Last, s., p. Witham Brooks [Wickam] 24 June 1739
John Everett, b., p. Hingham, & Elizabeth
    Jacob, s. .. .. 7 Feb. „
William Jaggard, b., p. Thetford, & Pearthy
    [*sic*] s., p. Mildenhall .. .. 21 Apr. 1740
Mr. Thomas Everson, b., p. Thetford, & Mrs.
    Bridgett Denton, s., p. Brandon .. 30 Apr. „
Richard Collin, b., p. Iglinghay, & Rachell
    Hill, s., p. Brandon .. .. .. 8 July „
John Pooley & Ann James, s., both p. Felt-
    well .. .. 30 Sept. „
William Horn, b., & Alice Rayne, w. .. 16 Nov. „
Joseph Taylor, b., & Mary Willett, w., both of
    Stoak .. .. 28 Mar. 1741
William Cock, b., & Margaret Cook, s., both
    of W. .. .. 11 Oct. „
William Lalham, b., & Catharine Prior, s.,
    both p. Great Saxham, co. Suffolk .. 30 Mar. 1742
John Davy, b., & Anne Cock, s. .. .. 7 July „
Thomas Cock, b., & Elizabeth Lancaster, s. 5 Oct. „
Richard Wright, p. Thetford, & Frances
    Cobham, s. .. .. .. 21 Feb. „
Thomas Potter, b., & Anne Seccrar, both p.
    Eshiell [?], co. Suffolk .. .. 8 Mar. 1743
        [1744, *no entry.*]
Henry Antony, b., & Jane Cary, s. 2 Oct. 1745

Thomas Coggan, w., & Sarah Eldred, w., both
    p. Stoak Ferry   ..   ..   ..   7 Nov. 1746

All Saints' Parish,

1561 to 1653.

VOLUME II.

Henry Pricke & Agnes Sampson ..	..	18 May 1561
Edmund Bullimore & Cicely Steed ..	..	22 May „
Thomas Woodward & Agnes Church	..	25 Oct. „
Alexander Maister & Cicely Long, w.	..	19 Jan. „
William Bateman & Katherin Cotton	..	28 Nov. 1563
Robert Rumbelow & Margaret Mays	..	18 June 1564
William Miller & Jone Lock ..	..	17 Dec. „
William Reynes & Margaret Rumbelow, w. ..		26 Jan. 1565
William Bateman & Dorothy Lord, w.	..	12 May 1566
John Childe & Margaret Wheatley ..	..	16 Oct. 1567
John Miller & Grace Cockerey ..	..	12 Jan. „

Roger, s. of William and Margaret Arrett, &
    Beatrix, d. of William and Margaret
    Wace .. .. 23 May 1568

Gregory Drinkmilk & Margaret Mower	..	29 Oct. 1570
Richard Francklyn & Mary Sam ..	..	20 Nov. „
John Aylmer & Elizabeth Button ..	..	7 May 1571
Richard Aylmer & Margaret Dearson	..	8 Aug. „
Laurence Fuller & Agnes Fitte ..	..	25 Oct. „
William Long & Agnes Chapman ..	..	6 Oct. 1572

[1573, *no Marriages.*]

William Miller & Marian Hagges ..	..	20 Oct. 1574
Edmund Bullimer & Helene Gunthorpe	..	14 Apr. 1575
John Haylett & Helene Harrison ..	..	20 Aug. „
Robert Bateman & Elizabeth Large	..	2 Jan. „
John Cowper & Margaret Samson ..	..	10 Jan. „
Robert Sommers & Katherin Noxe	..	16 Dec. 1576
Thomas Butler & Anne Burton ..		19 Dec. „
Thomas Bateman & Agnes Turner	..	20 May 1577
Leonard Dawghton & Francis [*sic*] Miles	..	29 July „
John Mandall & Margaret Master ..	..	6 Oct. „
William Oxborow & Annie Chicken	..	12 Sept. 1578
Thomas Walman & Alice Campe ..	..	4 Oct. „

John Samson & Susan Hill	17 Feb. 1578
John Sparrow & Phillip [*sic*] Webbe	30 Sept. 1579
John Scroggs & Grace Maye	25 Oct. „
Henry Skinner & Margaret Pattison	17 July 1580
William Raynes & Mary Hill	29 Jan. 158½
Edward Nobes & Jane Egle	23 Aug. 1582
William Mopted & Margaret Samson	15 Oct. 1583
Robert Rosby & Elizabeth Garter ..	30 Jan. 158¾
Nicholas Smith & Wydow Rumbold, w.	11 June 1584
Roger Clerke & Helene Arnold	10 May 1585
Raphe Johnson & Margery Parfe ..	31 May „
Robert Johnson & Susan Samson, w.	3 Sept. „
James Mawling & Elizabeth Selby ..	18 Jan. 158⅚
Thomas Harkwood & Margaret Hayn	15 May 1586
Richard Barker & Margery Fitte ..	17 Sept. 1587
Edmund Cadge & Ciceley Cele	30 Jan. 158⅞
John Aylmer & Sarah Loke	6 June 1588
Lawrence Lawrence & Alice Mower	10 June „
Adonie Bowlter & Mary Sellers ..	14 July „
Thomas Balden & Margaret Minnick	25 July „
Thomas Miller & Jane Barton	20 Oct. „
William Harrison & Margaret Oxborow	10 Nov. „
Thomas Tivie & Brigide Mais	25 Feb. „
Ambrose Eldred & Jone Pricke ..	8 June 1589
Thomas Balden & Agnes Stevenson	19 Nov. „
Edward Nicolls & Alice Sargeant ..	8 Jan. 15⁸⁹⁄₉₀
Henry White & Annie Emmes	13 Jan. „
Thomas Kydde & Emma Oxborow	26 Feb. „
Robert Middleton & Katherin Wace	26 Apr. 1591
Thomas Tivie & Helene Preety ..	6 Sept. „
Richard Clerke & Margaret Drinkmilke, w. ..	11 Oct. „
Raphe Johnson & Margery Buller ..	23 Dec. „
John Wace, ye elder, & Awdry Gunthorpe ..	12 Oct. 1592
William, ye younger, & Elizabeth Fisher ..	4 Oct. 1593
William Eldred, ye elder, & Alice Newell, w.	24 Oct. 1594
William Cocke & Jone Bloome	3 Oct. 1596
Thomas Miller & Dionise Wade ..	5 June 1597
William More, of Wrethin, & Anne Walker ..	26 June „
Richard Eldred & Helene Newell ..	21 Sept. „
Henry Miller & Brigide Miller	20 Feb. 159⁸⁄₉

Thomas Reade & Jone Allen	1 Feb.	159⁸⁄₉
Edmund Silvester & Cecily Potterell ..	20 Feb.	„
Jeoffrey Nobes & Mary Muriell	14 Oct.	1599
[1600, *no Marriages*.]		
Roger Clerke, w., & Alice Nicolls, w. ..	19 Apr.	1601
Richard Delfe, b., & Rose Yeongs, s. ..	3 Aug.	„
James Russell, b., & Agnes Wilkenson, s., of		
Bromehil	19 Nov.	„
William Barre, S. Marie's, & Katherin Newell,		
All Saints'	21 Oct.	1602
Richard Cocke, w., & Margaret Harison, w...	20 Feb.	„
Thomas Lincolne, b., & Mary, d. of James		
Malling, s.	3 Oct.	1603
Thomas Bayly, b., & Phillis Silverston, s., of		
Hengrave, Suff.	24 Oct.	„
William Eldred, elder, w., & Barbara Cooper,		
of Wralton [?], w.	26 July	1604
John Butler, w., & Agnes Russell, w. ..	30 Oct.	1606
Robert Cusseyn, b., & Elizabeth Penny, w. ..	1 Feb.	„
Lawrence Bayly, b., & Elizabeth Osberne, s.	17 May	1607
John Davye, b., & Katherin Wilkinson, s. ..	24 June	„
Abraham Fisher, b., & Thomasine Rous, both		
of Weting Mary	21 Jan.	„
John Reddish, b., & Helene Catewade, w., of		
Brandon, Suff.	8 Feb.	„
Froxmere Cockett, of Brunsthorpe, gent., b., &		
Brigide Fowler, of Bromehill, s. ..	25 May	1608
Thomas Jacob, shepheard, b., & Margery		
Baker, s., of Wilton	2 Oct.	„
William Raynes, b., & Agnes Harison, s., of		
Fordham, in Cambridgeshire ..	16 Jan.	„
Richard Browne, of St. Marie's, b., & Rose		
Cocke, s.	11 Jan.	„
Steven Johnson, of Hockwold, b., & Elizabeth		
Cateward, of Bromehill, s.	30 July	1609
Lancelot Jakes, b., & Jone Samson, s. ..	29 Nov.	„
John Seely, b., milner, & Sarah Baise, of		
Bromehill, s.	7 Oct.	1610
George Bennett & Mary Philips, both of		
Broomhill	18 Oct.	„

Philip Poole, of Flitcham, b., & Martha Clerke,
  of this p., s. .. .. .. 26 Jan. 1611
James Malling, b., & Mary Brand, s. .. 5 Apr. 1613
William Clerk, w., of Mildenhall, & Julia
  Miller, w. .. .. 6 May „
William Lerner, shepherd, w., & Jone Bate-
  man, s. .. .. 30 May „
Roger Shafting, b., & Margaret Raynes, s. .. 24 Aug. „
Thomas Dey, b., & Agnes Robinson, s. .. 3 Nov. „
Thomas Faux, w., & Agnes Seckar, of Sheep-
  ham [?], w. .. .. .. 7 Feb. 161⁴
Thomas Jacob, shepherd, b., & Agnes Philip, s. 6 Oct. 1614
Richard Barker, jun., of St. Marie's, b., &
  Marion Drewry, s. .. .. .. 30 Oct. „
Roger Raynes, b., & Grace Petche, of Milden-
  hall, s. .. .. 2 Feb. 161⁴
John Bateman, s. of Robert, & Anne Gooch,
  of Wangford, Suff., w. .. .. 9 Feb. „
Thomas Bayly, jun., w., & Cecilie Cadge, w. 21 May 1615
Jo. Rumbold, sen., w., & Agnes Jacob, w. .. 1 May 1616
Richard Wright, w., & Elizabeth Mason, s. .. 21 July „
Richard Key, b., & Agnes Warner, s. .. 15 Sept. „
Richard Driver, b., & Agnes Eldred, s. .. 19 Sept. „
Thomas Barker, of Norgate, b., & Amy Aylmer,
  of Southgate, s. .. .. .. 13 Oct. „
George Calverley, w., & Mary Seckar, of
  Shepham, s. .. .. .. 13 Feb. „
George Scarpe, of St. Mary, b., & Thomasin,
  d. of Robert Barker, jun. .. .. 1 May 1617
John Aylmer, w., & Emma Drinkmilke, s. .. 21 May „
Henry Bateman, b., & Mary Rushbrooke, s. .. 2 Oct. „
Ambrose Catiwade, of Thetford Peter, b., &
  Dorcas Fysher, s. .. .. .. 12 Oct. „
John Aylmer, w., & Cecily Ems, s. .. .. 8 Oct. 1618
William Raynes, w., & Agnes Smith, w. .. 2 Feb. „
John Walbey, shepheard, b., & Margaret, d.
  of Henry White .. .. .. 20 June 1619
Thomas Spencer, b., & Elizabeth Barker, s.,
  both of Santon .. .. .. 3 Oct. „
George Cap, of Brandon, b., & Dionyse Myller, s. 27 Dec. „

Richard Scrivener, b., & Anne Estgate, s., both of this p.	28 Feb.	1619
John Birde, of Brandon Fery, b., & Emme Spencer, of Bromhill, s.	20 Aug.	1620
Edmund Butler, b., & Susan Jordan, s. ..	1 June	1621
William Raynes, w., & Alice Bowliner, s. ..	13 Sept.	„
Thomas Eldred, b., & Alice Barker, s., *lic.* ..	21 Oct.	1622
George Scarpe, w., & Anne Fyson, s. ..	30 Oct.	„
Roger Copley, b., & Dorothea, d. of Jo. Cricke, s.	25 Sept.	1623
Robert Bell, of Norwold, b., & Tryphena Callow, s.	7 Dec.	„
Henry White, w., & Dionyse Goodwin, w. ..	20 Sept.	1624
William Fuller, w., & Martha Bellamy, s. ..	24 Oct.	„
Thomas Cadge, b., & Brigide Wace, s. ..	21 Apr.	1625
Matthew Eldred, b., & Susan Seckar, s. ..	19 Oct.	„
William Meade, b., & Mary Halls, w., *lic.* ..	20 Feb.	„
Thomas Barker, of Gooderston, w., & Margery, w. of William Cocke	29 June	1626
William Maney, b., of Broomhill, & Alice Page, s.	1 Oct.	„
Richard Driver, w., & Dorothie Mershe, s., of Bromhil	23 Apr.	1627
William Rhaines, w., & Elizabeth Bolter	20 June	„
Jeremy Meade, s., & Elizabeth Eldred, w.	4 Feb.	„
Thomas Lane, b., & Elizabeth Mawling	15 June	1628
William Cocke & Katherine White, s. ..	19 Oct.	„
James Seckar, b., & Ruthe Philips, s. ..	28 Oct.	„
Thomas Ollett, of Brandon, b., & Emma Richards, of Bromhill, s.	20 Jan.	„
John Bridges & Sara Arrets, of Bromehill ..	6 Apr.	1629
Francis Parlett, s., & Margaret Balam, w. ..	8 Apr.	„
Edward Peck, b., of Norwich, & Mary Fowler, s.	6 June	„
Thomas Barker, w., & Elizabeth Wattes ..	2 Feb.	1630
William Hardy, of Brandon, w., & Susan Moore, of Bromehill, w.	31 May	1631
John White & Elizabeth Mandall	19 Feb.	1632
Robert Morley, w., & Frances [Hill ?], s. ..	27 May	1633
Jacobus Baldwyn, w., & Elizabeth Fisher, w.	20 June	„
Edmund Walker & Anna Faux, of Weeting	29 Sept.	„

Randolph Lawson, b., & Elizabeth [——gton]	21 Oct. 1633
John Banks, b., & Susanna Kirkham, s. ..	25 May 1634
John Shafton, w., & Alice Uttinge, s. ..	30 July 1635
Stephen Towler, b., & Anna Bayly, s., both of this p.	27 July 1636
Thomas Lane & Elizabeth Cooke ..	24 Aug. 1637
Thomas Mannings & Agnes Mopted ..	21 Apr. 1639
Jacob Secker & Agnes Porter	13 [?] ,,
John Reeve & Elizabeth Journygoe ..	11 Apr. ,,
Edmund Newell & Marie Goole	28 June 1641
John Wright & Marie Mandall	28 Oct. ,,
Robert Raines & Jane Rumbelow ..	26 Nov. ,,
George Bennet & Anne Garrard	3 Feb. ,,
Robert Porter & Anna Coats	4 Oct. 1643
John Pricke & Elizabeth Eldred	18 May ,,
John Fenne & Marie, servant to Abigale Mundford	11 June 1644
John Barker & Dorithy Butler	7 Apr. 1645
John Pooly & Elizabeth Butler	16 Oct. ,,
John Barefoote & Katherine Tilshed	10 June 1647
William Shafton & Grace Raynes	25 Jan. ,,
Richard Baker & Elizabeth Newton ..	10 Aug. 1648
John Fues & Ellen Prat	8 Feb. ,,
John King & Alice Seago	27 Sept. 1649
John Page & Elizabeth Jackson	25 Jan. ,,
John Chapman & Anna Wivens	13 Feb. ,,
William Barker & Anna Newton	1 Apr. 1650
Robert Parker & Anna Robinson	7 Apr. ,,
Robert Wentland & Amie Coward ..	10 June ,,
John Spink & Margaret Huns	12 Oct. ,,
Nicolas Edowes & Margaret Hopkin ..	25 Feb. ,,
Simon Delf & Judith Tuck, w.	24 June 1651
Robert Hodg & Anna Delf	14 Jan. ,,
John Holmes & Mary Edowes ..	26 Jan. ,,
Thomas Lane & Anne Bennet ..	26 July 1652
Simon Pussey & Elizabeth Prat ..	13 Dec. ,,
John Fit & Anna Huns	7 June 1653
Robert Smith & Anna Butler	14 July ,,

[VOLUME II *is continued on page* 56.]

St. Mary's and All Saint's,

1653 to 1660.

VOLUME III.

"All the mariages, births, and burialls wh. have beene in both the parishes of Weeting since these wh. are here registered until the year 1659, are to be found in that new Register booke, wh. was by a new authority provided on purpose to register them in."

Thomas Lowly, w., & Anne Salter, w.	3 Jan.	1653
Roberte Yongs & Jane Dorking	26 Jan.	„
William Driver & Francis [*sic*] Barker	1 Feb.	„
William Moad & Anne Cap, s.	28 Mar.	1654
Edmund Wright, b., & Judith Barfold, s.	30 Mar.	„
Richard Wright, w., & Dorothe Ketteringham	24 Apr.	„
Henry Killingworth & Margaret Boswell	15 May	„
John Wright, b., & Francis [*sic*] Benet	16 May	„
John Brigis & Dorothe Barker	3 July	„
John Clarke & Margarett Barrett	7 Aug.	„
Robert Watts & Mary Newell	21 Sept.	„
Richard Fisher, gent., & Priscilla Russell	9 Nov.	„
Samuell Meads & Mary Muffitt	28 Jan.	„

[1655, *no Marriages.*]

William Beeton, of W., b., & Alice Tovy, p. Hockold, s.	7 Apr.	1656
Laurence Cadge, of W., b., & Margarete Thompson, of Fouldon, s.	9 Oct.	„
Frauncis Ollet, of W., b., & Jane Nobbes, of Standford, s.	9 Oct.	„
Robert Kinge, of W., & Tryphena Sutton, of Brandon, w.	1 Oct.	„
John Pooley, of W., b., & Elizabeth Nobbes, of Bromhill, s.	6 Nov.	„
Luke Aburne, b., & Margarett Mortlock, w., both of Brandon	14 May	1657
Robert Suckerman, p. Mildnall, co. Suff., w., & Anne Sicklemoore, of same [*sic*], co. Norf., s.	2 July	„
William Smyth, w., & Anne Chapman, s., both p. Brandon, co. Suff.	14 July	„

William Mead, of W., b., & Margarett
Starlynge, p. Wangford, co. Suff., s.,
mar. at Wilton   ..   ..   .. 16 Sept. 1657
Thomas Fish, b., & Mary Ashley, s., both p.
Foulden, co. Norf. ..   ..   .. 24 Sept. „
Thomas Mann, of W., b., & Rose Fytt, of
[———] ..   .. 3 Oct. „
Francis Bennet, b., & Elizabeth Lingwood, s.,
both p. Foulden, co. Norf.   ..   .. 22 Feb. „
Frauncis Honnes, b., & Dorothy Elyngton, s.,
both of W.   ..   ..   .. 3 Oct. „
Thomas Bell, p. W. All Saints', co. Norf., w.,
& Fraunces Clarke, p. Brandon, co.
Suff., w. ..   .. 10 May 1658
John Paisley, p. Feltwell, co. Norf., w., &
Dorothy Wright, of W., w. ..   .. 25 Oct. „
Clement Thompson, p. Great Cressingham,
co. Norf., w., & Susanna Sell, of
W., w. ..   .. 5 Apr. 1659
Thomas Thompson, p. Great Cressingham, b.,
& Elizabeth Sell, of W., s.   ..   .. 23 May „
Thomas Bell, w., & Anne Mead, w., both
of W.   ..   .. 21 June „
George Leach, p. Cranhouse, w., & Elizabeth
Hall, w., of W.   ..   ..   .. 6 Sept. „
Richard Shinkfield, p. Methwold, co. Norf., w.,
& Amy Butcher, of W., s.   ..   .. 8 Sept. „
Thomas Lovell, w., & Anne Crane, w., both p.
Mildenhall, co. Suff.   ..   .. 13 Sept. „
Thomas Learner, p. Downham, co. Suff., w.,
& Esther Drinkmilke, p. Hockold, co.
Norf., w. ..   .. 15 Sept. „
John Geson, p. Northwold, co. Norf., w., &
Tryphena King, of W., w. ..   .. 22 Sept. „
John Barance, p. Estwell, co. Suff., b., & Mary
Lane, p. Brandon, co. Suff., s.   . 3 Oct. „
William James & Jane Costin, w., both p.
Brandon, co. Suff. ..   ..   .. 29 Nov. „
Nicholas Howell, b., & Amy Leigh, s., both p.
Hockold, co. Norf. ..   ..   .. 26 Dec. „

John Playfield, p. Feltwell, co. Norf., b., &
    Thomasine Throward, p. Northwold, s.   5 Jan. 1659
William Thornton, w., & Jane Stallinge, both
    p. Hockold, co. Norf.   ..   ..   16 Jan.   „

All Saints' Parish: VOLUME II *continued.*

John Bell, of Norwold, & Anna Fit, of Bran-
    don, w.   ..   ..   11 Oct. 1659
William Humfrey & Elizabeth Fit, both of
    Brandon ..   ..   11 Oct.   „
Robert Fuller & Alice Smith, both of Brandon   19 Oct.   „
Francis Huns & Anna White   ..   ..   5 Sept. 1661
Samuel Wright & Anna Morley   ..   ..   28 Jan.   „
John Dennys & Dorothy Secker, both of
    Hockwold   ..   ..   ..   3 Nov. 1663
Thomas Walman & Katherin Cooper   ..   28 Apr. 1664
William Lewis & Margaret Cooke ..   ..   3 May   „
John Haen & Mary Monings   ..   ..   19 May   „
John Cock & Margaret Russell   ..   ..   2 June   „
John Middleton & Anna Mark   ..   ..   20 Sept.   „
Richard Leban & Margaret Beeton   ..   8 Dec.   „
Robert West & Mary Beeton   ..   ..   31 Jan.   „
Thomas Sexton & Clemens Heed ..   ..   5 Oct. 1665
William Driver & Mary Ailmer   ..   ..   1 Nov.   „
Henry Ollet & Anna Heywood   ..   ..   19 Nov.   „
Thomas Cook & Thomasin Russell   ..   21 Nov.   „
Abraham Cock & Rose Rands   ..   ..   18 Apr. 1667
William Drinkmilk & Elizabeth White   ..   2 July   „
Edmond Crow & Mary Windout   ..   ..   2 July   „
William Armiger & Anna Reines   ..   ..   1 Aug.   „
John White & Rose Corner   ..   ..   7 May 1668
Joseph Michell & Anna Armiger   ..   ..   12 May   „
Valentine Richardson & Ann Cap ..   ..   12 Sept. 1671
John Steele, of Feltwell, & Elizabeth Wilson,
    of Wilton ..   ..   17 Sept. 1672
Thomas Thickpenny, of Hockwold, & Elizabeth
    Mandall, of Weeting   ..   ..   15 Oct.   „
John Adams & Mary Corner   ..   ..   31 Mar. 1673
Thomas Humphry, of Foulden, & Bridget
    Sancroft   ..   ..   2 Oct.   „

Christopher Hobard & Dorothy White	..	2 Dec. 1673
Thomas Lea & Mary Brooke	.. ..	4 Oct. 1674
William Elmer & Susan Heynor, of Hockwold		5 Nov. „
Richard Miller & Susan Rix	.. ..	26 July 1675
John Duffeild & Priscilla Rod		6 Apr. „
Thomas Dey & Anne Starling	.. ..	23 Apr. 1676
Edmund Nunne, of Northold, & Jane Raynes		15 Feb. „
John King & Mary Ollet ..	.. ..	21 Sept. 1677
Mr. William Holley & Mis. Katherine Bell ..		4 Mar. 1678
Thomas Johnson & Mary Bell	.. ..	19 Oct. 1679
James Gatherwale & Ann Booty ..	..	19 Apr. 1680
John Bladnell & Ann Cooke	..	6 May „
William Bampton & Deborah Feild	..	13 May „
Robert Barre & Ann Baker	..	24 June „
John Seke [?] & Margaret Corner ..		4 Oct. „
Thomas Spurn & Widow Ann Wright		14 Aug. 1681
Osbert Denton & Ann Bell	.. ..	8 Apr. 1684
John Barker & Elizabeth Capp, of Bromhill ..		26 Apr. „
Robert Gerard & Susan Woods	..	20 May 1685
John Capp & Ann Faux, of Bromehill	..	1 Jan. „
Robert Fenton & Mary Steward	.. ..	27 Mar. 1686
Thomas Spurn, w., & Ann Armiger, w.	..	25 July 1687
William Clark & Susan Madwell, of Brandon		23 Apr. 1688
John Marsh & Margaret Huns	.. ..	29 Oct. „
Francis Cann & Sarah Pattle	.. ..	11 Dec. „
Thomas Squire & Jane Hetherset, *lic.*	..	11 Apr. 1689
Richard Bacon & Stephany Huns ..		29 Sept. „
Thomas Docking & Ann Russel .		29 Mar. 1692
Richard Denton & Margaret Starling		9 Oct. „
John Gore & Elizabeth White	..	17 Jan. „
Richard Johnson & Ann Dye	..	30 Dec. 1694
John Loads & Ann White		28 Mar. 1695
George Fuller & Rachel Reynolds ..	..	15 July „
Thomas Huns & Mary Lane	.. ..	25 Aug. „
Thomas Armiger & Ann Reynolds	..	3 Oct. „
James Waman & Bridget Whitebread	..	21 Nov. „
Clement Prank & Bridget Cadge, w.		1 June 1697
Francis Ollet & Mary Hipkin, w.	..	4 Nov. „
John Secchar & Elizabeth Miller	..	2 Feb. „
John King & Elizabeth Sherman ..		9 July 1699

Robert Cook & Mary Minns	17 Oct.	1699
Thomas Cook & Mary Neal	11 Feb.	„
John Coningham & Mary Faux	12 Feb.	„
Isaac Thaunton & Frances Knights ..	23 Feb.	1700
Thomas White & Elizabeth Jordan ..	9 June	1701
William Man & Sarah Tenihee	30 Dec.	1703
Edmund Sibbs & Susan Knights	17 Aug.	1708
Robert Lindsey & Mary Hipkin	23 June	1713
John Knights & Amy Carter	16 Nov.	1714
Edward Sedon & Mary Mandal	24 June	1717
John Mash, jun., b., & Elizabeth White, w. ..	6 June	1718
William Baker & Rose White, s.	28 Oct.	„
Thomas Salmon, of Thetford, & Mary Jacob	19 Apr.	1720
Thomas Norman & Anne Loads	10 Nov.	„
Roger Bullock & Anne Walman	1 Nov.	1721
John Loads, jun., & Elizabeth Morley ..	21 June	1722
John Ward & Jane Howlett, s.	16 Oct.	1723
Austin Howlett & Margaret Docking ..	8 Dec.	„
William Baker, w., & Frances West, w. ..	2 Jan.	„
William Cob, of Brandon, w., & Anna Hooker, s.	26 Dec.	1724
John Knights, w., & Anne Armiger, w. ..	28 Dec.	„
John Turner, b., & Elizabeth Ollett, s. ..	12 Oct.	1725
Lawrence Bayly, b., & Jane Armiger, s. ..	13 Oct.	„
John Pooly, b., & Anne Ollett, s.	13 Jan.	1728
John Cadge, b., & Anne Bullock, w. ..	21 May	1729
John Gore, w., & Anne Greengrass, w. ..	23 Oct.	„
Henry Jarvis, b., & Mary Loads, s. ..	31 Mar.	1730
William Armiger, w., & Mary Ollett, w. ..	22 Sept.	„
Christopher Docking, b., & Anne Howlett, s.	11 Feb.	„
John Jacob, b., & Susannah Sayer, s. ..	2 Oct.	1734
John Child, b., & Mary Bullock, w. ..	8 July	1735
John Barton, b., & Mary Armiger, w. ..	18 Sept.	„
Daniel Leech, b., & Charity Nichols ..	8 Oct.	1736
John Mandal & Margaret Bowers, s. ..	13 Apr.	1737
Thomas Stuart & Mary Mandal, s.	7 Nov.	„
John Laws, b., & Jane Chising [?], s. ..	14 Sept.	1738
John Howard, b., & Honory Docking, s. ..	23 Dec.	„
John Knights, w., & Amy Whitham, s. ..	28 Aug.	1739
Matthew Dent, b., & Ann Howlett, w. ..	1 Oct.	„
Richard Knights, b., & Elizabeth Soden, w. ..	29 May	1740

William Palmer, w., & Elizabeth Cromer, w.	19 Apr.	1742
Francis Bullock, b., & Elizabeth Skipper, w.	15 July	„
Thomas Harrison, b., & Mary Tid, w. ..	19 Nov.	„
Henry Seeckar, b., & Mary Chalice, s. ..	8 Feb.	„
William Ottly, w., & Katharine Docking, s. ..	21 June	1743
Nicholas Tilbrooke, b., & Amy Mash, w. ..	2 Nov.	1744
William Palmer, w., & Mary Cany, w. ..	25 Aug.	1745
John Knights, w., & Margaret Laws, w. ..	30 Mar.	1746
John Whistler, b., & Elizabeth Rawling, s. ..	8 June	1747
John Cadds [?], w., & Margaret Knights, w. ..	28 June	„
John Skeete, w., & Sarah Walman, w.	7 Aug.	„
Sylvester Spinks, b., & Mary Seckar, s. ..	3 Oct.	„
Richard Butter, b., & Ann Wetherell ..	10 Apr.	1748
Francis Sturgeon & Mary Spinks	6 June	„
John Coates, of Wainford, w., & Frances Mussell [?], w.	2 Oct.	„

St. Mary's and All Saints': Volume IV.

Richard Butter & Mary White	29 Mar.	1749
George Davis & Elizabeth Cattes, p. All Saints'	11 Sept.	„
Zacharias Wilson & Ann Buckle, p. St. Mary	1 Oct.	„
William Jewel & Mary Turner, p. St. Mary	2 Oct.	„
Hugh Chilvers & Rose Ash, p. All Saints' ..	3 Feb.	„
John Chesten & Sarah Butter, p. St. Mary ..	8 Oct.	1750
Francis Jacob & Elizabeth Gore, p. St. Mary	30 Oct.	„
John Woods & Mary Baily, p. All Saints' ..	8 Apr.	1751
Francis Holmes & Ann Jewell, p. All Saints'	21 July	„
John Hardy & Margarett Rouse, p. All Saints'	30 Sept.	„
Nicholas Dickson & Mary Kidd, p. All Saints'	26 Mar.	1752
Thomas Butter & Mary Lewis, p. St. Mary ..	13 Nov.	„
John Gore & Lydia Say, p. All Saints' ..	5 July	1753
John Jewell & Lydia Gore, p. St. Mary ..	25 Oct.	„
John Russells, p. Feltwell, & Mary Pooley ..	*11 Feb.	1754

Volume V.

Francis Skinner, p. Downham Market, Norf., & Lætitia Minter, *lic.*	19 Oct.	1754
Benjamin Challess & Sarah Rust	29 Dec.	„

* After this date, unless otherwise stated, the parties are invariably of Weeting, and bachelor and spinster respectively.

John Tayler & Ruth Challess	29 Dec.	1754
John Malt & Sarah Torrington, *lic.* ..	24 Jan.	1755
Richard Chelson & Mary [Sarah] Church, *lic.*	29 Jan.	1756
John Tuck, p. Hockwould, & Mary Denton ..	16 June	„
Robert Arnol, w., & Elizabeth Tidd ..	10 Oct.	„
James Godferry & Anne Rolfe	10 Oct.	„
Robert Jackson, w., p. St. James', Bury St. Edmunds, & Fanny Musset, *lic.* ..	27 Feb.	1758
Andrew Rolph, w., p. Lakenheath, co. Suff., & Elizabeth Musset, *lic.*	27 Feb.	„
William Hardy & Sarah Durrant	3 Oct.	„
William Murrell, p. Caston, co. Norf., & Frances Neal, *lic.*	26 Mar.	1759
James Morley, p. Lakenheath, co. Suff., & Mary Mead, w., *lic.*	21 Aug.	„
John Mayes & Elizabeth White	12 Oct.	„
Richard Spinkfield, p. Feltwell, co. Norf., & Elizabeth Youngs	24 Oct.	„
John Denton, p. Stowlantoft, co. Suff., & Margaret Denton, *lic.*	26 Dec.	„
Robert Fletcher & Ann Pooley	10 June	1760
Thomas Russell & Hannah Anantrum ..	21 July	„
John Gore & Sarah Fowler, *lic.*	6 Oct.	„
Thomas Jacob, w., p. Wilton, co. Norf., & Sarah Gore, *lic.*	6 Oct.	„
James Sexton, p. Santon, Norf., & Sarah Fison	16 Dec.	„
Robert Boughen & Susanna Wright, both of Brumwell	27 Apr.	1761
Edmund Larkam, w., & Mary Hall ..	26 July	„
John Stimpson, p. Feltwell, & Ann Ash ..	31 Dec.	„
Francis Diggon, p. Brandon, co. Suff., & Frances Durrant, *lic.*	18 Oct.	1762
Michael Hardy, p. Methwold, co. Norfolk, & Ann Rotherham	20 Oct.	„
John Fisher, p. Brandon, & Jemima Roddell	1 Nov.	„
William Willet & Ann Jemson	17 Oct.	1763
William Macrow, p. Coolidge, co. Suff., & Mary Tuell	19 Nov.	„
William Feetom & Mary Turner	24 Apr.	1764
Edmund Preston & Sarah Roddell ..	28 May	„

John Younge & Mary Pymer, *lic.* ..	26 Nov.	1764
Joseph Frost & Elizabeth Duke	9 Dec.	,,
Duffield Billow, p. Taunton, & Jane Felgate, *lic.*	18 Jan.	1765
John Turner, p. Colchester, co. Essex, &		
Frances Pettit	12 Oct.	,,
William Fuller & Margaret Gathercole ..	12 Oct.	,,
William Burrows [*signs* Buroughs], & Ann		
Guttridge	3 Feb.	1766
Simon Wilkin, p. Brandon, & Sarah Loads,		
lic.	5 Apr.	,,
Thomas Butter, w., & Elizabeth Brown	1 Aug.	,,
Francis Jacob, w., & Ann Shingfield ..	6 July	1767
Ambrose Barton & Rachel Fuller	1 Nov.	,,
[1768, *no entry.*]		
Samuel Dolton & Elizabeth Sewell ..	15 Jan.	1769
Thomas Jacob, p. W. St. Mary's, & Sarah		
Miller, p. W. All Saints', *lic.* ..	24 May	,,
William Currey, p. Bromhill, & Mary Pymer	12 Feb.	1770
Thomas Hinard & Mary Spinks	11 July	,,
Jonathan Gostalan, p. Reresby, co. Lincoln, &		
Mary Spikin, *lic.*	17 Oct.	,,
John Newell & Diana Armiger	18 Oct.	,,
John Folks & Sarah Youngs	23 Oct.	,,
Joseph Frost, w., & Sarah Fuller, w.	1 Apr.	1771
John Cadge, w., & Mary Knights, w. ..	1 Apr.	,,
John Debenham, surgeon, p. Feltwell St.		
Mary's, & Amy Pymer, *lic.*	4 July	,,
William Potter & Mary Young	18 Oct.	,,
John Baldrey, w., & Susannah Gore, *lic.* ..	28 Dec.	,,
Steed Arnold & Ann Pate	11 Feb.	1772
Edmund Swan, p. West Dereham, & Sarah		
Gray	12 May	,,
William Goat, w., & Ann Painter, w. ..	6 July	,,
Edmund Preston, w., & Ann Barton ..	7 Aug.	,,
John Fisher & Ruth Younge, w.	30 Nov.	,,
Thomas Osbourn, w., & Elizabeth Mounson, w.	23 July	1773
Francis Jacob, w., & Ann Baldry	6 Sept.	,,
William Pymer & Mary Jewell	17 Sept.	,,
William Crow & Ann Youngs	29 Oct.	,,
William Pymer & Rachael Curry, *lic.* .	23 Dec.	,,

Thomas Bretnall & Susanna Whidby	..	27 Dec. 1773
Thomas Smith, p. Beechamwell, & Ann Dale		7 Feb. 1774
Thomas Veal & Mary Sanders	.. ..	6 June „
Joseph Bumstead, w., & Sarah Malt	..	2 Aug. „
Joseph Neale & Elizabeth Nash	.. ..	17 Oct. „
Charles Bumstead & Susannah Lodes, *lic.*	..	1 Nov. „
William Dyer, w., & Margaret Hardy	..	14 Nov. „
William Lee & Mary Butter	.. ..	14 Nov. „
James Pett & Mary Cadge, w.	.. ..	21 Nov. „
Robert Spalding & Dorothy Dey ..	..	12 Jan. 1775
James Morley, w., & Elizabeth Pooley	..	13 Feb. „
Isaac Turrington & Susan Bland	.. ..	20 Feb. „
William Bell & Ann Oliver	.. ..	5 Mar. „
Geofry Malt & Mary Hill ..	.. ..	10 Oct. „
Thomas Sucker & Sarah Warner	..	20 Nov. „
John Butter & Ann Whistler	.. ..	14 Feb. 1776
Joshua Denton, p. St. Martin's, co. Middlesex, & Martha Leech, *lic.*	.. ..	15 Apr. „
Robert Fletcher, w., & Ann Newell, *lic.*	..	20 Sept. „
Thomas Smith, w., p. Bitchamwell [*sic*], & Ann Youngs, w., *lic.*	.. ..	31 Dec. „
*Robert Owen, p. Brandon, co. Suff., & Ann Spink, *lic.* ..	.. ..	23 June 1777
William Bolton, b., of W., & Elizabeth Drew, s., p. Brandon, co. Suff., *lic.* ..	..	22 Aug. „
Thomas Butter, b., & Elizabeth Butter, s., both of W.	.. .. ..	21 Feb. 1778
Roger Watts, b., p. Brandon, & Mary Frost, s., of W. ..	.. .. ..	11 Oct. „
Samuel Jarvis, b., & Elizabeth Sands, s., both of W.	.. .. ..	12 Oct. „
Edmund Parker & Ann Tuck	.. ..	28 Oct. 1778
Thomas Steward, p. Brandon, co. Suff., & Ann Leech, *lic.*	.. .. ..	29 Dec. „
John Bright & Alice Warner	.. ..	9 Sept. 1779
John Feetham, p. Methwold, & Elizabeth Worman ..	.. .. ..	18 Sept. „

* NOTE.—Robert Owen's "Licence", entered in Marriage Register, is probably a mistake, as the banns were published, and they were married the day after they were out.

Thomas Bretnal, w., p. Feltwel St. Mary, &
    Alice Rayner .. .. .. 28 Dec. 1779
John Harrod & Elizabeth Cornell, *lic.* .. 29 Dec. „
John Malt & Amy Mason, *lic.* .. .. 31 Mar. 1780
John Bond & Catherine Mead .. .. 5 Oct. „
William Collins & Alice Bright, w. .. 12 Oct. „
Joshua Nunn, w., p. Rockland St. Andrew, co.
    Norf., & Ann Salisbury, *lic.* .. .. 2 Sept. 1781
John Malt, w., & Mary Allison, p. Brandon, *lic.* 6 Jan. 1782
William Dell, p. Brandon, & Martha Curry,
    lic. .. .. 6 July „
Nathaniel Bacon & Catharine Sallett .. 29 Oct. „
John Speed & Flora Towler, *lic.* .. .. 4 Jan. 1783
Thomas Gamble & Catharine Bond, w. [*sic,*
    out of order], *lic.* .. .. .. 28 Nov. 1793
    "Here new Register stamped with 3d. duty."
John Rayner, w., & Mary Hunns .. .. 23 Feb. 1784
Richard Hubbard, w., p. Foulden, co. Norf., &
    Elizabeth Jewell, w., *lic.* .. .. 24 Feb. „
Robert Fletcher, w., & Jane Lorrimer, w.,
    lic. .. .. 5 Mar. „
William Wakeford, p. Christchurch, co. Surrey,
    & Frances Murrell .. .. .. 13 Apr. „
Robert Shaldon, w., & Sarah Frost, w. .. 17 June „
Robert Towler & Amy Malt, w. .. .. 25 Oct. „
George Kitson & Mary Jacob, *lic.* .. .. 8 Feb. 1785
John Lawrence, w., & Mary Harwood, w. .. 14 Feb. „
William Ward & Mary Lea, w. .. .. 23 Sept. „
George Turner & Susannah Mays .. .. 4 Nov. „
Samuel Rayner & Mary Towler .. .. 17 Oct. 1786
Francis Fincham, p. Feltwell St. Nicholas, &
    Mary Fuller .. .. .. 17 Nov. „
William Lawrence, p. Croxton, & Elizabeth
    Newton .. .. 5 Dec. „
Thomas Allard & Mary Fincham .. .. 8 Dec. „
    [1787, *no entry.*]
John Holmes, w., p. Wangford, co. Suff., &
    Mary Hynard, w. .. .. .. 23 Jan. 1788
Edmund Jacob & Elizabeth Dixon .. .. 24 Jan. „
Henry Judd & Mary Wiseman .. .. 2 June „

Peter Garner, p. Little Cressingham, co. Norf.,
    & Mary Newell .. .. 10 June 1788
John Armiger & Anne Painter .. .. 20 June „
William Harvey, p. Maney, in Isle of Ely, co.
    Cambridge, & Martha Neale, *lic.* .. 7 Oct. „
William Townsend, p. Fornham All Saints',
    co. Suff., & Ann Chilvers .. .. 1 Dec. „
James Gant & Eliza Maria Jacob .. .. 2 Feb. 1789
Richard Wiseman & Mary Feetham 1 July „
William Neale & Ann Farrow .. .. 17 Dec. „
James Armiger & Elizabeth Miller .. 15 Feb. 1790
John Mash, w., & Susannah Cane, w. .. 28 Sept. „
James Jacob & Jane Bradfield, p. Stoke, co.
    Norf., *lic.* .. .. 7 Oct. „
William Hewitt & Mary Preston, *lic.* .. 1 Jan. 1791
    "Stamped Register ends here."
William Fuller & Lydia Arnold .. .. 13 Feb. „
Charles Saunders, esq., & Sarah Bradfield, p.
    Stoke, co. Norf., *lic.* .. .. 10 Mar. „
Joseph Watson & Mary Catton, *lic.* .. 10 Mar. „
Robert Harrood & Ann Jee, p. Igburgh, co.
    Norf., *lic.* .. .. 10 Mar. „
Simon Hensby, p. St. Peter's, Thetford, co.
    Norf., & Mary Barton .. .. 21 Mar. „
John Malen, p. Chippenham, co. Cambridge,
    & Susan Morley .. .. .. 9 Jan. 1792
Robert Bullock & Mary Bell .. .. 5 Nov. „
James Thompson, p. Mendham, co. Norf., &
    Lydia Willett .. .. .. 29 Dec. „
John Whisker, p. Brandon, co. Suff., & Ann
    Youngs, *lic.* .. .. .. 16 Jan. 1793
Valentine Leach & Jane Stackwood .. 26 Jan. „
George Grigson, w., p. Eriswell, co. Suff., &
    Elizabeth Hood, *lic.* .. .. 8 Apr. „
Robert Carter, p. Culford, co. Suff., &
    Margaret Fuller .. .. .. 15 May „
Thomas Gamble [*inserted after* 1783, *which see*] 28 Nov. „
John Eagle & Elizabeth Barton .. .. 29 Dec. „
Robert Everett, p. Swaffham, & Elizabeth
    Wellingham, *lic.* .. .. .. 19 Mar. 1794

Francis Diggins [*signs* Diggons], p. Brandon,
   & Mary Jee, *lic.* ..   ..   ..   3 Apr.   1794
John Tuck & Jane Short ..   ..   ..   10 Apr.   „
John Evered & Ann Fitt ..   ..   ..   8 Dec.   „
John Parker, p. Whivestone, & Susannah
    Chelvers ..   ..   29 Dec.   „
Thomas Dent & Elizabeth Pooley, *lic.*   ..   15 Oct.   1795
James Andrews, p. Timworth, & Mary Hem-
    ington, w., *lic.*   ..   ..   ..   31 Mar.   1796
William Darkens & Elizabeth Drew   ..   30 Apr.   „
Samuel Dalton & Sarah Youngs, *lic.*   ..   21 Aug.   „
Benjamin Webb & Eleanor Neal ..   ..   27 Nov.   „
James Arnold, p. Santon, & Sarah Newel   ..   29 Nov.   „
John Jewell & Sarah Folks   ..   ..   13 Feb.   1797
John Pooley & Jane Jee, *lic.*   ..   ..   9 Oct.   „
John Newton & Elizabeth Wiseman   11 Nov.   „
John Hudson & Susannah Malt ..   ..   13 Mar.   1798
James Roper, p. Brandon, & Elizabeth
    Pymore ..   ..   11 Sept.   „
John Butters & Mary Lee   ..   ..   16 Apr.   1799
Abraham Higham, p. Stutton, co. Suff., &
    Phœbe Rounce, *lic.*   ..   ..   23 July   „
Benjamin Challess & Mary Almer ..   19 Oct.   „
John Everet & Elizabeth Nicholls ..   ..   28 Oct.   „
John Land, p. Stoke Dereham, & Susannah
    Bradfield, *lic.*   ..   ..   ..   20 Nov.   1800
William Newell & Sarah Hubbard   ..   13 Dec.   „
William Winderston, p. Torrington, & Mary
    Jarrad   ..   ..   5 Jan.   1801
Thomas Newton & Mary Salter   ..   ..   9 May   „
John Pymore & Mary Rampling, *lic.*   ..   16 Sept.   1802
John Howard, p. Westley, & Margaret Dalton,
    lic.   ..   ..   7 Oct.   „
Henry Malt & Elizabeth Fisher   ..   ..   12 Oct.   „
James Dyer & Elizabeth Tuck   ..   ..   6 Nov.   „
Henry Whistler & Hannah Greenfield   ..   11 Jan.   1803
John Greenfield & Susan Whistler   ..   9 May   „
Edward Bullock & Lydia Spalding   ..   27 June   „
John Harply & Sarah Secker   ..   ..   12 Dec.   „
Benjamin Petitt, w., & Hannah Ellington   ..   9 Apr.   1804

John Armanger, w., & Mary Bone, w. ..	3 July	1804
John Green & Phyllis Wallum, w.	5 Feb.	1805
James Gathercole & Susan Palmer, banns and		
consent of parents	28 Sept.	1806
William Arnold & Anne Ashby, p. Brandon	12 Oct.	„
William Nichols & Elizabeth Osborne ..	19 Oct.	„
Thomas Spencer & Alice Collins	1 Dec.	,.
James Hunt, p. Wilbraham Prior, co. Cam-		
bridge, & Susan Young, aged 21 years, *lic.*	5 Feb.	1807
John Arminger, w., & Ann Arnold, w. ..	9 Mar.	„
John Wade & Elizabeth Towler, w., *lic.* ..	5 May	„
Frances Tuddenham Snare, p. Brandon, &		
Margaret Roberts Richardson ..	13 Oct.	„
Francis Jacob, w., p. Northwold, co. Norfolk, &		
Sarah Cornell, *lic.*	14 Jan.	1808
Edward Laws & Mary Bowers .. .	15 May	„
John Breese & Maria James	29 Jan.	1809
William Moody & Mary Heigham	20 Nov.	„
Roger Gee [*signs* Jee], & Susan Cooper, *lic.*	25 Oct.	1810
Mark Leak & Frances Collings	6 Nov.	„
Robert Kent, p. Brandon, & Ann Culingford,		
banns and consent of parents ..	11 June	1811
William Thompson & Frances Russell ..	12 Aug.	„
James Secker & Alice Alerson	8 Nov.	„
John Bowyer, p. Poslington, co. Suff., & Ann		
Gant	11 Feb.	1812
George William Cockrell, p. Wisbeach, Isle of		
Ely, & Jemima Knock	29 Dec.	„

Marriages at Carleton Rode,

1560 to 1812.

NOTE.—The Marriages of Carleton Rode, near Attleborough, are contained in four volumes.

Volume I measures 14 in. by 7¾ in., and contains thirty-three leaves of parchment, generally in very good order. This volume contains the Marriages 1560 to 1637, as well as the Baptisms 1560 to 1653, and Burials 1560 to 1650.

Volume II measures 12¼ in. by 8½ in., and contains forty-two parchment leaves. In it are recorded the Marriages 1654 to 1706, but it is deficient 1638 to 1653 inclusive. It also contains Baptisms and Burials from 1654 to about 1706.

Volume III contains fifty-eight leaves, and contains the Marriages from 1710 to 1754, with Baptisms and Burials 1710 to 1797.

Volume IV contains Baptisms and Burials only, from c. 1796 to 1812; about a dozen leaves have been cut away which possibly contained the missing Marriages 1802 to 1812.

Volume V is the usual book of printed forms, and contains the Marriages 1754 to 1802.

These Marriages have been most obligingly transcribed from the original Register by W. T. Bensly, Esq., LL.D., F.S.A., assisted by the Rev. A. J. Back, Rector of Carleton Rode, by whose permission they are now printed. The entries have been carefully collated with the original books by Mr. Frederic Johnson, of Norwich.

VOLUME I.

John Bannock & Ellen Durante, w.	..	22 Sept. 1560
Stephen Pyle & Agnes Browne	.. ..	3 Nov. ,,
Thomas Carter & Isabell Racle	.. ..	7 Dec. ,,
John Browne & Isabell Wilson	..	16 Jan. ,,
John Maliet & Joane Tayler, w.	..	26 Jan. ,,
Robert Swanton & Ales Sherwin	..	10 Feb. ,,
Thomas Rudd & Joane Beymont	..	17 Feb. ,,
Martyn Sewell & Emme Curling	..	26 Apr. 1561
Stephen Long & Matha Smith	..	8 June ,,
Thomas Smith & Isabell Ringold	..	24 Aug. ,,
Robert Lewold & Kirchin Drake	..	14 Sept. ,,
Thomas Jubye & Isabell Page	..	2 Nov. ,,
William Kempe & Margaret Britwin	..	25 Apr. 1562

Stephen Smith & Margaret Palmer	..	7 Sept. 1562
John Cole & Agnes Cornwell	.. ..	7 Sept. „
John Clifton & Margery Youngman	..	12 Dec. „
Thomas Lycenz & Cathcrin Gonne	..	28 Jan. „
Edward Fuller & Margaret Palmer	..	1 July 1563
Thomas Briggs & Margaret Youngman	..	7 Oct. „
Thomas Suckling & Ellen Youngman, w.	..	13 Oct. „
John Fullwood & Joane Waynford	..	17 Oct. „
Clement Raynolds & Margaret Youngman	..	14 Nov. „
Thomas Lincolne & Agnes Randell	..	4 June 1564
Willam Boule & Agnes Waynford	..	25 June „
John Edwards & Katherin Gosfeld	..	24 Sept. „
William Parish & Marion Bowle	.. ..	12 Oct. „
William Lincolne & Elsabeth Mufforth	..	9 Feb. „
William Fuk & Margaret Longe	.. ..	8 July 1565
Robert Edwards & Elsabeth Hinde	..	29 July „
John Kempe & Joane Juby	..	11 Oct. „
John Moyes & Ursula Cocke	..	23 Feb. „
Robert Joell & Elizabeth Baxter	..	28 Apr. 1566
William Briggs & Elsabeth Daniell	..	3 Sept. „
Stephen Britwin & Thomasin Goldsmith	..	19 Sept. „
Robert Juby & Agnes Page	..	6 Oct. „
Clement Smith & Mary Briggs	..	12 Feb. „
Robert Symons & Mary Daynes	..	26 May 1567
William Longe & Rose Gosfeld	..	2 Oct. „
Thomas Youngman & Margaret Boule	..	5 Oct. „
Richard Briggs & Ales Rogell	..	23 Apr. 1568
William Page & Martha Denne	..	4 June „
Stephen Ringold & Frances Smith	..	18 July „
Robert Juby & Anne Tottell	..	1 Aug. „
Robert Nune & Dorothe Juby	..	23 Sept. „
Peter Poll & Isabell Youngman	..	2 Oct. „
Richard Juby & Margaret Edwards	..	24 Oct. „
Richard Hurning & Margerie Youngman	..	9 Oct. 1569
Thomas Fuller & Mary Twogood	..	14 Oct. „
Robert Starling & Katherin Cliffer	..	27 Oct. „
Thomas Edwards & Margaret Howlit	..	27 Nov. „
Clement Smith & Jelyon Wells	..	28 Jan. „
Thomas Blood & Margaret Youngman	..	4 May 1570
Jeremy Eldred & Katherin Baxter	..	28 May „

Stephen Smith & Alis Ringold	18 June 1570
William Juby & Anne Youngman	24 Sept. „
Thomas Heyward & Cecily Youngman ..	25 Oct. „
Thomas Smith & Margaret Feeke	29 Oct. „
Clement Barber & Dorothe Woods ..	28 Apr. 1571
William Bannister & [———] [———] ..	17 June „
Barthelmew Osborne & Agnes Brette ..	1 Jan. „
Sergent Raynolds & Alis Bannester ..	8 June 1572
Robert Brytiff & Isabell Briggs	14 Sept. „
Robert Joell & Cecily Smith	30 Sept. „
Thomas Longe & Agnes Andrewes ..	2 Oct. „
John Poynter & Mary Bemont	9 Oct. „
Frances Cobb & Agnes Machin	2 Nov. „
John Bannister & Kirchin Briggs	8 Dec. „
Henry Miles & Dorothe Britiff ..	9 May 1573
Thomas Youngman & Faith Newby ..	28 June „
Richard Kempe & Joane Edwards . ..	23 Aug. „
William Edwards & Mary Cundall ..	18 Oct. „
Mathew Curling & Martha Raynolds ..	20 June 1574
John Longe & Isabell Youngman	3 Oct. „
Miles Buxton & Avis Youngman	2 Nov. „
Benet Brytiff & Brigit Shyrife	22 Nov. „
Thomas Brett & Agnes Handford	30 Mar. 1575
Robert Swanton & Elsabeth Buttle ..	29 May „
Thomas Youngman & Margaret [———] ..	26 June „
Clement Smith & Joane Lewold	30 Sept. „
Thomas Fell & Agnes Newby	9 Oct. „
Nicholas Palmer & Margaret Kempe ..	23 Oct. „
Thomas Billand & Joane Thunder ..	7 Nov. „
John Kempe & Agnes Partryck	7 Feb. „
John Koggell & Kirchin Youngman ..	1 July 1576
Thomas Baxter & Elsabeth Buttell ..	21 Oct. „
William Henry & Maute Youngman ..	17 Dec. „
John Burges & Maring Page	12 Feb. „
Richard Vinne & Elsabeth Denne	2 May 1577
Gregory Sherwin & Dorothe Garham ..	11 Aug. „
Henry Benet & Margaret Martyn	11 July 1578
Frances Howell & Elizabeth Machin ..	3 Aug. „
John Newby & Mary Gray	26 Oct. „
John Longe & Anne Sparow	14 June 1579

William Youngman & Isabell Sherwin	..	21 June 1579
Robert Lucas & Katherin Thirketle	..	20 Sept. „
Henry Brigs & Elizabeth [———] ..	..	25 Oct. „
Richard Newnam & Joane Bret ..	..	15 May 1580
Richard Briggs & Anne Partrick ..	..	31 July „
John Metlesse & Elizabeth Bunne ..	..	9 Oct. „
Mathew Pyle & Alis Waynford ..	..	27 Nov. „
Thomas Youngman & Cecily Carter	..	16 Jan. „
Robert Norton & Margaret Smith ..	..	26 June 1581
Thomas Baldry & Elizabeth Crickmer	..	10 July „
Thomas Newby & Margaret Ungar	..	13 Aug. „
Nicholas Spane & Alis Pyle ..	..	15 Oct. „
Thomas Feeke & Oliva Partricke ..	..	13 Oct. 1582
Henry Machine & Anne More ..	..	17 Oct. 1583
Stephen Feeke & Oliva Hamont ..	..	4 May 1584
George Evans & Margaret Canne ..	..	10 May „
Gerrad Goldspin & Agnes Hartly ..	..	29 June „
Richard Gratie & Agnes Blome ..	..	19 Dec. „
William Myllet & Elizabeth Lewold	..	— — „
Henry Youngman & Alis Taylor ..	..	15 May 1585
Richard Youngman & Katherine Weeks	..	30 May „
Francis Edwards & Faith Clarke ..	..	30 Aug. „
Richard Carter & Katherine Boule ..	..	28 Dec. „
William Duson & Anne Benet ..	..	3 Apr. 1586
Robert Feeke & Margaret Punder ..	..	16 Apr. „
William Shirwine & Isabell Briggs	..	7 June „
John Harling & Frances Ryminton	..	31 July „
Thomas Hamont & Margaret Kempe	..	16 Sept. „
James Skeete & Anne Goosse ..	..	13 Oct. „
William Buttell & Katherine Blome	..	26 Oct. „
Nicholas Partrick & Margaret Grene	..	6 Feb. „
Thomas Sparow & Margaret Briggs	..	24 Aug. 1587
Edward Kempe & Kirchin Longe ..	..	21 Sept. „
Thomas Carter & Anne Smith ..	..	28 May 1588
Edward Murton & Margery Feeke ..	..	10 Oct. „
Thomas Longe & Alis Sparow ..	..	21 Oct. „
Stephen Sherwine & Martha Pyle ..	.	19 Nov. „
John Dobbes & Joane Juby ..	..	16 Dec. „
Edward Rushbrocke & Margaret Briggs	..	24 June 1589
Anthoney Britwine & Joane Kerrison	..	5 Aug. „

John Poll & Joane Briggs	..	.. 14 Oct. 1589
Thomas Feeke & Margaret Sparow		.. 28 Oct. „
Richard Nudds & Anne Sparke		.. 27 Dec. „
John Dymont & Agnes Parker	..	.. 29 Dec. „
Thomas Machine & Emme Clarke	..	.. 12 Feb. „
John Sherwine & Prudence Lynet		.. 21 Apr. 1590
John Briggs & Cecilye Raynolds	..	.. 8 June „
Thomas Briggs & Isabell Poll	..	29 Sept. „
John Lewold & Agnes Palmer	..	.. 20 Oct. „
John Sherwine & Marye Skote	..	.. 14 Feb. „
Stephen Kempe & Agnes Alexander		.. 25 July 1591
William Briggs & Elizabeth Poll	..	.. 10 Aug. „
William Juby & Joane Miller	..	.. 18 Oct. „
Robert Long & Martha Bowle	..	.. 30 Oct. „
John Lancer & Margaret Balden	..	.. 8 Feb. „
Richard Nudds & Agnes Raynolds		.. 28 Mar. 1592
Mathew Woods & Agnes Youngman		.. 27 July „
Robert Juby & Elizabeth Britwin	..	.. 4 Aug. „
John Kempe & Margaret Wodshed		.. 10 Oct. „
Sergent Raynolds & Agnes Poll	..	.. 28 Nov. „
John Pyle & Martha Page	..	.. 13 Aug. 1593
Gregory Walter & Joane Buttell	..	.. 29 Aug. „
Walter Diamont & Agnes Rosweth		.. 29 Sept. „
John Youngman & Elizabeth Edwards		.. 10 Oct. „
Robert Claxton & Grace Machen	..	.. 24 June 1594
John Sparow & Anna Barker	..	1 Aug. „
John Machen & Bridgit Hewke	..	14 Aug. „
Robert Machen & Margaret Norton		.. 28 Oct. „
Thomas Machen & Dorothe Feek	..	.. 1 Nov. „
William Buttell & Agnes Lewold	..	.. 29 Sept. 1595
Robert Flecher & Joane Walter	..	.. 28 Oct. „
Robert Longe & Margaret Neave	..	.. 28 Oct. „
Thomas Lytle & Agnes Smith	..	.. 10 Nov. „
Gregory Sherwin & Elizabeth Smith		.. 16 Jan. „
John Davy & Anne Watson	..	.. 21 Jan. „
Edmund Sowden & Katherin Frarie		.. 30 May 1596
Thomas Sparow & Sara Blome	..	.. 21 Sept. „
Robert Smith & Anne Bannocke	..	.. 30 Sept. „
Stephen Chapman & Anne Briggs	..	.. 24 Aug. 1597
William Archer & Agnes Girling	..	.. 7 Jan. „

William Randall & Margarete Reynolds	..	30 July 1598
Stephen Greve & Mary Edwards ..	..	5 Oct. ,,
Thomas Heiward & Agnes Archer, w.	..	8 Aug. 1599
Edmund Gosfield [?] & Margery Barber	..	25 Aug. ,,
Richard Briggs & Margarete Poll ..	..	20 Sept. ,,
Stephen Pyle & Isbell Britwine ..	..	8 Nov. ,,
Richard Page & Martha Yelverton ..	..	2 Jan. ,,
William Cliffon & Anne Juby	..	12 Aug. 1600
Robert Miles & Siblye Leman	..	14 Sept. ,,
William Long & Mathew Reynolds	..	25 Sept. ,,
Gregorie Carter & Frances Nunam	..	15 Dec. ,,
Thomas Malster & Margaret Barber	..	22 Jan. ,,
John Norman & Margaret Skeper ..	..	17 Sept. 1601
Hamnet Hyde & Anne Juby	..	3 Nov. ,,
John Brightin & Alis Briggs	..	— — ,,
John Winter & Katerine Nunham ..	..	27 June 1602
Richard Brighten & Margaret Edwards	..	29 June ,,
Robert Kempe & Mary Winder	..	4 Sept. ,,
John Carman & Mary Youngman ..	..	21 Sept. ,,
Richus Briggs & Fortune Wade	..	13 Nov. ,,
Nicholas Walter & Mary Nuby	..	22 Dec. ,,
William Week & Martha Long	..	3 Jan. ,,
Thomas Youngman & Amy Pile ..	..	6 Jan. ,,
Robert Punder & Margaret [—— ?]	..	— — ,,
William Sage, of Aslacton, & Martha, d. of		
John Long, sen., this p. ..	..	28 June 1603
Richard Brightin & Margaret Kempe	..	24 Aug. ,,
Richard Jex & Thomasin Dunkhorne	..	12 Mar. ,,
Thomas Kempe & Mathy Chapman	.	3 July 1604
Sergeant Brightin & Elizabeth Rangs	..	19 July ,,
Steven Kempe & Alis Chapman ..	..	— — 1605
Richard Palmar & Isabell Brighten	..	26 Sept. ,,
John Nuby & Alis Harman	..	17 Oct. ,,
John Baxter & Margaret Smith ..	..	22 Oct. ,,
Gregory Feeke & Elizabeth Charnell	..	27 Oct. ,,
John Long, jun., & Margaret Singleton	..	2 June 1606
John Beales & Margaret Sadde ..	..	21 Aug. ,,
John Briggs & Elizabeth Wade ..	..	24 June 1607
Daniell Warbutton & Joane Wase	..	— June 1608
Stephen Feeke & Elizabeth Eldred	..	25 Jan. ,,

Daniell Siclemore & Mary Youngman	24 Apr.	1609
Guliclmus Fecke & Isabel Clerke ..	14 Sept.	,,
Richardus Graty, jun., & Margaret Youngman	1 May	1610
William Punder & Elizabeth Stooks	12 June	,,
Henry Coper & Anne Brightin	26 June	,,
William Punder & Elizabeth Stokes	12 June	,,
Stephen Brightine & Emme Palmer	3 Sept.	,,
John Narford & Mary White	22 Aug.	1611
Gregorie Sherwin & Maria Pytman	10 Oct.	,,
Thomas Estow & Jane Gratie	17 Mar.	,,
Joseph Snelling & Mary Miles	30 Sept.	1612
Stephen Wade & Alis Brighten, w.	25 May	1613
John Nunam & Katerine Lator	20 June	,,
William Long & Anne Weeks	18 Sept.	,,
Robert Sheley & Elizabeth Churchman	21 Sept.	,,
William Parish & Elizabeth Woodshet	11 Nov.	,,
Thomas Yowngman, s. of John Yowngman, & Alice, d. of Jo. Dover, gent.	27 Jan.	,,
Henry Holden & Frances Adams ..	3 July	1614
John Gosling, *alias* Gislingam, & Susan Sherwen ..	31 May	1615
John Long & Elizabeth Feke	9 June	,,
Daynell Yongman & Elizabeth Marten	27 July	,,
John Newbye & Priscill Butell	17 Sept.	,,
Peter Pooll & [———] [———]	— Sept.	,,
Daynell Myllett & Esbell Pylle	— Oct.	,,
Richard Leader & Janne Anolde	15 Jan.	,,
John Kempe & Martha Carter	20 May	1616
William Miles & Elizabeth Kempe ..	24 June	,,
Robert Machin & Margery Dauson	29 July	,,
Nathan Youngman & Trephena Allan	2 Oct.	,,
William Page & Elizabeth Youngman	12 Oct.	,,
William Long & Mary Tuffts	22 Oct.	,,
John Smith, *alias* Foulsham, & Alice Newnham	29 Oct.	,,
John Herne & Elizabeth Hubberd, w.	4 Mar.	,,
William Brytayne & Martha Chapman	1 May	1617
Thomas Garrard & Elizabeth Jubie	19 June	,,
Thomas Longe & Dorithe Kempe ..	24 June	,,
Robert Sharp & Alice Gold	21 Aug.	,,

William Buttall & Joane Pile	.. ..	10 Dec. 1617
Elias Youngman & Anne Bulman ..	..	4 June 1618
William Mathew & Christian Long	..	30 July „
William Champlin & Elizabeth Youngman	..	4 Oct. „
Henry Miles & Anne Pile ..	.. ..	30 Nov. „
Richard Buttall & Anne Briggs	..	10 Dec. „
Sydraac Armes & Jone Browne	..	29 Mar. 1619
Stephen Long & Katherine Feeke ..		30 Mar. „
Robert Adoms & Grace Greanewaie	..	23 June 1620
John Chapman & [———] [———]		14[?] Aug. „
Victor Pursor & Elizabeth Smithe	..	5 Oct. „
John Newnham & Marye Juby	.. ..	15 Oct. „
John Youngman & Ann Florie	.. ..	20 Oct. „
John Youngman & Susan Vinyor ..	..	12 Nov. „
Stephen Youngman & Fides Nubie	..	2 Oct. 1621
Richard Juby & Mary Feeke	..	11 June 1622
Francis Bullen & Mary Bowgen	.. ..	2[?] Aug. „
Robert Smith & Mary Briteing	.. ..	13 Aug. „
John Reyner & Dorothy Smith	.. ..	13 Aug. „
Gregory Carter & Jone Smith	.. ..	12 Sept. „
Christopher Pinder & Mary Norgett	..	4 May 1623
Richard Jubie & Mary Kempe	.. ..	28 Sept. „
John Canne & Susan Punder	.. ..	2 Oct. „
Stephen Pile & Alice Reeve	.. ..	6 June 1624
Thomas Feeke & Ann Smith	..	28 Sept. „
Stephen Long & Barbara Reeve ..	..	20 Aug. 1625
Firmin[?] Greenwood & Elizabeth Millett	..	26 Nov. „
Daniell Smith & Avicia Miller	.. ..	29 June 1626
Richard Brigges & Mary Carter	..	15 Aug. „
Nicholas Walter & Margaret Staffie	..	24 Nov. „
Edward Kempe & Grace Parker	..	29 July 1627
Robert Jubie & Mary Brigges	..	9 Sept. „
Francis Jubie, w., & Margaret Browne, w.	..	9 Sept. „
John Jubie & Jane Machin	.. ..	25 Sept. „
Thomas Youngman, w., & Margaret Brigges	10 Nov. „
Richard Ince [?] & Elizabeth Edwardes	..	12 Nov. „
Thomas Machin & Bridget Jackson	..	26 Nov. „
John Nicolas & Mary Winter	.. ..	14 Jan. „
John Waters & Susan Youngman ..	..	24 Apr. 1628
John Rivett & Annisia Youngman ..	..	30 June „

Thomas Kempe & Elizabeth Kempe	..	29 July	1628
William Kempe & Elizabeth Punder	..	23 Sept.	,,
William Jubie & Ann Lister	.. ..	30 Sept.	,,
Robert Clifton & Elizabeth Eldred	..	16 Oct.	,,
Thomas Carter & Susan Kempe	.. ..	2 Feb.	,,
Stephen Chapman & Mary Saboth		9 July	1629
Thomas Machin & Ann Eldred	.. ..	29 Sept.	,,
John Norton & Elizabeth Hill	.. ..	8 Feb.	,,
Edward Browne & Ann Brice	..	11 July	1630
Richard Osborne & Mary Bond, w.	..	10 Aug.	,,
James Greme & Mary Wade	..	24 Aug.	,,
Thomas Waller & Ann Hall	.. ..	5 Sept.	,,
Philip Sparrow & Elizabeth Bullen	..	10 Oct.	,,
Thomas Parsie [? Pursie] & Ann Brigges	..	2 Nov.	,,
John Foyster & Margaret Barbar	.. ..	29 Jan.	,,
John Danie [? Dauie], w., & Rose Sharpe, w.		24 Feb.	,,
Richard Hind & Elizabeth Browne	...	12 Apr.	1631
John Garrad & Elizabeth Long	..	15 July	1632
Stephen Shirwin & Bridget Flatman	..	22 July	,,
John Nixon & Mary Hamond		25 Sept.	,,
Henry Barnes & Faith Palmer	.. ..	27 Sept.	,,
Richard Jubie & Elizabeth Moore	.. ..	10 Jan.	,,
William Parson & Dorothy Bullen	..	11 Feb.	,,
Miles Wittam & Faith Machin	.. ..	22 Apr.	1633
William Buttall & Mary Kempe	..	27 May	,,
Thomas Brightayne & Mary Long	..	24 June	,,
William Wellam & Margaret Newnham		28 Oct.	,,
Thomas Poll & Sarah Briggs	..	26 Jan.	,,
Thomas Heyward & Susannah Wade	..	10 Feb.	1634
William Cooke & Alice Cooke		7 Apr.	1635
William Page & Alice Woolstone	..	3 Oct.	,,
Robert Lincolne & Mary Brighten		19 Apr.	1636
John Filbye & Mathea Youngman	..	15 Aug.	,,
Christopher Lincolne & Phebe Kemp	..	18 Oct.	,,
Nicholas Walter & [———] Barton, w.	..	22 Feb.	,,
Nathan Panton & Elizabeth Osborne, w.	..	11 Apr.	1637
Nicolas Palmer & Mary Brigtinge	.. ..	30 May	,,
Edmond Nortton & Mary Masteres	..	2 Oct.	,,
Robert Grene & [———] Breffe, w.		30 Nov.	,,
Richard Kempe & Mary Sewell	.. ..	25 May	,,

Richard Brighting & Elizabeth Poll   .. 29 June 1637
[*Deficient from 1637 to 1654.*]

Volume II.
Robart Juby, b., & Elizabeth Rust, s., p.
  Lopham ..   .. 24 Apr. 1654
Edward Kempe, b., & Alice Kempe, s.   .. 10 Oct. „
Tobias Barnard, p. Skeyton, clarke, & Dorothie
  Howse, s., p. Carlton, by consent of
  parents ..   .. 10 Jan. „
Steaphen Kemp, b., & Mary Longe, s.   .. 16 Apr. 1655
Thomas Carter, b., & Martha Hacon, s., p.
  Tybinham   ..   ..   .. 6 Sept. „
Richard Nuby, b., p. Moulton, & Mary
  Girling, s.   ..   ..   .. 2 Oct. „
William Gallard, b., & Margarett Potter, s., p.
  Bestrop ..   .. 29 Apr. 1656
John Tayler, b., & Elizabeth Poll, s., both p.
  Bunwell ..   .. 19 Aug. „
William Britinge, w., & Mary Revitt, w.   .. 23 Jan. „
Richard Baxter, w., p. Tevetshall, & Prudence
  Fullcher, s.   ..   ..   .. 24 Jan. „
Richard Grenewode, b., & Elizabeth Woodes, s. 19 May 1657
William Kempe, b., & Bridgitt Cushing, s. .. 4 Aug. „
Henry Warde, b., p. Tibinham, & Dorothy
  Longe, s. ..   .. 8 Sept. „
William Michell, b., & Mary Cann, s.   .. 27 Oct. „
Dannell Smyth, b., & Allen Sparrow, s.   .. 1 Dec. „
Edward Palmer, b., & Margarett Warbutton,
  s., p. Bunwell   ...   . 15 Apr. 1658
John Howse & [——] [——] ..   .. 17 Sept. —
[*No entries from 1658-1663.*]
William Brightene & Margett Pallmer   .. 15 Apr. 1663
John More & Sarah Baxter   ..   .. 30 Sept. „
John Juby & Margaret George   ..   .. 15 Oct. „
Isaac Pitcher & Ann Everett   ..   .. 17 Dec. „
Richard Palmer, jun., & Elizabeth Bazely .. 29 Dec. „
Richard Mayes & Alles Lemans ..   .. 31 May 1664
Robert Yoll & Alles Tallyer   ..   .. 23 June „
William Martin & Mary Knights ..   .. 17 Oct. „

Stephen Poll & Mary Pallmer	15 Nov.	1664
Vallintine Kempe & Mary Pallgrave	12 Jan.	„
Robert Clifton & Elena Bacely	2 May	1665
Francis Edwards & Elizabeth Clifton	15 Nov.	„
George Battelle & Elizabeth Rowet	26 Apr.	1666
Thomas Everet & Elizabeth Pallmer	1 May	„
John Parker & Elizabeth Billard	1 May	„
Richard Parrish & Elizabeth Youngman	3 May	„
Thomas Kempe & Jane Sparke	4 June	„
Thomas Quaintrell & Dorcus Read	4 June	„
John Funnell & Mary Watts	27 Sept.	„
Robert Gallard & Elizabeth Jolly	1 Nov.	„
Titus Browne & Anne Welch	8 Nov.	„
Thomas Eles & the Widow Youngman	6 June	1667
John Lyncolne & Mary Smith	21 Sept.	„
Isake Thirstone & Susan Page	8 Oct.	„
Robert Birgess & An Battell	7 Nov.	„
Richard Smith & Elizabeth Dawdry	19 Nov.	„
William Badwell & Margett Brighting	19 June	1668
Simon Barton & Susan Kitte	4 Oct.	„
Samuell Warkes & Rebecka Talyer	6 Oct.	„
Mr. Clement Kempe & Mrs. Ann Wilton	4 Oct.	1669
Peter Poll & Mathew Kemp	5 Apr.	1670
William Dixon & Wille Blake	10 Oct.	„
James Youngman & Elizebeth Sherein	6 Sept.	1671
John Smith & Martha Brightinge	29 Sept.	„
William Rivitt & Margatte Wattson	3 Oct.	„
Edward Poll & Mary Smith	3 Oct.	„
William Brightinge & Margette Pallmer	10 Oct.	„
Stephen Baxter & Mary Smith	28 Jan.	„
John Dye & Mary Carter	24 Sept.	1672
William Dawdrye & Margett Youngman	10 Oct.	„
Anthony Holden & Frances Briggs	31 Sept.	„
George Doged & Elizebeth Poll	3 Feb.	„
Robert Buttell & Mary Martin	4 Feb.	„
John Briggs & Mary Grattle	5 Feb.	„
John Die & Susen Wavers	8 Jan.	1673
Robert Wix & Marget Moore	1 Oct.	1674
John Beets & Elizabeth Wix	27 Nov.	„
William Townsen & Mary Howchen	29 Jan.	„

Thomas Buttle & Sarah Daynes ..	.. 18 Oct.	1675
Samuel Cartter & Elizabeth Carter	.. 25 Oct.	,,
Thomas Long & Elizabeth Burrows	.. 6 Feb.	,,
William Filbye & Audrye Dawdrye	.. 3 Oct.	1676
John Pitcher & Anne Johnsonn ..	.. 6 Oct.	,,
John Mane & Susan Youngman ..	.. 2 Jan.	,,
William Marton & Elizebeth Tallyer	.. 28 Dec.	,,
John Rivitte & Francis Talyer ..	.. 21 Jan.	,,
Thomas Hearde & Bridgett Coe ..	.. 16 Apr.	1677
Richard Germene & Jane Brighteing	.. 17 Apr.	,,
Daniell Lyncolne & Anne Ficher ..	.. 8 May	,,
William Lyncolne & Elizebeth Brighting	.. 28 June	,,
Mills Rivitte & Mary Casen ..	.. 30 Sept.	,,
John Dentt & Abbigall Matha ..	.. 4 Oct.	,,
John Elder & Margarett Pillgrime ..	.. 18 Oct.	,,
Francis Brighting & Margarett Clarke	.. 5 Nov.	,,
Thomas Funnell & Susan Youngman	.. 6 Nov.	,,
Raff Cockell & Susan Spinke ..	.. 5 Dec.	,,
Micac[?] Tollver & Susan Youngman	.. 6 Dec.	,,
Daniell Sturman & Katherine Whittine	.. 23 Apr.	1678
William Filbye & Susan Poll ..	.. 20 May	,,
Thomas Page & Elizebeth Gallyard	.. 20 May	,,
Francis Kempe & Anne Gill ..	.. 25 July	,,
Henry Denny & Dorithy Wiffin ..	.. 3 Oct.	,,
Joseph Parson & Lidia Newbye ..	.. 11 Nov.	,,
John Croch, p. Bunwell, & Sarah Smyth	.. 24 Aug.	1679
John Warns & Maria Thurston ..	.. 4 Sept.	,,
Robert Hardaman & Susan Hardaman	.. 16 Sept.	,,
John Lea & Elizabeth Sherring ..	.. 30 Sept.	,,
Robert Maching & Maria Carter ..	.. 22 Feb.	,,
Richard Kempe & Maria Warbuten	.. 20 Oct.	1680
Henrey Dixson & Elizabeth Purcer	.. 9 Nov.	,,
Anthony Rookes & Elizabeth Littleproud ..	14 Feb.	,,
Mr. William Holmes & Mrs. Tabitha Howse	15 Feb.	,,
Robert Brigting & Sarah Palmer ..	.. 3 Apr.	1681
William More & Katharine Hargrave	.. 14 Apr.	,,
Robert Woodcock & Ann Clarke ..	.. 19 Apr.	,,
Edward Davy & Mary Chamberlane, w.	.. 24 Apr.	,,
William Booth & Sarah Buttell, w.	.. 23 May	,,
Mr. Rowland Cockey & Mrs. Ann Howse ..	14 July	,,

Josias Wood & An Hall	26 July	1681
Thomas Girling & Elizabeth Elsy	26 Aug.	,,
Richard Galard & Frances Briggs	20 Oct.	,,
Andrew Ayton & Mary Cooke	27 Nov.	,,
Richard Knights & Ann Aylmer ..	9 Jan.	,,
William More & Elizabeth Watts	15 Feb.	,,
John Tayler & Mary Wix	18 Apr.	1682
William Buttle & Margreat Woodes, w. ..	1 May	,,
James Witherby, p. N. Buckenham, & Elizabeth More, p. Bunwell	22 May	,,
John Silom & Martha Smith	23 July	,,
John Sherwine & Hannah Badcock	3 Oct.	,,
Edward Armanger & Sarah Fulcher ..	25 Oct.	,,
Nickles Elet & Frances Carter	12 Nov.	,,
Samuel Dardary & Mary Buttel	30 Nov.	,,
John Ogger & Mary Kempe ..	1 Dec.	,,
Robert Curtis & Bridgett Wattson, w. ..	1 Jan.	,,
Richard Kempe & Elizabeth Marten, w. ..	14 Feb.	,,
Thomas Tebbe & Elizabeth Cooper ..	20 May	1683
Robert Buckenham & Dorothy Gray ..	25 June	,,
William Doll & Elizabeth Dow	19 Aug.	,,
John Britting & Susan Smyth	24 Aug.	,,
Thomas Kempe & Elizabeth Parrish ..	3 Oct.	,,
James Youngman & Mary Yewles ..	8 Nov.	,,
Robert Bibye & Elizabeth Pilgrim ..	25 Feb.	,,
William Goodwine & Ann Tostock ..	22 May	1684
John Rix & Elizabeth Lea ..	3 June	,,
Robert Wix & Sarah Kerrison	24 June	,,
Charles Buxton & Margarett Barton, p. New Buckenham	18 Sept.	,,
John Filby & Mary Kemp	23 Sept.	,,
Robert Hardiman & Susan Filby	7 Oct.	,,
John Briting & Ann Dover	21 Oct.	,,
Thomas Self & Dorothy Harman	17 Sept.	1685
Robert Longe & Isabell Jesop	15 Oct.	,,
Samuel Barnard & Elizabeth Champlin ..	12 Nov.	,,
Stephen Brightinge & Mary Spencer ..	27 May	1686
Richard Richards & Mary Sharpe ..	27 June	,,
Thomas Briggs & Dorothy Smyth	22 Aug.	,,
John Addis & An Bolton	27 Sept.	,,

Stephen Kemp & Margaret Hales ..	..	27 Nov. 1687
John Neave, jun., & Ann Armes ..	..	26 Dec. „
Edmund Adams & Mary Johnson ..	..	30 Jan. „
Mr. William Gosling & Mrs. Susan Howse ..		18 Apr. 1688
Henry Poll & Elizabeth Everitt ..	..	18 Oct. „
James Edwards & Alice Youngman	..	9 Feb. „
Mr. John Howse & Mrs. Mary Jubbs	..	28 May 1689
Thomas Taylor & Mary Kemp ..	..	29 Sept. „
Johnathan Neve & Anne Scar ..	..	17 June 1690
Sammuel Hastings & Elizabeth Sides ..		1 May 1691
Robert Burr & Sarah Sanders ..	..	25 May „
John Shirewin & Elizabeth Rivet ..	..	16 June „
John Steward & Mary Youngman ..	..	17 July „
Valentine Kemp & Margaret Brightwin	..	4 Aug. „
Richard Philips, jun., & Ann Cullyer		18 Aug. „
Henry Clerke & Sarah Sharp ..	..	30 Sept. „
James Watson & Mary Jenyson ..		12 Jan. „
Joseph Augus & Elizabeth Neave .	..	22 June 1692
Thomas Smith & Ann Wily ..	..	23 June „
Robert Fulcher & Dorothy Smith ..	..	26 June „
Robert Oakly & Susan Richards ..	..	22 Sept. „
John Buxton & Ann Blith ..	..	22 Sept. „
John Thirston & Katherine Dow ..	..	9 Oct. „
Mr. Isaac Parke & Mrs. Frances Atkinson ..		17 Nov. „
Robert Filby & Dorothy Daudry ..	..	3 Jan. „
William Boast & Mary Downs ..	..	13 Apr. 1693
Francis Neve & Marget Bardwell ..	..	25 Apr. „
Richard Maire & Sarah Briting ..	..	25 July „
John Wicks & Alis Grange ..	..	12 Oct. „
Thomas Briting, jun., & Elizabeth Adcock ..		23 Oct. „
Osborne Betts & Ann Daudry ..	..	2 Nov. „
Robert Juby & Lydia Muddiclift ..	..	24 May 1694
John Smith & Frances Gallard ..	..	14 June „
Thomas Burges & Susan Litewine ..	..	2 July „
James Edwards & Mary Ellis ..	..	24 July „
Mr. Elisha Phillippo & Mrs. Frances Garrould		5 Sept. „
Richard Youngman & Sarah Youles ..	..	4 Oct. „
James Howse & Mary Brooke ..	..	13 Oct. „
Samuell Parsons & Mary Wicks ..	..	18 Oct. „
William Briting, senr., & Mary Wicks ..		27 Oct. „

William Buxton & Margaret Matthews	..	18 Dec. 1694
William Filbey & Mary Gleed	.. ..	26 Dec. ,,
Mr. Thomas Walne & Mrs. Susan Blake	..	2 May 1695
Hezikiah Neve & Elizabeth Filby	.. ..	28 July ,,
Richard Smith & Mary Knights	.. ..	1 Oct. ,,
Jeremiah Leverett & Hannah Oakely	..	2 Oct. ,,
John James & Susan More	..	10 Oct. ,,
Thomas Spurling & Mary Sparrow	..	2 Jan. ,,
Richard Payn & Sarah Adcock	.. ..	6 Jan. ,,
John Sparrow, sen., & Susan Briten	..	19 May 1696
William Bele & Mary Adcock	.. ..	29 June ,,
Edward Stebbin & Lydia Vincent	.. ..	14 Aug. ,,
Samuel Flower & Mary Daudery	.. ..	1 Sept. ,,
William Harvy & Martha Youngman	..	1 Oct. ,,
Richard Carter & Elizabeth Wix	.. ..	4 Nov. ,,
Henry Warnes & Elizabeth Brighten	..	11 Nov. ,,
Robert Poll & Amy Parson	.. ..	23 Feb. ,,
John Bubbins & Mary Falk	.. ..	18 May 1697
Christopher Freree & Jane Sattifat	..	27 Aug. ,,
John More, jun., & Elizabeth Howel	..	7 Nov. ,,
John Osborn & Elizabeth Barber	.. ..	27 Dec. ,,
William Howlet & Elizabeth Carter	..	3 Jan. ,,
Robert Brighting, b., & Catherine Carter, s., both this p.		17 Sept. 1699
Thomas Parsonns & Ann Herd, both of Tacolneston, *lic.*		16 Oct. ,,
James Briggs & Sarah Knights, w., both p. Old Buckenham, *lic.*		22 Oct. ,,
John Smyth & Susan Parish	.. ..	11 Feb. ,,
Edward Palmer & Mary Dixon	.. ..	22 July 1700
Robert Wicks & Sarah Arminger	..	26 Sept. ,,
Robert Briting & Margaret Kemp	..	10 Dec. ,,
William Colman & Mary Aldred	.. ..	6 Feb. ,,
John Briggs & Margaret Kemp	.. ..	6 Feb. ,,
Nathanael Goodings & Katherine Tooke	..	6 Feb. ,,
Richard Kemp, sen., & Margaret Hammond		3 June 1701
Robert Scurles & Elizabeth Wicks	..	2 Oct. ,,
Edward Woodrow & Mary Betts	.. ..	20 Apr. ,,
Thomas Buttall & Ann Steward	.. ..	21 Nov. ,,
John George & Mary Wicks	.. ..	26 May 1702

Robert Plowman, p. Forncett S. Peter, &
    Margaret Buxton, w.　　..　　..　　2 June 1702
Thomas Mellows, p. E. Harling, & Ann
    Watson ..　　..　　..　　..　　27 Dec. „
Jonathan Neeve & Elizabeth Feet ..　　..　　29 Dec. „
Edward Rudland & Alice Kemp, both p. New
    Buckenham　　..　　..　　..　　1 Jan. „
Thomas Dalling, gent., p. Denton, & Ann
    Cockey, w.　　..　　..　　..　　27 May 1703
John Briggs & Catharine Butterham　　..　　1 Apr. 1704
Philip Smith & Jane Morphew　　..　　..　　5 June „
George Chamberlayn & Mary Crook　　..　　30 June „
Cristopher Baylie, gent., & Elizabeth Jubbs ..　　10 Aug. „
Richard Stepny & Mary Hardy　　..　　..　　13 Sept. „
James Stimpson & Elizabeth Ellder　　..　　28 Sept. „
Robert Smith & Mary Booth　　..　　..　　28 Sept. „
Robert Buttall, p. Gillingham, & Mary
    Daines, w.　　..　　..　　..　　8 Oct. „
Edward Stannard & Margaret Mayhew [?] ..　　9 Jan. „
Daniel Shardelow & Frances Warnes　　..　　6 Mar. „
John Palmer & Ann Poll ..　　..　　..　　1 May 1705
John Kett, p. New Buckenham, & Elizabeth
    Wade　　..　　..　　..　　..　　4 June „
John Elder & Esther Brighting　　..　　..　　1 Oct. „
John Brighting & Ann Smith　　..　　..　　12 Dec. „
Richard Briting & Susan Oakely　　..　　..　　30 Mar. 1706
Thomas Dains & Mary Machen　　..　　..　　8 Dec. „
    [*From* 1706 *to* 1710 *deficient.*]

VOLUME III.

Christopher [———] & Frances Curtois　　..　　24 June 1710
William Kemp & Mary Woodrow ..　　..　　16 Sept. 1711
Robert Poll & Mary Lee ..　　..　　..　　27 Sept. „
Thomas Smith & Mary Lewel　　..　　..　　21 Oct. 1712
William Feek & Hannah Rudrock ..　　..　　21 Jan. „
Samuel Smith & Hannah Feek　　..　　..　　4 May 1713
William Rogers & Elizabeth Smith　　..　　15 Oct. „
George Dawdry & Frances Goodchild　　..　　11 Oct. „
John Spurlin & Elizabeth Howse ..　　..　　27 Nov. „
John Bunn & Lucy Brown　　..　　..　　5 Aug. 1714

Samuel Hastings, jun., & Rebeckah Ward	..	5 Aug. 1714
Samuell Woommock & Elizabeth Pitcher	..	10 Aug. „
William Brighting & Ann Smith	.. ..	23 Dec. „
Emanuel Briggs & Elizabeth Elvin	..	16 Apr. 1715
Samuel Briggs & Mary Smith	.. ..	2 May „
Silvester Goldworth & Dorothy Smyth	..	30 Sept. 1717
John Bell & Anne Long	.. .. ..	14 Oct. „
Lewellin Rieve, of Eye, & Mary Ellsey	..	13 Nov. „
[1718, *none*.]		
Robert Brighting & Elizabeth Tayler	..	15 Sept. 1719
Sherebiah Smyth & Mary Ellder	..	14 Oct. „
Reuben Whiting & Faith Bowing	.. ..	20 Oct. „
James Kushen & Mary Sparrow	.. ..	19 Dec. „
Stephen Palmer & Elizabeth Everet		29 Dec. 1720
Thomas Auger & Mary Clifton	..	2 May 1721
John Moor, w., & Frances Barker	..	13 May 1722
Thomas Morphew & Elizabeth Gratea	..	10 June „
Richard Gratea & Anne Lunn	.. ..	7 Aug. „
Thomas Everitt & Sarah Able	.. ..	9 July 1723
Francis Hastins & Martha Godfrey	..	5 Dec. „
Nathaniel Porter & Elizabeth James	..	7 Apr. 1724
Samuel Hastings, jun., & Mary Neve	..	15 June „
Amos Potter & Sarah Briggs	.. ..	6 Oct. „
Joseph Ward & Elizabeth Daniell	.. ..	30 Sept. 1725
Richard Smyth & Elizabeth Poll	.. ..	10 Nov. „
William Neve & Mary Everett	.. ..	4 Apr. 1727
Richard Everett & Bridget Watson	..	— — „
John Chabman & Lydia Edwards	.. ..	30 May „
Stephen Palmer & Elizebeth Wicks	..	28 Sept. „
William Woodrow & Elizabeth Read	.	24 Dec. „
John Rouse, of Crownthorp, & Mary Briggs,		
of Carlton		28 July 1728
John Auger & Mary James	.. ..	9 Sept. „
Francis Hastings & Susan Bush	.. ..	2 Dec. „
Thomas Willson & Elizebeth Allen, both p.		
Bunwell		2 Feb. 1729
Thomas Tayler & Elizabeth Sowell	..	22 May „
John Bond & Mary Woodrow	.. ..	29 June „
Joseph Pearson & Elizabeth Shering, w.	..	13 July „
Samuel Right & Bridget Everet	.. ..	3 Nov. „

William Trundell & Liddia Chapman, w. ..	7 Dec.	1729
Thomas Daines & Elizabeth Egmore ..	18 May	1730
Lyas Browne & Elizebeth Oakeley ..	18 May	„
Thomas Okely, of Attleburgh, & Mary Bird	7 June	„
John Briggs & Mary Stone	1 Oct.	„
John Spurling & Mary Kemp	30 Jan.	„
John Tayler & Abigail Elliner	26 Apr.	1731
James Drane & Abigail Palmer	9 May	„
Robert Bybie & Elizabeth Morphew ..	3 July	„
Francis Betts & Rachell Rushmore ..	5 Oct.	„
William Scott, b., & Mary Knights, s., both this p.	17 Dec.	„
William Smith, b., & Elizabeth Oakly, s. ..	1 July	1732
Robert Clifton, b., & Bridget Pyggot, s. ..	2 Oct.	„
James Bircham, of Bunwell, w., & Margaret Daudery, this p., s.	20 Oct.	„
Daniel Neve, b., & Martha Barnes, s. ..	3 Apr.	1733
Joseph Scott, b., & Sarah Briting, s., both this p.	17 Apr.	„
John Leader, of Banham, b., & Amy Steward, this p., s.	14 May	„
Richard Youngman, of Bunwell, b., & Mary Cheny, this p., s.	9 Oct.	„
William Smith, b., & Tabitha Dawdery, s., this p.	15 Oct.	„
John Moore, w., & Anne Newby, w. ..	26 Aug.	1734
Thomas Foyster, b., & Hannah Everett, s. ..	29 Sept.	„
William Farrow, b., & Martha Poll, s., both this p.	14 Oct.	„
John Elder, b., & Mary Moor, s., both this p.	14 Oct.	„
John Stevenson, b., & Sarah Youngman, s., both this p.	11 Nov.	„
Jeremiah Wilson, b., & Elizabeth Bowles, s., both this p.	9 Jan.	„
Thomas Oakly, b., & Sarah Cheney, s., both this p.	13 Feb.	„
William Scot, w., & Elizabeth Balls, s., both this p.	4 Mar.	„
Benjamin Bernard, b., & Anne Heath, s., both this p.	24 Apr.	1735

Robert Handyman, this p., b., & Susannah
    Richards, of Bunwell, s.   ..   ..   24 July 1735
John Potter, b., & Susannah Briggs, s., both
    this p.   ..   ..   19 Oct. ,,
Richard Woodcock, b., this p., & Sarah
    Baldwin, of Bunwell, s.   ..   ..   21 Oct. ,,
Thomas Oakley, w., & Susan Hubbard, s.,
    both this p.   ..   ..   ..   30 Oct. . ,,
William Greenwood, b., & Elizabeth Buxton,
    s., both of New Buckenham ..   ..   6 Sept. 1736
James Elder, of Hetherset, b., & Anne Mark-
    ham, this p., s.   ..   ..   ..   28 Sept. ,,
Thomas Goddard, w., & Margaret Fincham, s.,
    both of Snitterton ..   ..   ..   29 Sept. ,,
William Bardwell, of Tacolneston, b., & Sarah
    Hastings, this p., s.   ..   ..   31 Dec. ,,
Robert Hammond, b., & Susannah Mundford,
    s., both of Bunwell ..   ..   ..   2 Jan. ,,
John Smith, b., & Frances Daudery, w., both
    this p.   ..   ..   16 Feb. ,,
William Greengrass, b., & Frances Carleton,
    s., both this p.   ..   ..   ..   27 Oct. 1737
Robert Briggs, b., & Anne Palmer, s., both
    this p.   ..   ..   31 Oct. ,,
Peter Buck, b., & Anne Castleton, s., both of
    Bunwell ..   ..   9 Jan. ,,
William Elder, b., & Charlotte Bird, w., both
    this p.   ..   ..   1 Apr. 1738
Joseph Knights, b., & Mary Wittham, s., both
    this p.   ..   ..   6 July ,,
William Blake, b., & Honour Briting, s., both
    this p.   ..   ..   27 Oct. ,,
John Parsons, b., & Sarah Smith, s., both
    this p.   ..   ..   26 Dec. ,,
Stephen Filby, b., & Sarah Daudery, w., both
    of Bunwell   ..   ..   ..   25 Jan. ,,
John Shepheard, b., & Mary Smith, s., both
    this p.   ..   ..   30 Jan. ,,
John Palmer, b., & Elizabeth Knights, s., both
    this p.   ..   ..   6 Feb.· ,,

Richard Howse, of Tibenham, b., & Sarah
    Elliot, of Bresingham, s.   ..   ..   14 Aug. 1739
Daniel Clifton, of New Buckenham, b., & Mary
    Bennet, this p., s. ..   ..   30 Sept. „
Edward Palmer, b., & Mary Kemp, s., both
    this p.   ..   ..   ..   12 Oct. „
Amias Briggs, b., & Mary Self, s., both this p. 29 Oct. „
Robert Barnes, b., & Abigail Kemp, s., both
    this p.   ..   ..   ..   9 Nov. „
John Dale, w., & Esther Elder, s., both this p. 7 Jan. „
John Grey, b., & Mary Rich, s., both this p. ... 26 May 1740
Francis Clark, of Sudbury, co. Suffolk, b., &
    Anne Terrey, of Diss   ..   ..   20 July „
John Palmer, of New Buckenham, b., & Sarah
    Kemp, this p., s. ..   ..   ..   8 Oct. „
John Palmer, b., & Mary Briggs, s., both this p. 9 Oct. „
Nicolas Leader, b., & Mary Brothers, s., both
    this p.   ..   ..   ..   30 Mar. 1741
John Elder, w., & Elizabeth Brown, w., both
    this p.   ..   ..   ..   15 Feb. „
Robert Oakly, b., & Elizabeth Palmer, s., both
    this p.   ..   ..   ..   25 Feb. „
John Carman, b., & Sarah Mendham, s., both
    this p.   ..   ..   ..   19 Apr. 1742
Seth Rout, b., & Susannah Sharing, w., both
    of Banham   ..   ..   ..   30 June „
John Barnes, b., & Elizabeth Burton, s., both
    this p.   ..   ..   ..   8 Nov. „
John Sherman, b., & Alice Riches, s., both
    of Bunwell   ..   ..   ..   6 Jan. „
Richard Kemp, b., & Elizabeth Bell, s., both
    this p.   ..   ..   ..   27 Jan. „
George Daudery, b., & Elizabeth Hill, s., both
    this p.   ..   ..   ..   2 May 1743
Paul Baxter, of Keninghall, w., & Margaret
    Yell, this p., w. ..   ..   ..   11 July „
Robert Long, b., & Sarah Daudery, s., both
    of Bunwell   ..   ..   ..   29 Nov. „
John Greengrass, b., & Lydia Barnes, s., both
    this p.   ..   ..   ..   8 Dec. „

James Watson, b., & Phillis Jordan, s., both
  this p.   ..   ..   19 Apr. 1744
George Lee, b., & Sarah Steel, w., both of
  Quidenham   ..   ..   ..   24 June „
Robert Read, b., & Mary Woodrow, s., both
  this p.   ..   ..   16 Sept. „
Richard Watson, w., & Martha Kemp, s., both
  this p.   ..   ..   20 Sept. „
John Bate, of Tibenham, b., & Lettice Francis,
  this p., s. ..   ..   24 Sept. „
James Moor, b., & Martha Neave, w., both
  this p.   ..   ..   8 May 1745
Samuel Smith, b., & Mary Dunnet, s., both
  this p.   ..   ..   21 May „
Robert Stone, b., & Elizabeth Barnes, s., both
  this p.   ..   ..   30 Sept. „
Edward Bridges, b., & Deborah Ludbrook, s.,
  both this p.   ..   ..   ..   1 Oct. „
Nicholas Wrackham, b., & Elizabeth Foyster,
  s., both this p.   ..   ..   ..   9 Oct. „
Isaac Rich, b., & Jane Blake, s., both of Bun-
  well   ..   ..   27 Oct. „
John Beales, b., & Judith Dally, s., both of
  Bunwell ..   ..   27 Oct. „
Robert Barnes, w., & Mary Tailor, s., both
  this p.   ..   ..   13 Nov. „
James Filby, b., & Elizabeth Tailer, s., both
  this p.   ..   ..   27 June 1746
Richard Bly, of Topcroft, b., & Anne Tight,
  of Pulham, s.   ..   ..   ..   4 Oct. „
James Foyster, b., & Eleanor Smith, s., both
  this p.   ..   ..   12 Dec. „
James Howse, w., & Anne Mendham, s., both
  this p.   ..   ..   31 Mar. 1747
Edward Clark, b., & Elizabeth Smith, s., both
  this p.   ..   ..   11 May „
Jeremiah Beales, of Bunwell, b., & Elizabeth
  Ebrons, this p., s. ..   ..   ..   14 July „
William Feak, b., & Anne Daudery, s., both
  this p.   ..   ..   27 Sept. „

James Child, b., & Martha Jourdan, s., both
this p.   ..   ..   10 Nov. 1747
John Greengrass, b., & Susannah Gowin, s.   5 Jan.   „
Abraham Lonsdale, of New Buckenham, b., &
Mary Poll, this p., s.   ..   ..   21 Aug. 1748
John Kemp, b., & Elizabeth Pottle, s., both
this p.   ..   ..   26 Sept. „
William Read, b., & Margaret Ives, s., both
this p.   ..   ..   30 Sept. „
John Tight, b., & Sarah Foister, s., both this p.   30 Sept. „
Edward Woodrow, b., & Elizabeth Keely, s.,
both this p.   ..   ..   ..   13 Nov. „
Henry Raggs, b., & Anne Dale, s., both this p.   18 June 1749
John Thurston, b., & Mary Stevenson, s., both
this p.   ..   ..   25 July „
Simon Pottle, b., & Sarah Dawdery, s., both
of Bunwell   ..   ..   ..   31 Dec. 1750
Thomas Sharp, b., & Elizabeth Turner, s.,
both of Bunwell   ..   ..   ..   27 July 1751
John Kemp, b., & Mary Woodrow, s., both
this p.   ..   ..   2 Sept. „
Thomas Whyat, b., & Sarah Allen, s., both
this p.   ..   ..   21 Oct. „
William Kemp, b., & Lydia Rowse, s., both
this p.   ..   ..   3 Dec. „
George Ward, b., & Elizabeth Scott, s., both
this p.   ..   ..   6 May 1752
William Barnes, b., & Mary Poll, s., both this p.   8 Oct. „
William Mallows, of Attleborough, b., &
Susanna Porter, this p., s.   ..   ..   14 Oct. „
Richard Neave, b., & Mary Dove, s., both this p.   18 Dec. „

[1753, *none.*]

VOLUME IV.

Thomas Powter, b., & Mary Leman, s., both
of Carleton   ..   ..   ..   *4 Feb. 1754
Thomas Blake, of Bunwell, & Jemima Dale, *lic.*   20 Sept. „

---

* After this date the parties are invariably of Carleton Rode, and
bachelor and spinster respectively, unless otherwise described.

Robert Biby & Mary Ives	5 Nov. 1754
Edward Stubbings & Elizabeth Goss	2 Dec. „
Henry Manclark, of Tacolneston, & Martha Bunn, w., *lic.*	12 Dec. „
John Kemp & Mary Crucknall, *lic.*	11 Feb. 1755
John Briggs & Mary Wright, *lic.*	25 Feb. „
Gabriel Briggs & Elizabeth Smith, *lic.*	19 Mar. „

" N.B.—There was no service performed in the Parish Church of Carleton from April 1755 to Feb. 1758."

Robert Harrison, of Old Buckenham, & Mary Hart	8 May 1758
Jonas Brighting & Sarah Steemson	12 June „
Thomas Kemp & Sarah Knave	14 Aug. „
Jacob Moor & Tabitha Bush	12 Oct. „
Ralph Lincoln, of Bunwell, & Margret Read, w.	12 Oct. „
Benjamin Wright & Ann Scott	27 Nov. „
Thomas Turner & Sarah Johnson	5 Jan. 1759
Samuel Allen & Martha Farrer	15 Jan. „
Richard Dover & Mary Chestnutt	3 Aug. „
Samuel Farrer & Mary Rogers	12 Aug. „
Thomas Quantrel, w., & Sarah Stone	24 Sept. „
Robert Lewell, of Tibbenham, & Jemima Woodward	30 Sept. „
James Warne, of Moulton, & Ann Francis	11 Oct. „
Joseph Chilves, of Tibbenham, & Margret Dawson	4 Nov. „
Samuel Steemson & Elizabeth Pooley	29 Jan. 1760
John Abons, w., this p., & Mary Barnard, of Bunwell	28 Mar. „
William Parson, of Bunwell, & Judith Sparkal	6 Apr. „
Robert Bowen, w., & Rebecca Moor, w.	22 Apr. „
Samuel Franklin, w., & Mary Wiggiten	15 Sept. „
David Bird, w., & Phillis Riches	4 Nov. „
John Bond & Ann Britin	11 Jan. 1761
Thomas Frost & Elizabeth Poll, w.	26 Jan. „
Richard Kemp & Mary Howes, *lic.*	15 Apr. „
John Matthews & Sarah Lane	11 Aug. „
Richard Kemp, w., of Bunwell, & Elizabeth Rogers	17 Sept. „
William Whyatt & Susan Clears	7 Oct. „

Robert Feak & Dorcas Scott ..	13 Oct.	1761
William Tunmore & Mary Ryol	26 Oct.	,,
Abraham Lansdell, w., & Ann Greaty	25 Nov.	,,
Stephen Brown & Mary Briggs	8 Jan.	1762
John Smith & Hannah Musket	1 June	,,
John Ringbell, of Old Buckenham, & Mary Kemp, w.	10 Aug.	,,
Samuel Wright, this p., & Susan Knave, of Old Buckenham	7 Oct.	,,
Thomas Adcock & Sarah Hardy	21 Oct.	,,
John Limmer, this p., & Lucy Clark, of Besthorpe	2 Nov.	,,
Thomas Frost, w., & Catherine Franklin, w.	19 Dec.	,,
John Palmer, w., & Lydia Riches	12 Jan.	1763
Charles Howes, of Besthorpe, & Elizabeth Pymer	15 Feb.	,,
Samuel Parsons & Mary Sparkal	2 Mar.	,,
John Boodle, this p., & Ann Warming, of Banham	19 July	,,
John Stumoon & Mary Brigs	11 Oct.	,,
George Dawdry & Mary Wilson	11 Oct.	,,
Jonathan Musket & Mary Read	25 Nov.	,,
John Dawson, w., & Elizabeth Osborn, w. ..	16 Apr.	1764
James Philippo, w., this p., & Margaret Warnes, w., of Gissing	27 Apr.	,,
Richard Graty, p. Forncett S. Peter, & Lydia Parson	1 May	,,
Richard Smith, w., & Elizabeth Kiband, w. ..	10 May	,,
John Spawl & Mary Barns, w. ..	12 June	,,
George Wright & Charlotte Scott	12 Sept.	,,
Francis Fisher & Ann Dordery	19 Dec.	,,
Thomas Ockley & Martha Briggs	4 Jan.	1765
Samuel Briggs & Rebecca Scott	31 Jan.	,,
Robert Lebbon & Elizabeth Prundle ..	6 May	,,
Amyas Briggs & Susan Pearson	21 May	,,
John Sturman, of Bunwell, & Rachael Stevenson	27 May	,,
John Torbold & Mary Palmer	16 July	,,
John Neve, of Bunwell, & Phœbe Sparkall ..	14 Sept.	,,
William Knott & Mary Vines	14 Oct.	,,

Daniel Redgrave & Mary Poll, w.	5 Nov.	1765
Marlborough Rush & Ruth Moore	16 Dec.	,,
Robert Briggs, of Aslacton, & Anne Bligh ..	16 Feb.	1766
John Stephenson, of Besthorpe, & Elizabeth Beales	24 Mar.	,,
Stephen Taylor, of Bunwell, & Mary Lane, w.	20 Apr.	,,
George Rode & Mary Blake	28 Apr.	,,
John Smith & Elizabeth Scott	13 June	,,
John Colyer, w., of Attleburgh, & Elizabeth Dawson, w.	15 Aug.	,,
Calver Walne, of Starston, & Sarah Kemp ..	2 Oct.	,,
Robert Bowen & Deborah Bridges ..	3 Nov.	,,
Robert Vince & Frances Allen	18 Nov.	,,
Robert Hart & Mary Rowse	21 May	1767
John Large, of Attleburgh, & Mary Sparkhall	13 Oct.	,,
James Quadling & Lydia Briggs	23 June	1768
Nathaniel Plumton & Lucy Hardy .. .:	11 Oct.	,,
Robert Thompson, a minor, with consent of his father, & Sarah Adams, w. ..	9 Feb.	1769
Robert Quantrell, of Bunwell, & Elizabeth Alden	17 Apr.	,,
John Rose, of Besthorpe, & Anne Austin ..	29 May	,,
Thomas Clarke, of Wymondham, & Elizabeth Thompson	25 Sept.	,,
James Glover, New Buckenham, a minor, & Elizabeth Brighting, w.	11 Oct.	,,
James King, of Ashwell Thorpe, & Lydia Scott	24 May	1770
William Dawdry, of Bunwell, & Elizabeth Nudds	28 May	,,
Francis Long & Jane Moore	15 Oct.	,,
James Woods, of Attleburgh, & Elizabeth Hardy	16 Oct.	,,
Benjamin Barnes & Elizabeth Bird ..	21 Oct.	,,
William Snelling & Mary Lewell	12 Nov.	,,
Malachi Sturman & Lydia Stimpson ..	12 Nov.	,,
Jeremiah Smith & Mary Watson	10 Dec.	,,
John Rainer & Mary Woodrow	13 Dec.	,,
Richard Kemp & Mary Bird	21 Jan.	1771
Davy Ong, w., of New Buckenham, & Mary Warns	20 Feb.	,,

Samuel Smith, of Besthorpe, & Mary Olley ..	8 Apr.	1771
John Neve, w., this p., & Judith Webster, w., of Attleburgh	15 Apr.	,,
James Burton, of Wreningham, & Elizabeth Austin	6 Jan.	1772
Robert Barnham & Elizabeth Culyer ..	13 Jan.	,,
Thomas Smith & Elizabeth Hardy ..	2 Mar.	,,
James Clarke & Ann Ockley	13 May	,,
John Jefferys & Hannah Parsons	26 May	,,
Joseph Scott & Amy Everett	26 May	,,
Richard Smith & Mary Neve	5 Aug.	,,
John Gray & Mary Kemp	27 May	1773
Anthony Hardy, w., & Margaret Philippo, w.	2 June	,,
James Briggs & Mary Pottle	23 Aug.	,,
John Boodle, w., & Elizabeth Thurston ..	18 Oct.	,,
Richard Scott & Mary Arnold	25 Jan.	1774
John Spink, of Wymondham, & Elizabeth Bush	10 Mar.	,,
Fuller Warnes & Elizabeth Brown ..	10 Nov.	,,
William Hardy & Susan Parson	1 Jan.	1775
John Long & Sarah Woodrow	3 Jan.	,,
Robert Feake, w., & Mary Trundle .	22 Jan.	,,
Benjamin Rowe, w., & Susannah Poll ..	24 Feb.	,,
Charles Browne, p. Forncett S. Peter, & Sarah Parson	28 Apr.	,,
William Leader & Ann Mountain	13 Aug.	,,
James Tite & Susan Burton ..	2 Oct.	,,
Edward Bridges & Elizabeth Warrington ..	11 Oct.	,,
Abraham Landsdale & Mary Austin ..	21 Nov.	,,
James Castleton, of Bunwell, & Sarah Everett	5 Feb.	1776
Stephen Cheney & Ann Smith	2 Mar.	,,
Thomas Austin & Elizabeth Claxton ..	10 June	,,
George Linstead, of Roydon, & Elizabeth Smith	12 July	,,
Richard Kemp, w., this p., & Mary Brown, w., p. S. Giles, Norwich	29 July	,,
Joseph Rainer & Sarah Betts	18 Aug.	,,
John Osborn, Keswick-with-Intwood, & Elizabeth Poll	14 Oct.	,,
John Briggs & Jane Clarke	25 Dec.	,,
Richard Neve & Elizabeth Bligh	6 Jan.	1777

Richard Kemp, w., & Lydia Scott ..	9 July	1777
Robert Love & Sarah Bass ..	15 Aug.	„
Thomas Frost, w., & Tabitha Halls ..	22 Sept.	„
William Dawdrey & Lydia Turner ..	10 Oct.	„
James Stevenson & Honour Turner	24 Apr.	1778
John Bales, w., & Mary Barnes ..	11 Oct.	„
Thomas Ockley & Judith Beales ..	25 Nov.	„
Robert Woodrow & Alice Malowes ..	2 Aug.	1779
James Watson, of Hethersett, & Lydia Palmer	19 Oct.	„
Isaac Lebbell, minor, with consent, & Mary Castleton ..	13 Dec.	„
Thomas Beast, w., of Palgrave, & Elizabeth Adams, a minor, with consent of her mother	24 Dec.	„
William Barham, of Kenninghall, & Sarah Moore, *lic.*	9 Jan.	1780
Miles Stanley, of Wymondham, & Elizabeth Kemp	21 Feb.	„
James Woodrow & Ann Brooks ..	27 Mar.	„
John Abon, of Bunwell, & Ann Stevenson	20 Apr.	„
Maladi Sturman, w., & Sarah Ockley, w. ..	11 July	„
Edward Palmer, of Bunwell, & Susanna Hinchley ..	5 Oct.	„
Benjamin Barcham & Mary Poll ..	13 Oct.	„
Thomas Hastings & Honour Wirr ..	19 Oct.	„
John Brighting [*signs* Briten] & Elizabeth Everitt	26 Oct.	„
William Kemp & Ann Woodrow ..	3 Dec.	„
William Grey & Elizabeth Briggs	4 Jan.	1781
John Burton, w., & Mary Bunn, *lic.* ..	5 Apr.	„
George Everitt, w., & Sarah Stevenson, w. ..	12 Apr.	„
Edmund Hart & Elizabeth Stevenson ..	19 Apr.	„
William Woods, w., & Mary Bird	23 May	„
Richard Nave, w., & Mary Dawdrey, w., *lic.*	31 Aug.	„
Henry Kemp & Phœbe Bird ..	7 Oct.	„
John Bridges & Elizabeth Thompson ..	7 Oct.	„
James Smith, of Wymondham, & Martha Arnold	11 Oct.	„
Simon Blazey, of Morley, & Mary Royal ..	11 Oct.	„
Peter Poll & Ann Freake	16 Oct.	„

William Sherring & Rebecca Turner ..	12 Nov.	1781
Henry Thrower & Elizabeth Lebbell ..	24 Nov.	„
William Phillippo & Mary Ann Browne ..	1 Jan.	1782
William Cream & Mary Briggs, w., *lic.* ..	14 Jan.	„
Thomas Bird, of Besthorpe, & Sarah Cook ..	28 Jan.	„
Thomas White & Mary Elmer	21 Apr.	„
John Cannom, of Tacolnestone, & Elizabeth		
Quantrall	23 May	„
William Burns & Mary Ringer	3 June	„
John Hunt, jun., of Old Buckenham, & Mary		
Kemp, *lic.*	8 Oct.	„
James Foster & Elizabeth Shimpton ..	14 Oct.	„
Robert Hardy & Sarah Crowe	15 Oct.	„
Richard Kemp & Bathulia Natt, w. ..	11 Nov.	„
George Ward, w., & Sarah Kemp, w. ..	18 Nov.	„
John Boodle, w., & Frances Bush	24 Nov.	„
Robert Downs & Ann Page	3 Mar.	1783
Timothy Kemp & Mary [*or* Ann] Dawdry ..	3 Mar.	„
Henry Dunster, of Camberwell, co. Surrey, &		
Rebecca Palmer, *lic.*	4 Mar.	„
William Abon, w., & Elizabeth Smith ..	12 Oct.	„
Samuel Stevenson, w., & Mary Woodrow ..	8 Dec.	„
James Ward, of Tibbenham, & Elizabeth		
Ruddock, *lic.*	12 Dec.	„
John Turner & Mary Chapman . ..	12 Oct.	1784
Noah Cannom & Lydia Quantrel	18 Oct.	„
John Woodrow & Elizabeth Wright ..	9 Nov.	„
Thomas Green, w., & Mary Bales	14 Dec.	„
Richard Foyster & Tabitha Brown ..	10 Jan.	1785
James Barnes, of Old Buckram [? Buckenham],		
& Deborah Parson	4 Apr.	„
Andrew Browne & Susanna Lond	11 Apr.	„
Samuel Cooper & Lydia Nudds	17 Oct.	„
John Sparling & Sarah Redgrave	7 Nov.	„
James Lewell & Sarah Warnes	14 Nov.	„
John Bales, w., & Mary Hart, w.	14 Nov.	„
William Smith & Sarah Kemp	20 Nov.	„
John Everett & Honor Brighton	16 Jan.	1786
Micheal Fox, of Ingrave, co. Essex, & Lucy		
Hardy	25 Jan.	„

William Parson, w., of New Buckenham, &		
Lydia Palmer, w.	21 Feb.	1786
Ellis Gapp, of Besthorpe, & Esther Royal ..	28 Sept.	„
Jonathan Knights & Phœbe Hinchley ..	26 Nov.	„
John Abon, w., of Bunwell, & Hannah Cable	22 Jan.	1787
Elisha Briggs & Charlotte Wright	20 Feb.	„
Henry Burton & Jane Stacey	16 July	„
Isaac Stephenson & Susanna Turner ..	20 Aug.	„
Mark Briggs & Ann Thompson	28 Oct.	„
Fuller Warne, w., & Hannah Warne ..	5 Nov.	„
Samuel Farrow & Alice Elmer	4 Dec.	„
James Boice, of Besthorpe, & Hannah Feek ..	25 Dec.	„
Philip Browne, w., & Susanna Elmer ..	18 June	1788
William Ellis, of Brissingham, & Ann Royall, *lic.*	24 Sept.	„
William Robert Kemp, New Buckenham, &		
Sarah Adcock, *lic.*	9 Dec.	„
Rodament Hastings & Mary Dawdry ..	22 Mar.	1789
William Turner, w., & Lucy Brown	5 Apr.	„
Henry Andrews & Sarah Youngman ..	12 Apr.	„
Robert Pretty, *or* Prighty, of Winfarthing, &		
Martha Parson	16 June	„
George Osborn & Frances Stevenson ..	17 Aug.	„
Benjamin Burcham, w., & Keziah Knowls ..	15 Oct.	„
Richard Sutton & Sarah Quantril	30 Nov.	„
Robert Briggs & Ann Garland	31 May	1790
John Baker, of Tibbenham, & Sarah Stone ..	22 June	„
Robert Allum & Elizabeth Howard ..	15 Sept.	„
Anthony Abell, of South Burgh, & Martha		
Kemp, *lic.*	7 Oct.	„
John Brooke & Diana Kemp	12 Jan.	1791
Isaac Hardy, p. Forncett St. Peter, co. Nor-		
folk, & Elizabeth Adcock	8 Sept.	„
Stephen Taylor, w., & Ann Wright, w. ..	6 Oct.	„
Francis Abon, w., of Bunwell, & Alice Head	10 Oct.	„
Benjamin Burcham, w., & Sarah Jackson ..	13 Oct.	„
John Muskett & Mary Hart	24 Oct.	„
John Briggs & Lydia Ann Briggs, w. ..	5 Dec.	„
Jeremiah Smith, w., & Sarah Sharp ..	21 Feb.	1792
William Smith & Mary Fisher	30 Apr.	„
John Reynolds, of Banham, & Prudence Briggs	16 July	„

Robert Ayton, of Wymondham, & Elizabeth Page, *lic.*	30 July	1792
William Hawes & Mary Smith	15 Oct.	„
Benjamin Wright & Ann Green	26 Nov.	„
John Royal & Sarah Muskett, *lic.*	7 Dec.	„
William Muskett & Elizabeth Bennett ..	29 Apr.	1793
John Limmer, of Banham, & Sarah Thompson	3 May	„
William Wright & Sarah Clark	23 July	„
John Briggs & Elizabeth Lawrence ..	25 Aug.	„
John Barnard & Ruth Rush	18 Sept.	„
William Cole, of Mourningthorpe, & Catherine Brown, *lic.*	26 Sept.	„
John Locke & Elizabeth Huggins	24 Oct.	„
William Ringer & Mary Wright	12 Nov.	„
George Dordery & Jane Couzins	22 Nov.	„
William Hall & Charlotte Bennet	17 Jan.	1794
John Wells, Wymondham, & Sarah Burton ..	19 Feb.	„
Isaac Finch, Attleborough, & Rebeckah Dent	4 Mar.	„
Samuel Muskett & Kezia Howes	29 Apr.	„
Joseph Plumpton & Mary Garner	11 Sept.	„
Charles Bennett & Honour Knights ..	3 Oct.	„
Elisha Briggs, w., & Mary Smith	7 Oct.	„
William Crane, w., & Elizabeth Knights ..	16 Oct.	„
John Briggs, w., & Mary Ellis	16 Oct.	„
John Briggs & Elizabeth Bridges	10 Nov.	„
Benjamin Hunt & Frances Taylor	10 Nov.	„
John Cann & Mildred Bales	20 Nov.	„
Joseph Howlett & Ann Roberts	20 Nov.	„
Richard Scot & Lidia Hart	29 June	1795
Henry Burton, w., & Mary Ann Randel ..	13 Jan.	1796
Abraham Hardyman & Mary Snelling, w. ..	12 Feb.	„
Richard Wright & Ann Briggs	14 Mar.	„
Jeremiah Smith, w., & Elizabeth Hardyman ..	19 Sept.	„
Thomas Bowing & Mary Snelling	26 Sept.	„
William Howes & Esther Warns	12 Oct.	„
Benjamin Wright & Lydia Hawes	31 Oct.	„
Samuel Farrow, w., & Mary Byby, w. ..	14 Dec.	„
Henry Hilling, w., & Ann Alexander, *lic.* ..	19 Jan.	1797
John Brundle & Ruth Royal	25 Apr.	„
Archibald Hardyman & Elizabeth Whiterod, w.	4 July	„

Thomas Ockley, w., & Elizabeth Chalker, w.	12 Feb.	1798
Richard Briggs & Sarah Bennett	12 Mar.	„
George Briggs & Ann Bennett ..	12 Mar.	„
John Lincoln & Susan Woodrow	30 Oct.	„
Samuel Page & Rebecca Ayton	5 Nov.	„
Stephen Chaney, w., & Sarah Franklyn ..	5 Nov.	„
Henry Brickham & Mary Thurston ..	5 Dec.	„
Philip Turner, of Colchester, & Mary Wood-		
row, *lic.*	11 Dec.	„
Jonathan Bennett & Ann Austin	12 Feb.	1799
John Hart, of Tibbenham, & Ann Austin ..	26 Mar.	„
John Smith & Charlotte Knowles	22 Mar.	„
James Lewell, w., & Susannah Thurston, w.	3 May	„
Edward Manser & Mary Lansdell	18 June	„
Edward Holl, w., & Mary Browne, w. ..	24 June	„
Roger Nebbard, of Tibbenham, & Sarah Ellis	15 Oct.	„
John Glandfield, of Winfarthing, & Martha		
Fisher	24 Oct.	„
Jonathan Muskett & Judah Hart	24 Oct.	„
William Haws, w., & Mary Smith	22 Nov.	„
Joseph Snelling, of Tibbenham, & Martha		
Ockley	6 Feb.	1800
William Phillippo[? s] & Ann Dordery ..	3 June	„
Edward Bridges, & Mary Taylor	12 Oct.	„
James Page & Elizabeth Ayton, *lic.* ..	15 Dec.	„
Thomas Lewell & Mary Briggs, w., *lic.* ..	20 Mar.	1801
Marlborough Rush & Sarah Smith	4 Aug.	„
William Bloss Rudd & Ann Briggs, *lic.* ..	29 Sept.	„
William Trudgate & Ann Hart	29 Sept.	„
William Dordery & Elizabeth Warnes ..	2 Nov.	„
George Kerridge & Mary Foister	3 Nov.	„
Robert Kemp, this p., & Susan Raynes, p. New		
Buckenham, *lic.*	19 Jan.	1802
Francis Parkins, w., p. New Buckenham, &		
Elizabeth Morley	4 June	„
William Self & Susan Daudry	15 Nov.	„
Simon Oakley & Mary Rush	7 Nov.	„

[*No entries are to be found from* 1802 *to* 1812.]

Marriages at
Burnham Sutton with Ulph,

1653 to 1837.

NOTE.—The Weddings which follow are contained in four volumes, as
indicated below, but are entered in a very irregular manner, and
some of the entries are duplicated.
These extracts have been made by the Rev. Edmund Kinaston, and
are now printed under his supervision.

VOLUME I.

[1653, *no marriages.*]

Francis Leech & Elizabeth Broughton ..	24 Apr.	1654
John Clarke, of Holt, & Elizabeth [———] ..	19 July	„
Thomas Pyle & Ann Folyate [?]	7 June	1655
John Youngs & Edna Walker	23 May	„
William Skippoon & Elizabeth Bull ..	12 May	1656
Thomas Parry & Elizabeth Browne, of New Wallsingham	28 July	„
Abraham Hobart & Katherine Anbertt [?] ..	6 Nov.	„
Barnard Laveroth [?] & Ann Patts	26 Nov.	„
William [?] Gathergood & Lidia Collison, of Lidistron	13 Dec.	„
John Gunby & Jane Thurton	12 Apr.	1658
Thomas Houghton & Alice Godwin, of Docking	16 Nov.	„
Martin [Scotting ?] & [S]ary Widdons ..	11 Jan.	1662
[———] Julion & Sarah Loads [?]	1st day	1679
Francis Willyamson, of Burnham Westgate, & Margaret Andrews, of Nelhoughton	12 Feb.	„
Godfrey Hansell & Frances Hoolme ..	4 Apr.	1681
Edmundus Munyment & Elizabetha Suffield	20 July	1682
Thomas Dey & Elizabetha Hopper ..	12 Feb.	1683
Johannes Cleaver & Elizabetha Whiteing ..	25 Jan.	1686
Robertus Jennis & Elizabetha Cooke ..	2 Feb.	„
Rogerus Platten & Maria Moll	7 Nov.	1687

Johannes Waalton & Francisca Hansell .. 19 Aug. 1688
Thomas Dawle & Susanna Croome .. 22 Nov. „
David Thomson & Lydia Teel .. .. 14 Dec. 1721
[*Repeated below, with different day of month.*]
Thomas Chapling & Elizabeth Wallard .. 14 Feb. „

Volume II.

Godfrey Hansell & Widdow Golder . 2 Mar. 1666
Henricus Bowthorpe & Jana Folgate .. 16 Nov. 1668
Gulielmus Ward & Katherina Norman .. 4 Jan. „
Thomas Day & Bridgetta Lamkin .. .. 16 Nov. „
Benjamin Burrows & Jana Dathe [?] .. 10 Apr. 1670
Gulielmus Julian & Amia Chamberlaine .. 5 June 1671
Gulielmus Mitchell & Frances Wilson .. 30 July 1672
Jacobus Elliot & Jana Wiggon .. .. 31 Oct. [—]
Richardus Hubbard & Anna Heydon .. 24 Oct. 1680
Henricus Cademan & Rachel Angel .. 23 Sept. 1682
Franciscus Thimbler & Margeria Herring .. 8 Oct. „
Richardus [? Pinnock] & Margaretta Julian .. 10 Oct. „
Thomas Richman & Ellena Redding .. 3 Dec. „
Robertus Tilney & Sara Huggan .. 9 Oct. 1683
Johanes Parker & Dorothea Cooke .. 18 Nov. „
Robertus Wales & Anna Stuntley [?] .. 2 Dec. „
Johanes Doyle & Elizabetha Crawford .. 22 Apr. 1684
Johanes Clarke & Jana Waller .. .. 31 July „
Robertus Edmonds & Jana Rawlings .. 20 Aug. 1686
Gulielmus Curson & Elizabetha Scotten .. 23 Oct. 1687
John Bird & Barbara Wendham .. .. 22 Apr. 1690
Bassenbourn Browne & Thomasin Ginnis .. 28 Oct. 1691
Thomas Wakefeild & Sarah Willson .. 21 May 1693
John Palmer & Alice Bately .. .. 17 Jan. 1694
John Christmas & [———] Hall .. .. 24 May 1695
William Smith & Scotten Hare .. .. 20 Jan. „
John Bridges & Frances Woods .. .. 28 June 1696
William Farmer & Dorothy Kemp .. .. 26 Apr. 1697
William Purle & Elizabeth Flood, both of
Holkham .. .. 15 Oct. 1699
John Dunwell, of Burnham St. Andrews, &
Susan Wood .. .. .. 7 Sept. 1709
Richard Gurling & Alice Mason .. .. 29 Dec. „

Philip Creed & Elizabeth Gardiner, of Walsingham	22 Oct.	1710
John Paul & Bridget Rust	4 Mar.	1711
Thomas Pinnock & Martha Sheringham	25 June	1713
Thomas Sprag, of Wotton, & Jane Bingham, of N. Creake	15 Aug.	1714
Francis Hare & Anne Royston	27 Dec.	„
Benjamin Clarke & Bridget Atkins	6 June	1715
Edward Ringstead & Jane Fitt	4 Oct.	1716
George Carpin, of Wells, & Mary Smith	25 June	1717
John Billing & Jane Isaac [?]	17 Dec.	1718
Francis Rutland & Mary Chapman	29 Sept.	1719
William Mortimer & Anne Rainor	1 Aug.	1720
Nicholas Cutting & Mary Lynn	25 Dec.	„
David Thompson & Lydia Teel	11 Dec.	1721
Richard Pinnock & Frances Walker	26 June	1722
Thomas Oakes & Christian Woods	25 July	„
William Batley & Katharine Fisher	1 Aug.	1723
William Pilch & Mary Lattin	9 Apr.	1705
Andrew Hall & Ann Daniel, both of Docking	1 Jan.	1706
John Paul & Elizabeth Caudel	5 Nov.	1724
Edmund Ellit & Elizabeth Leaky	24 June	1725
John Smith, of Halkham, & Elizabeth Bell	31 Mar.	1730
John Cleaves & Frances Smith	22 Feb.	1731
Anthony Merrim, of Wortham, & Elizabeth Wallard	20 Sept.	1732
John Read & Anne Hare	4 June	1734
Thomas Browne & Susanna Heating	19 Dec.	„
William Groome & Mary Anne Golty	1 Apr.	1736
William Youngs & Sarah Smith	3 Feb.	1737
William Goggs & Catherine Walker, of Thorpe	5 June	1739
James Leeds & Mary Goggs, of Thorpe	26 Sept.	„
Henry Back, of Little Snoring, & Susanna Smith, of Lower Warham	25 Sept.	1740
Richard Francis & Catherine North, of Burnham Westgate	31 Jan.	1741
[1742, *none.*]		
Barnabas Boyden & Elizabeth Barker	3 Oct.	1743
William May & Philippa Farrow	30 Jan.	„
[1744 *to* 1747, *none.*]		

John Hinson & Jane Lee	26 Jan.	1748

[*1749 to* 1754, *none.*]

Edmund Fowle & Mary Cock, *lic.*	21 Oct.	1756
Matthew Grime & Clementine Jaggs, *lic.* ..	29 June	1758
Edward High & Rose Chaplin	19 Nov.	„
Joseph Buck, of Litcham, & Anne Sharpe, *lic.*	21 Mar.	1760
Bream Shotten [? Shetten], of Wells, & Mary Oldman, *lic.*	1 Mar.	1761
Richardson Miles & Ann Barefoot	5 Oct.	„
Robert Chadwick & Frances Chapman, of Burnham Westgate	22 Dec.	1762
Robert Dunwells & Elizabeth Clans [?] ..	22 Nov.	1763
Edward High & Mary Curtis	15 Oct.	1764
John Ellis & Mary Billing, *lic.*	25 Apr.	1765
Edmund Ellis & Alice Todd	17 Oct.	„
Edmund Bell & Mary Rawling	20 Oct.	1768
Thomas Rix, of Ryburgh, & Ellen Bell ..	20 Oct.	„
Thomas Hendry & Mary Ellis	2 Nov.	„
Edward Nobbs & Anne Mays	6 Nov.	„
Joseph Capps, of Walpole St. Peter, & Ann Oldman, *lic.*	1 June	1770
Thomas Bolding, of Holt, & Elizabeth Bell, *lic.*	13 Nov.	„
Thomas Lack, of Little Walsingham, & Elizabeth Oldman, *lic.*	9 Dec.	1771
William Johnson & Ann Rowe	25 Dec.	1779
William Hendry & Phoebe Creed	20 Mar.	1780
John Rogers & Ann Thurdon	31 Dec.	„
Thomas Stocking, of Burnham Westgate, & Susanna Smith, *lic.*	10 Aug.	1781
Thomas Hall & Mary Oakes	19 Nov.	1782
John Sadler & Ann Gillit	20 Jan.	1783
James Williamson & Susanna Worrel ..	21 July	„

VOLUME III.

John Sanders & Jane Ellis	21 Oct.	1784
Henry Bush & Ann Shore	25 Oct.	„
Matthew Harvey & Mary Lancaster ..	29 Nov.	„
Samuel Billing & Mary Gilson	10 Oct.	1785
Henry Barwick & Mary Margettson ..	17 Oct.	„

John Woodham, of St. Margaret's, Lynn Regis,
   & Mary Bunting .. .. .. 18 May 1786
Charles Simmons & Mary Vincent .. .. 5 June „
Peter Blackit, of Burnham Thorpe, & Sarah
   Bully .. .. 12 Sept. „
Richard Girling, of Burnham Westgate, &
   Catherine Hinson .. .. .. 19 Sept. „
Lee Moxen & Susanna Walker .. .. 20 Apr. 1787
William Parr & Ann Roston .. .. 17 Dec. „
Peter Fisher & Elizabeth Clark .. .. 5 Feb. 1788
Francis Cremer, of Burnham Westgate, & Amy
   Hamond .. .. 24 July „
William Parsons & Mary Skeet .. .. 10 Oct. „
Thomas Mitchell & Mary Kemp .. .. 14 Oct. „
Charles Newton, of St. James, Westminster,
   & Ann Raven, *lic.* .. .. .. 19 Nov. „
John Lewis & Ann Hendry .. .. 13 Aug. 1789
Henry Anderson & Elizabeth Dextern .. 12 Jan. 1790
John Hopper & Jane Williamson .. .. 11 Oct. „
James Parsons, of Easten, & Mary Pike .. 11 Oct. „
Robert Ward & Eleanor Savage .. .. 5 Jan. 1791
James Williamson & Rebecca Taylor .. 5 Oct. „
Robert Hazlewood, of Burnham Westgate, &
   Matilda Holmes .. .. .. 28 Oct. „
Benjamin Rogers & Elizabeth Dextern .. 7 Nov. „
William Woods & Frances Massingham .. 5 Nov. „
James Hendry & Sarah Harvey .. .. 2 June 1793
John Whidby & Sarah Hendry .. .. 2 June „
John Dunton, of Brancaster, & Ellen Hains .. 27 July „
James Lubbock & Elizabeth Elliott .. 28 July „
James Oxborough & Sarah Barnard .. 15 Oct. „
Robert Hendry & Ann Warns .. .. 16 Oct. „
John Tate & Elizabeth Vincent .. .. 4 Dec. 1794
Robert Pike & Ann Lewis .. .. 12 Jan. 1795
John Dybal & Lydia Howard .. .. 9 Feb. „
William Smith & Susannah Green, of Burnham
   Westgate .. .. 7 Dec. „
John Proudfoot & Ann Bennal .. .. 24 Dec. „
William Allen & Elizabeth Rogers .. .. 29 Dec. „
Thomas Rix & Joanna Allison, *lic.* .. 12 Jan. 1796

Roads Emms & Ann Bobbin	9 Feb.	1796
William Blyth & Sarah Dextern	9 Feb.	,,
Robert Anderson & Ann Hull Fiddaman, *lic.*	1 Mar.	,,
William Belding & Ellen Rawston ..	12 July	,,
William Spooner & Mary Billing	29 Aug.	,,
Richard Belding & Susannah King ..	15 Nov.	,,
Hendry Hudson & Ellen Thurlow	29 Aug.	1797
William Ringwood & Ann Tighe	24 Oct.	,,
Robert Gazely & Ann Mary Atkins ..	12 Dec.	,,
Joseph Suggett & Elizabeth Loades ..	11 Oct.	1798
Joseph Claxton, of Burnham Westgate, & Ann Johnson	25 Oct.	,,
Benjamin Marshall & Clarissia Shorten ..	2 Apr.	1799
Simon Glasscock, of Downham, & Elizabeth Thurlow, *lic.*	13 June	,,
Thomas Francis & Mary Pinnock	22 Oct.	,,
John Francis & Ann Gibson	12 Nov.	,,
Joshua Johnson, of Docking, & Rebekah Parrock, *lic.*	27 May	1800
Dennis Thurlow & Eleanor Scott, *lic.* ..	25 Sept.	,,
Francis Miller, of North Creake, & Esther Watts	17 Mar.	1801
Francis Young & Ann Handcock	30 Apr.	,,
Dennis Howard, of Burnham Thorpe, & Fanny Maria Foley	24 Nov.	,,
John Symonds & Elizabeth Pinnock ..	17 Nov.	1802
John Philap[s ?] & Anne High ..	22 Sept.	1803
John Faulconbridge, of Egmere, & Ann Toll, *lic.*	17 Dec.	,,
Charles Rust & Elizabeth Bell	19 May	1805
Adam Francis & Sarah Gazely	30 Oct.	,,
John Page & Maria Elliot	4 Nov.	,,
John Thurlow & Sarah Bennall	5 Nov.	,,
Thomas Pinnock & Mary Watts	27 May	1806
Henry Belting, of Burnham Westgate, & Elizabeth Hawes, *lic.*	18 June	,,
Jonas Pinnock & Susan Chilvers	7 Sept.	,,
John Hawes & Amy Hendry .. .	2 Dec.	,,
Richard Girdlestone & Mary Page, *lic.* ..	12 Dec.	,,
Joseph Sandford & Mary Watts	6 Jan.	1807
Thomas Turner & Ann Norton	20 Jan.	,,

Thomas Baily & Mary Wright	26 May	1807
George Cubit & Charlotte Dennis	3 July	„
Henry Anderson & Sarah Francis	13 Oct.	„
William Beck, of Great Bircham, & Charlotte Overman, *lic.*	2 Dec.	„
John Williamson & Maria Page	12 Jan.	1808
James Billing & Frances Plum	7 June	„
Edmund Ellis, of Burnham Thorpe, & Susan Walker, *lic.*	20 June	„
John Folker & Jane Holmes	22 Nov.	„
Frederick William Howitt & Jane Mearns ..	9 Jan.	1809
Joseph Dowdy & Elizabeth Marsh	6 Apr.	„
James Kendle, of Weasenham St. Peter, & Sarah Overman, *lic.*	25 Oct.	„
Robert Hawes & Mary Ann Riches ..	25 Nov.	„
John Bleasby & Jane Ellis	8 Jan.	1810
Robert Rout & Maria Hall	6 Mar.	„
Samuel Meek & Elizabeth Bobbin	22 Oct.	„
William Curzon & Alice Ellis	25 Dec.	„
Robert Bore & Maria Steel, of Burnham Westgate	14 Oct.	1811
Miles Waldon, of South Creake, & Susannah Riches	17 Aug.	1812
James Rudd & Frances Ellett	6 Nov.	„
William Hall & Mary Sapye	10 Nov.	„
Robert Pratt & Anne Waller	5 Dec.	„
Robert Taylor & Mary Hancock ..	21 Dec.	„

VOLUME IV.

Timothy Moxon & Matilda Hazlewood, of Burnham Westgate, *lic.*	23 Mar.	1813
Richard Belding & Esther Dent	7 June	„
Henry Harper & Anne Taylor	12 Oct.	„
William Plaice & Anne Ward, *lic.*	31 Oct.	„
Robert Taylor & Anne Balding	3 Feb.	1814
Thomas Brightmer & Anna Watts	11 Apr.	„
Robert Oughton & Charlotte Rodwell ..	12 May	„
John Clement Forster, of Brancaster, & Elizabeth Clamp, *lic.*	28 Oct.	„
Benjamin Nuds & Sarah Snell	22 Jan.	1815

John Brany & Mary Grimes	12 Oct.	1815
Samuel Spooner, of Docking, & Esther Isabella Stringer	13 Oct.	,,
John Nurse, of Bagthorpe, & Elizabeth Palmer	16 Oct.	,,
James Allen & Sarah Monument	2 Nov.	,,
John Ward & Elizabeth Williamson ..	7 Dec.	,,
William Roy & Martha Taylor	28 Dec.	,,
Robt. Hooks, of Holme, & Prudence Hooks, *lic.*	3 Dec.	1816
John Tinker & Anne Evetts	20 Jan.	1817
William Creak & Sarah Wright ..	22 Jan.	,,
Robert Beverley & Rebecca Taylor ..	17 June	,,
Thomas Moore & Mary Vincent	27 Oct.	,,
Aaron Wales & Margaret W. Sporne ..	8 Jan.	1818
John Sapey & Mary Kirk	23 Apr.	,,
William Allen & Anne Jarey	28 Apr.	,,
William Ward & Lydia Yeavem	4 May	1819
Francis Starkins & Sarah Oxburgh ..	15 July	,,
James Spink & Mary Curson ..	19 July	,,
John Kendal & Anne Shackcloth ..	10 Nov.	,,
Michael Allen & Anne Howard	11 Apr.	1820
Thomas Yearam & Jane Gazeley	3 Sept.	,,
Thomas Baldon & Ann Parsons	16 Oct.	1821
John Mitchley & Rose Mary Morley ..	5 Mar.	1822
George Wheatley & Margaret Allen ..	25 June	,,
Henry Blyth & Maria Hooks	8 Apr.	1823
John Barnes, of Snettisham, & Eliz. Palmer ..	13 May	,,
Thomas Strong & Maria Sadler	29 Sept.	,,
Zachariah Mitchley & Phoebe Stringer ..	13 Oct.	,,
John Rout & Phoebe Kirk	— —	,,
David Dowdy & Mary Grice Bird	4 Dec.	,,
Martin Allen & Frances Morris	28 Apr.	1824
Henry Allen & Susan Balls	8 June	,,
John Ford & Mary Martins	28 Oct.	,,
James Groom & Mary Turner	15 Apr.	1825
Robert Page & Elizabeth Gazeley	24 July	,,
Robert Hendrey & Sarah Thurlow ..	9 Aug.	,,
James Sapey & Sarah Gazeley	5 Sept.	,,
John Claxton & Catherine Fisher, *lic.* ..	6 Oct.	,,
Charles Margerson & Elizabeth Youngs ..	11 July	1826
William Groom & Anne Sporne	13 Sept.	,,

James Wilkin & Sarah Kirk	12 Oct.	1826
Henry Bush & Elizabeth Lavington	6 Dec.	,,
James Parsons & Mary Ann Thurlow	26 Sept.	1827
Charles Kirby & Hannah Hary	13 Oct.	,,
Jonathan Bond & Ann Seely	30 Oct.	,,
William Groom & Susan Arnold	10 Nov.	,,
Robert Simms & Jane Elizabeth Bird	15 May	1828
John Gowing, of Western Market, Suffolk, &		
Martha Malk, *lic.*	24 June	1829
Henry Cooper & Judy Blyth	8 Nov.	,,
John Peeps & Anna Sampher	21 Nov.	,,
John Hall & Rebecca Howell	1 Dec.	,,
Robert Hubbard & Susan Meek	29 Mar.	1830
James Gant & Mary Spoone	8 Apr.	,,
William Skeet & Sarah Booer	10 Apr.	,,
Edmund Graver & Sarah Meek	24 June	,,
Adam Francis & Mary Atkins	30 Nov.	,,
James Allen & Hannah Pettengale	27 Dec.	,,
Robert Nudds & Anne Hall	11 Jan.	1831
William Ringwood & Ann Trotting	25 Oct.	,,
Joseph Southgate & Elizabeth Pace	1 Nov.	,,
Thos. Millar, of Bircham Newton, & Sarah Rout	12 Nov.	,,
Henry Leverett & Mary Clarke	7 Dec.	1832
Ephraim Marsham & Frances Franklin	18 Dec.	,,
John Raven, of Brancaster, & Maria Groom	26 Jan.	1833
James Bowles & Martha Curson, *lic.*	18 July	,,
John Hill & Sarah Shore	10 Oct.	,,
John Farrow & Jessemine Thurlow	14 Nov.	,,
William Beverley & Sophia Bensly Sainty	19 Nov.	,,
Thomas Renaut & Caroline Thurlow	26 Aug.	1834
John Batterby & Patience Simmons	19 Oct.	,,
George Robinson, of Wells, Norfolk, & Sophia		
Thurlow	11 May	1835
Robert Booer & Harriett Frary	24 July	1836
William Raven & Elizabeth Wildbore	4 Nov.	,,
Samuel Meek & Mary Leveritt	19 Nov.	,,
Thomas Mitchell & Mary Langley	12 Feb.	1837
Samuel Fane, of St. Margaret, Kings Lynn, &		
Harriett Sampher	9 Apr.	,,

Marriages at Hickling,

1657 to 1812.

NOTE.—The Marriages at Hickling are contained in three books, viz.:
Vol. I is 1 ft. 4½ in. long, and 6 in. wide, and contains the Baptisms,
Burials, and Marriages from 1653 to 1716—the latter do not begin
until 1657. There are 47 leaves of parchment, of which the first
is a title page. The leaves have been numbered apparently in
error, as there is no leaf 16, although the entries follow on in date;
neither is there leaf 19, one side of 20 is blank, and there is no
leaf 22, but the entries follow on from leaf 21 to 23. There are no
leaves 24, 25, 26, or 33, and on page 27 the Weddings begin.
Vol. II consists of 28 leaves of parchment, which have been
numbered in ink, but there are no pages 14 and 15, although
the entries follow on in proper order: there is no leaf 20. The
same book contains Baptisms and Burials from 1716 to 1772:
the Weddings begin at page 17.
Vol. III is the usual volume of printed forms.
These extracts, from the original Register, were made by Mr.
Frederic Johnson, of Norwich, with the permission of Rev. A.
N. T. Crosse, Vicar, and are now printed under his supervision.

VOLUME I.

Thomas Rumball, w., & Ann Short, w.	8 Sept.	1657
George Palling, b., & Ann Welch, s.	21 Sept.	,,
William Tomson, b., & Ann Pratt, s.	21 Sept.	,,
Edward Heylocke, w., & Ann Watson, s.	16 Mar.	,,
James Watson, w., & Thomasin Johnsons, s.	7 June	1658
Edmund Burgis, clark, w., & Alice Barker, w.	17 June	,,
Robert Catt, w., & Isabell Beverley, s.	12 May	1659
Edmund Sumers, w., & Elizabeth Hamond, s.	12 May	,,
John Varley, b., & Ann Wenn, s.	8 June	,,
Richard Cutley [or Catley], w., & Elizabeth Underwoode, w.	15 June	,,
Thomas Hodds, b., & Ana Gedney, s.	2 July	,,
Thomas Callow, w., & Grace Jorden, s.	11 July	,,
Thomas Chitten, b., & Mary Palling, s.	31 Aug.	,,
James Ebbs, b., & Elizabeth Woolsey, s.	26 Sept.	,,
Robert Larwood, b., & Ann Riches, s.	3 Oct.	,,

William Paumor, w., & Elizabeth Leame, s. ..	1 Nov.	1659
Nicholas Beare, w., & Briget Prise, s. ..	9 Nov.	„
Thomas Bolt, b., & Hanna Bold, w. ..	3 Dec.	„
Christopher Grant, b., & Susan Bell, s. ..	10 Apr.	1660
Joseph Kirspe, w., & Garthrin Waters, w. ..	12 July	„
William Brady, w., & Elizabeth Steward, w.	14 Aug.	„
Richard Read, w., & Ann Lambert, w. ..	13 Sept.	„
Robert Atkins, w., & Susan Corps, w. ..	18 Sept.	„
Anthony Dinnis, w., & Mary Holtow, w. ..	2 Oct.	„
John Sageant, b., & Elizabeth Dennis, s. ..	2 Oct.	„
Thomas Howes, w., & Ursula Perse, w. ..	11 Oct.	„
William Randalls, w., & Ann Woods, s. ..	17 Jan.	„
Francis Stewardson, w., & Mary Cutloct, w.	11 Feb.	„
John Catt, w., & Rose Huggings, s. ..	25 Feb.	„
John Waters, w., & Rachell Spicer, s. ..	11 Mar.	„
John Bungay, w., & Prischa Smith, w. ..	10 Apr.	1661
Thomas Farrow, w., & Susan Kirspe, w. ..	15 Apr.	„
Joseph Kirspe, b., & Ann Dobson, s. ..	15 Apr.	„
John Norton, b., & Verely Randolls, s. ..	13 May	„
John Garrwood, b., & Elizabeth Stratford, s.	11 June	„
John Wolterton, b., & Elizabeth Apleton, s. ..	16 July	„
John Batton, b., & Cicely Smith, s.	23 July	„
John Mihill, b., & Ursula Fenn, s.	23 July	„
Thomas Bocking, b., & Sarah Astin, s. ..	1 Aug.	„
Joseph Boyse, w., & Ann Pallant, w. ..	8 Sept.	„
Mr. Peter Whitakers, b., & Mrs. Barbarah Calthorp, s.	9 Jan.	„
William Jewell, b., & Elizabeth Beeters [? Beebers], s.	11 Feb.	„
Richard Tomson, w., & Elizabeth Wolsie, w.	4 May	1662
Thomas Sheapheard, b., & Mary Baspoole, s.	20 Oct.	„
Robert Boys, b., & Ann Dennis, s.	6 Nov.	„
Thomas Gedney, w., & Love Crickmore, s. ..	13 Nov.	„
Edmund Foe, b., & Ciseley Gedney, w. ..	14 Jan.	„
William Lambert, b., & Abigall Skeete, s. ..	24 May	1663
Christopher Gillians, w., & Elizabeth Ebbs, w.	15 June	„
John Sumers, b., & Elizabeth Wolsie, s. ..	4 Aug.	„
Robert Randall, b., & Mary Faireweather, s. ..	5 Aug.	„
Peter Perse, w., & Mary Jay, s.	28 Mar.	1664
Thomas Claiton, b., & Judith Apleton, s. ..	28 Mar.	„

Nicholas Johnson, b., & Elizabeth Skeete, s. ..	18 May	1664
John Kirspe, b., & Baria [? Bethya] Emeris, s. ..	last of June	,,
Esdras Lambert, b., & Elizabeth Reade, s. ..	14 July	,,
William Corbett, w., & Susan Catt, s. ..	25 July	,,
Ralph Lisbey, w., & Sarah Palling, s. ..	2 Aug.	,,
Richard Reade, w., & Mary Pendalls, w. ..	2 Oct.	,,
Joseph Winkfield, b., & Mary Tilney, s. ..	12 Oct.	,,
Robert Skeete, b., & Mary Palling, s. ..	13 Oct.	,,
Henry Spooner, w., & Dorithy Foe, w. ..	6 Feb.	,,
Mr. John Utting, b., & Mary Lubbocke, s. ..	18 Apr.	1665
Thomas Shapard, w., & Marey Kinstone, s. ..	15 May	,,
Mr. John Husband, b., & Catherine Calthorp, s.	4 July	,,
John Summers & Ane, his wife	6 Sept.	,,
Edmund Artertun, b., & Christian Pawling, s.	14 Nov.	,,
Robert Bachelour, w., & Mary Elgur, w. ..	7 May	1666
[*Among the Burials for* 1667 *are the following Weddings.*]		
Willyam Haylett & Christierne Wolsey ..	4 June	1667
Richard Gibbes, w., & Elizabeth Lawson, w. ..	25 July	,,
Roger Som'ers, b., & Elizabeth Carre, s. ..	11 Nov.	,,
George Browne, w., & Sarah Dennys, s. ..	25 Dec.	,,
Willyam Haylett, w., & Margery Price, s. ..	2 Feb.	,,
Mr. Matthew Markham, b., & Mrs. Barbara Whitaker, w.	7 Apr.	1668
Samuel Howell, b., p. Palling, & Anne Foxe, s.	29 July	,,
John Catt, b., & Dorothy Fenne, s., both p. Hickling	10 Nov.	,,
Thomas Sheppard, w., & Elizabeth Sergeant, s.	14 Apr.	1669
Joseph Helmes, b., & Abigaile Smith, s. ..	20 Apr.	,,
John Myhill, w., & Abigaile Randalls, s. ..	20 Apr.	,,
Stephen Reading, w., & Martha Linstead, w.	23 June	,,
Thomas Marthason, b., & Love Gednye, w. ..	29 June	,,
Robert Reade, b., & Sarah Browne, w. ..	28 Oct.	,,
John Dawson, b., & Hannah Peck, s. 5 [*or* 6]	June	1670
Philippe Roberts, w., & Elizabeth Tompson, w.	26 June	,,
Stephen Baldwyn, w., & Susan Corbett, w. ..	12 July	,,
Isaack Boots, b., & Anne Hoddes, s. ..	3 Oct.	,,
Richard Gibbes, w., & Anne Sumers, w. ..	2 Nov.	,,
John Margettsonne, w., & Mary Fenne, s. ..	2 Nov.	,,
Wellyam Dengayne, w., p. Martham, & Elizabeth Marshman, w., this p.	17 Jan.	,,

John Calthorp, gent., this p., & Mrs. Elizabeth
   Cuddon, p. Shanfield, co. Suffolk, both
   single, were married there [*i.e.*, Shad-
   dingfield]   ..   ..   ..   7 Feb.   1670
John Warde, w., & Cicely Bolt, w., both p.
   Catfield   ..   ..   29 May   1671
Benjamin Dawson, b., & Alice Goose, w., both
   p. Ingham   ..   ..   ..   26 July   „
John Bacton, w., & Margery Haylett, w.   ..   1 Aug.   „
Willyam Coxton, b., & Anne Spicer, s.   ..   30 Oct.   „
Willyam Porter, b., & Elizabeth Cook, s., both
   p. Horsey   ..   ..   ..   1 Dec.   „
James Cubitt, b., this p., & Margarett Wright,
   s., p. Ingham   .   ..   ..   26 Dec.   „
Robert Grapes, w., & Anne Bongay, w., both p.
   Catfeilde   ..   ..   ..   31 Dec.   „
Willyam Cubitt, w., & Elizabeth Fuller, s.   ..   8 Jan.   „
Paul Fisher, b., & Elizabeth Stone, s.   ..   5 Feb.   „
Willyam Myhill, b., p. Catfield, & Elizabeth
   Empson, s., p. Potter Heigham   ..   3 Apr.   1672
Edmund Fenne, b., & Elizabeth Neve, s., this p.   3 Apr.   „
Solomon Dowe, b., & Margarett Cobbe, s.,
   both p. Catfield   ..   ..   ..   9 Apr.   „
Thomas Shorting, b., & Margarett Smith, w.   11 Feb.   „
Richard Johnson, b., & Margarett Johnson, s.   25 Nov.   1673
Nicholas Wright, b., & Margarett Johnson, w.   8 Jan.   „
Richard Pising, b., & Anne Allen, w.   ..   2 Feb.   „
John Bolt, b., & Mary Nuttell, s., both p.
   Palling   ..   ..   10 Feb.   „
Robert Ebbs, b., & Anne Manning, s.   ..   20 Apr.   1674
Nathaniel Neve & Mary Smith, both p. Great
   Yarmouth, *lic.*   .   ..   ..   8 June   „
Roger Sumers, w., & Mary Stewardson, s.,
   both this p.   ..   ..   ..   14 July   „
Thomas Burrage, w., & Elizabeth Gryffen, w.   15 Jan.   „
Samuel Fuller, b., p. N. Walsham, & Cicely
   Ebbes, s., this p.   ..   ..   ..   10 Aug.   1675
Anthony Steward, w., & Elizabeth Pollard, s.   14 Sept.   „
Samuel King, b., & Ann Gibbs, w. ..   ..   2 Feb.   1676
John Barker, w., & Alice Wincop, s., *lic.*   ..   13 Feb.   „

William Dawson, b., & Mary Pendall, s.	17 Apr.	1677
Nicholas Myhill, w., & Elizabeth Pye, s.	5 June	,,
John Ellis, b., & Joane Gambell, s. ..	5 June	,,
Robert Neave, b., & Alice Neave, s. ..	6 Nov.	,,
Robert Pye, w., & Elizabeth Morsses, w. ..	30 Nov.	,,
William Dawson, w., & Elizabeth Adkins, s.	21 May	1678
John Aylworth, b., & Mary Allen, s. ..	25 Aug.	,,
Thomas Keed, w., p. Tunstead, & Margaret		
Crane, s., p. Palling	3 Mar.	,,
Francis Standfeild, s., & Anne Crane, s., both		
this p.	4 Mar.	,,
John Catt, senr., w., & Elizabeth Summers, w.	29 Apr.	1679
Benjamine Callowe, b., p. Ingham, & Mary		
Backton, s., this p.	20 July	,,
James Sanders, w., p. Dilham, & Elizabeth		
Burrage, w., this p.	13 Oct.	,,
Thomas Cubitt, s., this p., & Anne Waters, s.,		
p. Reedham, *lic.*	2 Mar.	,,
Isaac Faireweather, b., & Elizabeth Digby, s.	18 May	1680
Stephen Reading, b., & Elizabeth Johnson, s.	19 May	,,
Phillip Roberts, w., & Elizabeth Julians, s. ..	14 Feb.	,,
John Bacton, w., & Frances Gates, s. ..	4 Apr.	1681
Stephen Fulcher, w., & Cicelie Hammond, w.,		
both p. Ludham, *lic.*	13 June	,,
William Martins, b., & Martha Pawling, s.,		
both this p.	5 Dec.	,,
John Summers, w., & Elizabeth Lambert, w.,		
both this p.	28 Feb.	,,
Thomas Breadye, b., & Amy Hodds, s., both		
this p.	17 Apr.	1682
William Hobart, w., p. Swanton Abbot, &		
Joan Tuck, w., p. Ludham	24 Apr.	,,
John Holton, b., & Anne Bray, s.	14 May	,,
John Thompson, b., p. Waxham, gent., &		
Elizabeth Calthorpe, s., this p., gentle-		
woman, *lic.*	27 Oct.	,,
Samuel Spanton, w., & Elizabeth Myhell, w.,		
both p. Pawling	31 Oct.	,,
Simon Haslewood, w., & Mary Pearse, w.,		
both this p.	20 Nov.	,,

John Robinson, b., p. Stalham, & Mary Read,
    s., p. Hickling .. .. .. 19 Dec. 1682
Robert Jackson, w., & Rachel Waters, s. .. 10 Apr. 1683
Thomas Hansell, b., & Mary Pightling, s.,
    both this p. .. .. .. 24 June „
Thomas Marthason, w., & Mary Waters, s. .. 9 Sept. „
Samuel Mack, b., & Ursula Pearce, w., both
    this p. .. .. 26 Dec. „
Henry Rolfe, b., & Esther Norgate, s., p.
    Ludham .. .. 14 Jan. „
John Holton, w., this p., & Jane Steward, w.,
    p. Ludham .. .. .. 21 Apr. 1684
James Ebbs, b., & Martha Wiseman, s., both
    this p. .. .. 6 May „
Robert Saunders, b., & Elizabeth Portar, w.,
    both p. Ludham .. .. .. 19 May „
Thomas Manne, b., & Mary Ebbs, s., p.
    Ludham .. .. 17 June „
Robert Margison, b., & Martha Leader, s.,
    both this p. .. .. .. 3 Aug. „
Anthony Graver, w., this p., & Anne Mickle-
    borough, w., p. Ingham .. .. 30 Sept. „
Valentine Gates, b., & Martha Margison, w.,
    both this p. .. .. .. 24 Nov. „
Adam Gates, w., & Lydia Hilderston, s., both
    p. Pawling .. .. .. 25 Nov. „
Thomas Lawes, b., & Alice Summers, s., both
    this p. .. .. 30 Apr. 1685
Elias Buttiphant, b., & Mary Wigger, both p.
    Ludham .. .. 4 May „
Francis Ormes, w., p. Great Yarmouth, &
    Anne Wilgresse, w., p. Martham .. 16 July „
John Russels, b., & Elizabeth Illbert, s., both
    p. Pawling.. .. .. .. 23 Aug. „
William Steward, w., & Thomasin Howes, s.,
    both p. Ludham, *lic.* .. .. 6 Jan. „
Thomas Clayton, w., & Margaret Thaxter, s.,
    both this p. .. .. .. 9 May 1686
Thomas Jackson, b., & Anne Hansell, s., both
    this p. . .. . 25 May „

Robert Gower, b., & Frances Baily, s., both p. Pawling, *lic.*	8 July	1686
Christopher Julians, b., & Lucie Cornwall, s., both this p.	30 Sept.	,,
Joseph Green, b., & Judith Lettice, s., both p. Ludham	30 Sept.	,,
Nathanael Wright, b., & Elizabeth Bowles, s., both p. Ludham	30 Sept.	,,
Richard Gilbert, b., & Sarah Faltrix, s., both p. Ludham	3 Oct.	,,
John Nobbing, b., & Anne Summers, s., both this p.	5 Oct.	,,
Robert Neave, w., & Mary Elworth, w., both this p.	19 Oct.	,,
Mr. Andrew Byng, b., & Sarah Lisbey, w., both this p., married at Norwich	24 Mar.	,,
Paul Fisher, w., this p., & Abigail Litler, w., p. Antingham	24 May	1687
William Coulsell, w., p. Hempstead, & Frances Lancaster, w., p. Hickling, *lic.*	14 June	,,
John Christmas, b., & Anne Noble, s., both p. Ludham	26 Sept.	,,
Salathiel Leame, w., p. Pawling, & Christian Haylet, w., this p.	18 Oct.	,,
Edward Underwood, b., & Susan Steward, s., both this p.	2 Nov.	,,
George Loads, b., & Elizabeth Sealey, s., both p. Ludham	7 Nov.	,,
Robert Allen, b., & Martha Dyball, s., both p. Ludham	21 Nov.	,,
Thomas Ormes, b., p. Great Yarmouth, & Mary Littlewood, s., p. Ludham	26 Dec.	,,
George Cooke, b., & Miriam Sadler, s., both p. Ludham	2 Jan.	,,
John Green, b., & Mary Brown, s., both p. Ludham	16 Feb.	,,
Samuel Haylet, b., & Frances Gower, w., both p. Pawling, *lic.*	27 Feb.	,,
John Annison, w., p. Billogby, & Elizabeth Milward, s., p. Ludham	16 Apr.	1688

Nathanael Haylet, b., & Anne Blogge, w., both
this p.   ..   ..   26 Apr.   1688
Daniel Taylour, w., p. Winterton, & Elizabeth
Steward, w., p. Pawling   ..   ..   11 June   „
Samuel Salman, b., p. Brumstead, & Alice
Lawes, w., p. Hickling   ..   ..   12 June   „
Stephen Holmes, w., & Elizabeth Haw, s.,
both p. Ludham   ..   ..   ..   18 Sept.   „
William Johnson, w., & Mary Slipper, s., both
this p.   ..   ..   9 Oct.   „
Charles Thompson, w., & Anne Greenaway, s.,
both p. Ludham   ..   ..   ..   23 Oct.   „
Samuel Wright, b., & Anne Summers, s., both
this p.   ..   ..   12 Nov.   „
John Catt, junr., w., & Elizabeth Allen, s.,
both this p.   ..   ..   ..   26 Nov.   „
Nicholas Tesdall, b., & Margaret Read, w.,
both p. Ludham   ..   ..   ..   27 Dec.   „
Paul Fisher, w., & Felicity Fuller, s., both
this p.   ..   ..   2 Jan.   „
Henry Manclark, w., & Alice Peterson, s.,
both p. Ludham   ..   ..   ..   1 Apr.   1689
Matthew Barker, b., & Prisca Atkins, s., both
this p.   ..   .. on Easter Monday,   1 Apr.   „
Thomas Tesdall, w., p. Catfield, & Anne Stain-
forth, w., this p.   ..   ..   ..   2 Apr.   „
Isaac Boots, w., & Mary Randals, w., both
this p.   ..   ..   23 Apr.   „
John Tuck, b., & Martha Empson, w., both p.
Ludham ..   ..   10 May   „
George Kendall, b., p. Thirne, & Mary Christ-
mas, s., p. Ludham ..   ..   ..   4 June   „
William Trollop, w., & Elizabeth Neave, w.,
both p. Ludham   ..   ..   ..   12 June   „
John Colbey, b., & Hannah Gray, s., both p.
Ludham ..   ..   29 July   „
William Boult, w., & Anne Dunham, w., both
p. Pawling   ..   ..   ..   26 Sept.   „
William Dawson, w., & Judith Sudbury, s.,
both this p.   ..   ..   ..   29 Sept.   „

John Breese, w., p. Stalham, & Christian
    Leame, w., this p. .. .. .. 3 Oct. 1689
Tobias Gilbert, b., & Mary Smith, s., both
    this p. .. .. 14 Oct. ,,
William Herbert, w., & Elizabeth Fuller, s.,
    both this p. .. .. .. 22 Oct. ,,
Roger Adams, w., & Abigail Ryall, w., both
    p. Ludham .. .. .. 20 Feb. ,,
William Vale, b., this p., & Alice Harding, s.,
    p. Ingham .. .. .. 21 Apr. 1690
William Johnson, w., & Mary Mason, s., both
    this p. .. .. 16 June ,,
Robert Harvy, b., & Mary Wasey, w., both p.
    Horning, *lic.* .. .. .. 24 June ,,
William Ulf, b., & Martha Ebbs, w., both
    this p. .. .. 2 July ,,
John Lomb, w., & Frances Wright, s., both p.
    Ludham .. .. 15 July ,,
John Holton, w., & Mary Crane, s., both
    this p. .. .. 3 Oct. ,,
William Jenkinson, b., p. Potter-Heigham, &
    Anne Backton, s., this p. .. .. 14 Oct. ,,
Thomas Harris, b., & Martha Jay, s., both
    this p. .. .. 30 Nov. ,,
Ambrose Gaul, b., this p., & Margaret Tuck,
    s., p. Ludham .. .. .. 5 Dec. ,,
William Meek, b., & Susan Cook, s., both p.
    Ludham .. .. 16 Dec. ,,
John Symonds, w., & Margaret Adams, s., both
    p. Ludham .. Easter Monday, 13 Apr. 1691
Joseph Thompson, w., & Jane Jordan, s., both
    p. Ludham .. .. .. 14 Apr. ,,
Thomas Myhill, b., p. Catfield, & Elizabeth
    Smith, s., this p., *lic.* .. .. 27 Apr. ,,
Edmond Gybbs, b., & Elizabeth Kirsp, s., both
    this p. .. .. 24 June ,,
Robert Cole, b., & Elizabeth Church, s., both
    this p. .. .. 2 Oct. ,,
Martin Youngs, w., & Mary Bird, s., both p.
    Ludham .. .. 22 Oct. ,,

Robert Moon, b., & Elizabeth Empson, s., both
    p. Ludham, *lic.* .. .. .. 24 Dec. 1691
John Moll, b., & Rebecca Mendham, w., both
    p. Ludham .. .. .. 26 Dec. „
Samuel Haylet, b., & Judith Cole, s., both
    this p. .. .. Shrove Tuesday, 8 Feb. „
Samuel Turner, b., this p., & Lettice Walker,
    s., p. Catfield .. .. .. 24 May 1692
Thomas Tracey, b., & Hannah Bailey, s., both
    p. Pawling .. .. .. 18 July „
Thomas Newbey, b., p. Palling, & Elizabeth
    Sudbury, s., this p... .. .. 4 Oct. „
Robert Trett, b., & Mary Popye, s., both p.
    Ludham .. .. 24 Oct. „
Paul Fisher, w., this p., & Briget Jay, s., p.
    Stalham .. .. 27 Nov. „
Edward Trett, b., & Margaret Connisby, s.,
    both this p. .. .. .. 27 Dec. „
John Russel, w., & Esther Shin, w., both p.
    Pawling .. .. 16 May 1693
John Mileham, b., & Mary Gray, s., both p.
    Ludham .. .. 5 June „
James Wright, b., p. Ingham, & Mary Stymp-
    son, s., p. Palling .. .. .. 25 June „
Richard Read, b., & Margaret Johnson, s.,
    both this p. .. .. .. 27 July „
John Bradley, b., & Jane Mickleborough, s.,
    both p. Potterheigham .. .. 19 Sept. „
Stephen Barnes, w., p. Stalham, & Mary
    Johnson, w., this p. .. .. 21 Sept. „
Thomas Empson, b., p. Pawling, & Anne
    Lambert, s., this p. .. .. 7 Nov. „
William Herbert, w., & Susan Shimpling, s.,
    both this p. .. .. .. 12 Nov. „
Thomas Swan, b., & Susan Helmes, s., both
    this p. .. .. 13 Nov. „
Matthew Barker, w., & Amy Fuller, s., both
    this p. .. .. 26 Dec. „
George Bayfield, b., & Elizabeth Thompson,
    both p. Ludham, *lic.* .. .. 19 Jan. „

Samuel Mack, w., & Mary Page, s., both
this p. .. .. 20 Feb. 1693
John Crisp, w., & Mary Margison, w., both
this p. .. .. 17 Apr. 1694
Joseph Boys, w., & Martha Bulliphant, w.,
both p. Ludham .. .. .. 28 May ,,
George Ellett, b., & Sarah Read, s., both this p. 5 Aug. .,
Nathanael Cann, w., & Mary Ryall, s., both
this p. .. .. 10 Sept. ,,
William Matthews, w., p. Hempstead, & Mary
Smyth, w., this p. .. .. .. 11 Sept. ,,
Daniel Davy, b., p. Ingham, & Mary Lisbey,
s., this p. .. .. 30 Sept. ,,
Christopher Ryall, w., & Martha Carter, w.,
both p. Ludham .. .. .. 13 Nov. ,,
Richard Bell, b., p. Ludham, & Margaret
Bernard, w., p. Frigby [Thrigby], *lic.* .. 2 Dec. ,,
Edmond Hamond, w., & Thomasin Steward,
w., both p. Ludham .. .. 27 Dec. ,,
Martin Calthorp, gent., b., & Mrs. Elizabeth
Wilkes, s., p. Satterley, in Suffolk,
married there .. .. .. 7 Jan. ,,
John Wigger, b., & Margaret Wiseman, s.,
both p. Ludham .. .. .. 3 July 1695
William Summer, b., & Elizabeth Pratt, s.,
both this p. .. .. .. 24 Sept. ,,
Stephen Fulcher, jun., b., & Thomasin Myhill,
s., both p. Ludham .. .. .. 3 Oct. ,,
John Smyth, b., & Margaret Myhill, s., both
this p. .. .. 23 Oct. ,,
William Summer, b., & Elizabeth Johnson, s.,
both this p. .. .. .. 23 Oct. ,,
William Coxton, w., & Abigail Jackson, w.,
both this p. .. .. .. 29 Oct. ,,
Francis Oakes, w., & Elizabeth Mohun, w.,
both p. Ludham .. .. .. 29 Oct. ,,
Robert Francis, b., & Judith Reeve, s., both
p. Ludham .. .. .. 30 Oct. ,,
John Gouge, b., & Ann Shanke, s., both p.
Ludham .. .. 8 Nov. ,,

William Mohun, b., & Mary Yembs, s., both
    p. Ludham   ..   ..   ..   12 Nov. 1695
Jacob Rouse, b., & Achsah Tate, s., both this p.   26 Dec.   „
John Waterson, b., & Jane Trivet, s., both p.
    Ludham ..   ..   4 Feb.   „
Robert Winter, w., & Mary Bunbury, w., both
    p. Ludham   ..   ..   ..   24 Feb.   „
John Dove, b., & Elizabeth Catt, s., both this p.   13 Apr. 1696
George Howel, w., & Elizabeth Spanton, w.,
    both p. Palling   ..   ..   ..   15 June „
Robert Walters, b., p. Hempstead, & Penelope
    Prior, s., this p.   ..   ..   ..   2 Oct.   „
Nicolas Pye, b., & Mary Falks, s., both this p.   20 Oct.   „
Thomas Empson, w., & Elizabeth Summer, s.,
    both this p.   ..   ..   ..   9 Nov.   „
Robert Allen, w., & Amy Ruddock, w., both
    p. Ludham   ..   ..   ..   13 Nov.   „
Thomas Tesdal, w., & Abigail Coxton, w., both
    this p.   ..   ..   15 Nov.   „
Robert French, b., & Mary Rogers, s., both p.
    Ludham ..   ..   11 Feb.   „
Robert Wright, b., & Mary Deynes, s., both p.
    Ludham ..   ..   30 Mar. 1697
Richard Russel, b., & Lydia Spanton, s., both
    p. Palling ..   ..   6 Apr.   „
John Ryall, b., & Margarett Margison, s., both
    this p.   ..   ..   18 Apr.   „
Samuel Thompson, b., & Judith Dawson, w.,
    both this p.   ..   ..   ..   19 July „
John Falks, w., & Elizabeth Gybbs, w.   ..   27 Dec.   „
Daniel Waller, b., & Elizabeth Dyball, s., both
    p. Ludham   ..   ..   ..   4 Mar.   „
Robert Worstead, b., labourer, & Elizabeth
    Watson, s., both p. Ludham ..   ..   27 Mar. 1698
Thomas Pollard, b., miller, & Mary Read, s.,
    both p. Ludham, *lic.*   ..   ..   14 June „
Robert Allen, w., labourer, & Mary Colbey,
    w., both p. Ludham   ..   ..   15 June „
Samuel Haylet, w., tailour, & Elizabeth Hodds,
    s., both p. Palling, *lic.*   ..   ..   29 July „

Thomas Pye, b., labourer, & Abigail Allen, s.,
  both this p.   ..   ..   ..   1 Aug.   1698
William Colls, b., labourer, & Elizabeth Bower,
  s., both this p.   ..   ..   ..   12 Sept.   „
Henry Sommer, b., labourer, & Margaret
  Martins, s., both this p.   ..   ..   7 Nov.   „
Jabez Holmes, b., labourer, & Mary Sarason,
  s., both p. Palling   ..   Easter Day, 9 Apr.   1699
John Howes, b., cordwainer, & Anne Larwood,
  s., both this p.   ...   .   10 Apr.   „
Luke Catt, labourer, & Elizabeth Jackson, w.,
  both this p.   ..   ..   ..   24 Apr.   1700
Simon Crow, b., husbandman, & Elizabeth
  Barns, of Stalham, married at Norwich   — — —
John Howes, cordwinder, & [———] [———]   — — —
William Margetson, labourer, & Ann Ilbrid,
  both this p., married at Sutton   ..   — Aug.   „
Thomas Hodeson, labourer, & Sarah Fuller,
  both this p.   ..   ..   ..   7 Oct.   „
Nichelass Case, thatcher, & Mary Jay, both
  this p.   ..   ..   29 Oct.   „
Henry Brooks, gardiner, & Elizabeth Read,
  this p., *lic.* ..   ..   9 Mar.   „
Robert Knave, w., & Mary Porter, both this p.   21 May   1701
John Bensly & Esther Amys, of Potter
  Heigham ..   ..   21 Oct.   „
William Ebbs, husbandman, & Mary Steward,
  both this p.   ..   ..   ..   28 Nov.   „
William Moon, b., husbandman, & Jane
  Welch, s. ..   ..   6 Apr.   1702
Samuel Paxman, labourer, & Elizabeth Borkin   19 June   „
Robert Nudd, miller, & Ann Smyth   ..   24 June   „
Henry Fenn, labourer, & Grace Cousins   ..   4 Oct.   „
Thomas Palling, w., labourer, & Mary Barker,
  w., married at Hempstead   ..   ..   5 Oct.   „
John Smyth, cordwinder, & Sarah Summers   1 Nov.   „
John George & Mary Catt   ..   ..   30 Mar.   1703
Edward Barker & Rebecca Moon ..   .   17 May   „
Stephen Johnsons & Ann Haylett ..   8 Oct.   1704
Edmund Gibbs & Ann Myhill   ..   ..   6 Nov.   „

Thomas Earle, w., & Elizabeth Jefery	..	29 May —
Thomas Bradley & Ann Each	.. ..	10 July —
John Woolstone & Ann Cubit	.. ..	31 July —
Robert Wade & Sarah [———]	.. ..	19 June 1708
John Flaxman & Mary Carter	..	23 May 1710
Thomas Bessy & Mary Dey	..	1 Nov. ,,
Richard Gibbs & Philippa Dingenary	..	12 Apr. 1711
Anthony Shekle & Margaret Ryal ..	..	28 May ,,
Henry Prat & Ann Cursp	..	29 May ,,
John Summers & Prudence Gaunt ..	..	18 June ,,
Samuel Howel & Mary Rust	..	9 July ,,
Samuel Ebbs & Ann Hall	..	7 Oct. ,,
Samuel Green & Elizabeth Cursp ..	..	8 Oct. ,,
David England & Ann Wright	..	15 Nov. ,,
Thomas Jackson & Margaret Dey ..	..	31 Dec. ,,
Christopher Shekle & Judith Winter	..	25 Feb. ,,
Robert Spanton & Hester Pixton ..	..	4 Mar. ,,
Samuel Savory & Hannah Weeds ..	..	2 Apr. 1712
John Summers & Martha Howes ..	..	29 Sept. ,,
Robert Nudd, w., & Margaret Thirkettle	..	29 Sept. 1713
William Moor & Elizabeth Witton ..	..	27 Oct. ,,
Thomas Pye & Elizabeth Colby	..	9 Nov. ,,
William Roe & Elizabeth Turner ..	..	8 May 1714
Henry Summers & Elizabeth Atkins	..	8 June ,,
John Fisher & Frances Cat	..	26 Dec. ,,
Anthony Shekle & Susanna [———]	..	17 Oct. 1715
Giles Stimpson & Elizabeth Cook ..	..	8 Dec. ,,
William Gibbs & Ann Ebbs	..	28 May 1716

Volume II.

Daniel Mears, w., & Frances Hodds, s., both p. Palling	26 Dec. 1716
Samuel Gillburd, b., & Elizabeth Ward, s., both this p.	13 May 1717
Anthony Shekle, w., & Mary Blogg, s., both this p.	15 May 1718
Samuel Haylett, b., & Elizabeth Stubbs, s., both this p.	9 June ,,
Isaac Myhill, w., & Elizabeth Case, w.	17 Sept. ,,

John Johnsons, b., & Elizabeth Dunham, s.,
  both p. Palling .. .. .. 3 Nov. 1718
John Houghton, b., & Elizabeth Crane, s. .. 28 Sept. 1719
John Barker, b., & Elizabeth Sumers, s. .. 10 Nov. „
John Mortar, w., p. Catfield, & Mary Keeler,
  this p. .. .. 17 Nov. „
Richard Gibbs, w., & Ann Ebbs, w. .. 24 Apr. 1720
Christopher Woolstone, b., & Elizabeth Bland,
  s., both p. Horsey, *lic.* .. .. 3 July „
Henry Dingenary, w., & Mary Neve, w. .. 17 Oct. 1721
George Teasdale, b., & Ann Massey, s. .. 23 Oct. 1722
William Ebbs, w., & Elizabeth Richmond, s. 12 Dec. „
John Boots, w., & Mary Callow, s. .. .. 7 Jan. „
Samuel Ward, b., p. Thirne, & Ann Dey, s.,
  this p. .. .. 29 Jan. „
Edmund Page, b., & Elizabeth Hunt, s., both
  p. Palling .. .. 23 Apr. 1723
Thomas Matthews, w., & Elizabeth Paxman, w. 6 June „
William Mowhaire, w., p. Sutton, & Rebecca
  Keeler, w. .. .. 12 Aug. „
John George, b., & Sarah Richmond, s. 3 May 1724
Joseph Stuard, b., & Mary Thaxter, s. 29 July „
Henry Summers, b., & Mary Chalders, s. .. 5 Oct. „
Edward Flogden, b., p. Somerton, & Sarah
  Robinson, s., p. Palling, *lic.* .. .. 10 Nov. „
Thomas Dove, b., p. Potter Heigham, & Joyce
  Crismas, s., this p. .. .. .. 22 Dec. „
Robert Woodrow, w., & Susannah Pye, s.,
  both p. Palling, *lic.* .. .. .. 28 Jan. „
Samuel Green, w., & Susannah Richmond, s. 12 Jan. 1725
William Ulfe, w., & Martha Gates, w. .. 10 Nov. 1726
Robert Read, b., & Phillipa Willes, s. .. 30 Apr. 1727
Thomas Empson, b., & Elizabeth Stimp-
  son, w. .. .. 2 Dec. 1728
Edmund Claxton, w., p. Ingham, & Ann
  Shevers [? Skevens], s. .. .. 16 Jan. „
Thomas Kidd, b., & Elizabeth Moon, s. .. 30 Sept. 1729
Anthony Sheckle, w., & Mary Breeze, s. [? 29 June] 1730
Robert Ward, b., & Elizabeth Cat, s. .. 29 June „
Benjamin Capps, b., & Elizabeth Crome, s. .. 5 Oct. „

Edmund Blackson, b., & Sarah Pye, s., both
this p. .. .. 3 Nov. 1730
Joel Myhil, b., & Mary Drake, s. .. .. 16 Nov. „
Simon Greenacre, w., & Mary Beverley, w.,
both this p. .. .. .. 30 Nov. „
John Turner, b., & Elizabeth Harding, s., both
this p. .. .. 6 Dec. „
Robert Moon, b., & Elizabeth Myhil, s. .. 28 Apr. 1731
Robert Nud, b., & Mary Bensley, s. .. 1 Oct. „
Samuel Roberts, w., & Esther Doughty, s. .. 8 Nov. „
Solomon Dowe [? Dove], b., & Ann Nudd [or
Rudd], s. .. .. 30 Nov. „
Nicholas Pye, w., & Elizabeth Johnson, s. .. 8 Dec. „
William Ebbs, b., this p., & Elizabeth Philips,
s., p. Havendem .. .. .. 26 Jan. „
Christopher Hows, b., & Sarah Boots, s. .. 20 Feb. „
Edmund Ebigail, b., & Sarah Bensley, s. .. 11 June 1733
John Margason, b., & Sarah Harvey, s. .. 12 Sept. „
Samuel Baker, b., p. Kirby Cane, & Mary
Worts, s., p. Roughton .. .. 17 Oct. „
John Summers, w., p. Ingham, & Hannah
Saunders, s., this p. .. .. 7 Oct. 1734
Edward Younge, b., this p., & Elizabeth
Hendry, s. .. .. .. 4 Nov. „
Robert Warnes & Elizabeth Watson .. 27 Jan. 173⁵⁄
Luke Catt & Easter Beverly .. 5 May 1731[*sic*]
William Duck & Hannah Witton .. .. 6 Dec. 1737
Edmund [? Gibbs] & [———] Riseborough .. 20 June 1738
Thomas Corbett & Hannah Somers .. 6 July „
Ed. [*sic*] Gilbert & Susannah Thaxter .. 4 Mar. „
Thomas Stimpson & Margaret Johnson .. 10 Oct. 1740
Samuel Coleman, b., & Margaret Fisher, w. .. 17 Oct. „
Robert Moon, w., & Anne Earl, s. .. .. 2 Nov. „
Robert Harvey & Susanna Everit .. .. 11 Nov. „
Joab Myhill & Elizabeth Freeman .. .. 13 Jan. „
John Bougin & Clementia Neal .. .. 11 Oct. 1741
Caleb Teasdale & Katherine Beest .. 17 Oct. „
William Cork & Elizabeth Tyler 3 May 1742
Richard Gibbs & Mary Harda .. .. 27 Oct. „
William Gibbs & Lydia Roberts .. .. 7 Nov. „

Samuel Ebbs & Margaret Crake	22 Nov.	1744
Caleb Teasdal & Mary Gedge	25 Nov.	„
John Flaxman & Ann Newton	21 Oct.	1745
Edward Flogden & Ann Myal	19 Nov.	„
John Lament & Elizabeth Wittledon ..	14 Apr.	„
John Fisher, this p., & Ann Harth, p. Gorlston	6 Oct.	1746
Simon Greenacre & Lydia Smith	6 May	„
John Mins & Elizabeth Miller ..	— Sept.	1747
William Richardson & Mary Stuard ..	— Oct.	„
John Hipper & Martha Teasdell	30 Sept.	1751
Samuel Haylett & Elizabeth Rutherford ..	1 Nov.	„
William Bully & Martha Haylett	26 Dec.	„
William Wells, b., p. Ingham, & Sarah Green-		
smith, s., this p.	6 Nov.	1752
John Gibbs & Elizabeth Kidd, both this p. ...	18 Oct.	1753
John Ward & Mary [*over* Elizabeth] Tomson,		
both this p.	— —	1754

Volume III.

John Beverly & Alice Neale	*29 July	1754
Samuel Turner & Mary Barrett, *lic.*, and		
woman's father's consent	17 Oct.	„
Richard Yaxley & Elizabeth Strange ..	25 Nov.	„
Samuel Ebbs & Sarah Mortemer, *lic.* ..	27 Jan.	1755
Thomas Stimpson, w., & Mary Allen ..	24 Mar.	„
Robert Barker & Hannah Wright, w., *lic.* ..	25 May	„
Thomas Pey, husbandman, & Mary Swallow	20 Oct.	„
Richard Barker & Mary Jarnakal	22 Feb.	1756
William Barker, w., this p., & Anne Sudberry,		
w., St. Martin at Palace, Norwich, *lic.*	5 July	„
Thomas Hutson & Sarah Strange	18 Oct.	„
John Woodrow, p. Bacton, & Elizabeth Barker,		
this p., *lic.*	25 Oct.	„
Jacob Andrews, p. St. Martin at Palace, Nor-		
wich, & Ann Bean, this p., *lic.* ..	1 Nov.	„
Edmund Gibbs, w., & Mary Cooper ..	8 Nov.	„
John Blaxen & Ann Kettle	29 Nov.	„

* After this date, unless otherwise stated, the parties are invariably
of Hickling, and respectively bachelor and spinster.

John Martins, w., & Eamey Bush	7 Feb.	1757
William Greenaker & Sarah Smith ..	6 Nov.	1758
John Turner & Mary Press	5 Dec.	„
Joel Myhill, w., & Elizabeth Haylet, w. ..	22 Jan.	1759
John Burton & Mary Duck	29 July	„
Thomas Hardy & Mary Stone, w., *lic.* ..	8 Oct.	„
Robert Batchelor & Elizabeth Summers, *lic.* ..	5 Nov.	„
John Houghton & Susan Blaxen	21 Jan.	1760
Thomas Barret & Elizabeth Gibbs	21 Jan.	„
Edward Bloom & Lettice Turner	14 Apr.	„
John Smith & Mary Strange	7 July	„
John Dyball, w., p. Southrepps, & Prudence Bates	14 July	„
John Smith, p. Wroxham, & Margaret Mack	6 Apr.	1761
Robert Westgate & Margaret Fisher ..	5 Oct.	„
John Crowe, p. Catfield, & Elizabeth Brooks, *lic.*	20 Oct.	„
Miles Wiseman & Anne Harrison	9 Nov.	„
John George & Elizabeth Ulph ..	19 Apr.	1762
Thomas Carter, w., & Alice Leech	5 July	„
John Burton & Anne Benstead, *lic.* ..	15 Nov.	„
James Harby, w., & Mary Hall, *lic.* ..	3 Jan.	1763
Simon Greenacre, w., & Hannah Corbett, w.	30 Apr.	1764
Robert Moore & Judith Hall, *lic.*	28 May	„
Richard Fabb & Elizabeth Moon, *lic.* ..	17 Dec.	„
Humphry Eglinton, p. Neatishead, & Hannah Passon, w.	9 Apr.	1765
Solomon Dove, w., & Mary Crane	27 May	„
Benjamin Passon, w., & Mary Bean, *lic.* ..	30 May	„
Samuel Pooley, p. St. Michael, Coslany, Norwich, & Sarah Moon	20 Jan.	1766
Aaron Willows & Ann Hall, *lic.*	4 Feb.	„
John Gaville & Mary Carter . ..	30 June	„
George Covel & Sarah Stimpson	14 Nov.	„
William Myhill & Mary Bougen, *lic.* ..	25 Feb.	1767
John Smith, w., & Sarah Passon	21 Apr.	„
Joseph Greenacre & Anne Brooke	15 June	„
John Conniard, w., p. Horning, & Sarah Croxton	16 June	„
William Gilbert & Mary Anne Hennant ..	12 Oct.	„
Thomas Durrant & Anne Hudson	5 Jan.	1768

William Thain & Martha Haddon	31 Oct.	1768
George Riches, p. Martham, & Elizabeth Bowgen, *lic*	30 Nov.	,,
Daniel Cook, p. Stalham, & Sarah Fisher ..	10 Oct.	1769
Nathaniel Cann & Mary Blackstone ..	23 Nov.	,,
John Hipper, w., & Elizabeth Breese ..	2 July	1770
Joseph Boyce, p. St. Clement, Norwich, & Mary Sudbury	16 July	,,
William Gibbs & Elizabeth Frances ..	22 Oct.	,,
William Mortar & Elizabeth Corbett ..	14 Jan.	1771
William Pilgrim & Sarah Brooks .. .	20 Feb.	,,
Samuel Burton & Mary Barker	17 June	,,
Thomas Bollom & Mary Coleman	30 July	,,
Benjamin Beates & Anne Bully	17 Sept.	,,
John Crean & Sarah Howse	5 Nov.	,,
Edward Arms & Amy Roll, *lic.*	16 Dec.	,,
John Francis & Anne Phillis Passon ..	23 Feb.	1772
William Cork, p. Great Yarmouth, & Mary Ann Langley	30 June	,,
Samuel Haylett, w., & Amy Martins, w. ..	23 Sept.	,,
Robert Nudd & Margaret Gibbs . ..	9 Nov.	,,
Valentine Gibbs & Sarah Cork	18 Nov.	,,
Samuel Flogden, p. Waxham, & Ann Durrant, *lic.*	26 Nov.	,,
Isaac Thompson & Sarah Trorey	26 Apr.	1773
James Allen, w., & Mary Howse	7 June	,,
John Gaze & Margaret Fisher	29 June	,,
William Howard & Martha Randels ..	1 Nov.	,,
William Grant, p. Great Yarmouth, & Phyllis Howse, *lic.*	22 Dec.	,,
Stephen Collyer, w., & Sarah Haylett ..	13 Jan.	1774
Matthew Gedge & Anne Gibbs	14 Apr.	,,
William Ebbs & Elizabeth Stone, *lic.*	18 Oct.	,,
James Rye & Anne Stone	27 Feb.	1775
Joel Miel [*signs* Myhill], w., & Mary Mounford [*signs* Munford], w.	10 June	,,
William Sadler, p. East Ruston, & Ann Cubitt *lic.*	21 Oct.	,,
Thomas Norgate, w., p. Smallburgh, & Mary Gibbs, w.	19 Feb.	1776

John Shreve & Sarah Wiseman	28 Apr.	1777
Artemis Wigg & Elizabeth Oakley ..	4 June	„
John Daniel, p. Great Yarmouth, & Susannah		
Cubitt, *lic.*	18 Nov.	„
Thomas Caulk & Elizabeth Woolstern ..	6 Apr.	1778
William Sloper & Margaret Gaze, w. ..	20 Apr.	„
John Wiseman & Rebecca Carter	12 Oct.	„
James Woodrow & Hannah Archer ..	2 Nov.	„
Robert Orstick & Hannah Morse	24 Nov.	„
Robert Mortar & Mary Burton	12 Jan.	1779
Samuel Thaine & Elizabeth Gibbs	29 Mar.	„
John Hotson & Mary Lacey	4 Nov.	„
William Jones & Mary Wiseman	21 Dec.	„
John Fisher & Elizabeth Martin	28 Feb.	1780
Benjamin Passons, jun., & Susannah Dutch-		
man, w., *lic.*	28 June	„
James Allen, w., & Elizabeth Gilbert ..	7 Oct.	„
Francis Linford & Mary Postle	16 Oct.	„
Thomas Gay & Elizabeth Webster ..	5 Nov.	1781
Samuel Ford & Mary Dove	9 Nov.	„
John Gaze, w., & Margaret Last, w., *lic.* ..	21 Nov.	„
John Gibbs, w., & Mary Thompson ..	14 Oct.	1782
James Bell & Mary Bully	14 Oct.	„
Thomas Howard & Sarah Fisher	18 Nov.	„
Lawrence Barker, jun., & Elizabeth Pratt ..	19 May	1783
Falock Randal & Dianah Mason	3 June	„
Robert Nichols & Elizabeth Houghton ..	9 June	„
John Fish, p. Burgh, & Thomesine Gibbs ..	13 Oct.	„
John Neave, p. Catfield, & Jane Bush ..	12 Nov.	„
Thomas Sizer & Elizabeth Cann, *lic.* ..	9 Jan.	1784
George Chase, w., & Susanna Holten, w. ..	20 Apr.	„
Richard Trorey & Elizabeth Gibbs ..	18 Oct.	„
William Beales [*signs* Bales] & Sarah Doughty	12 July	1785
Jeremiah Sufflen, p. Ludham, & Sarah Nudd	27 Dec.	„
Matthew Gedge, w., & Sarah Ward ..	2 June	1786
Alexander Siely, p. Happisburgh, & Ann		
Crowe, *lic.*	11 July	„
Philip Gibbs & Elizabeth Wiseman, w., *lic.* ..	29 Sept.	„
John Fish, w., & Sarah Steward	3 Oct.	„
William Flaxman & Elizabeth Martins ..	16 Oct.	„

John Sims & Ann Oakley, *lic.*	28 Feb. 1787
John Field & Phillis Jee	4 June „
John Dunn, w., & Susannah Elden, *lic.* ..	25 Sept. „
John Hicks & Ann Dow, *lic.*	2 Oct. „
Joseph Fox & Ann Bexfield	10 Oct. „
William Minner & Mary Mack, *lic.*	12 Feb. 1788
Samuel Beverly, p. Runham, & Sarah Greenaker	19 May „
John Orstick & Hannah Ward	11 Nov. „
Richard Lown, w., & Elizabeth Weales ..	29 July 1789
William Orstick & Ann George	5 Oct. „
Thomas Blackbone & Sarah Covell ..	23 Apr. 1790
Joseph Eaton & Sarah Kerrison, w., *lic.* ..	28 Apr. „
Thomas Amas & Frances Allen	2 June „
John Mason & Abigail England	11 Oct. „
John George & Elizabeth Ward	12 Oct. „
John Clark & Hannah Passon	14 Oct. „
Robert Batcheldor & Elizabeth Drooksher ..	10 Nov. „
John Gamble & Sarah Oakley, *lic.*	18 Nov. „
John Mayes & Anne Norman	20 Apr. 1791
James Thaine & Elizabeth Chapman ..	1 Aug. „
William Wall & Ann Corp, w.	8 Aug. „
Mark Bacon & Mary George	23 Jan. 1792
George Gibbs & Amies Burton	2 Apr. „
Samuel Jones & Ann Purt	9 Apr. „
John Dove & Alice Bird	11 Apr. „
Robert Moore & Mary Gibbs	18 July „
Samuel Nockels & Mary Goose, a minor, with consent of parents, *lic.*	23 July „
Robert Gibbs & Hannah Barker	14 Aug. „
James Nudd & Elizabeth Saunders ..	4 Feb. 1793
John Fisher, w., & Mary Dove, w.	26 Mar. „
John Bulley & Mary Oakely	22 Apr. „
John Nicholson & Elizabeth Howard ..	30 Apr. „
Jonathan Norman & Mary Lack	2 Oct. „
John Gaze & Elizabeth Thain, w.	13 Jan. 1794
William Caulk, w., & Hannah Adams ..	12 Feb. „
William Ward, w., & Elizabeth Sizar, w. ..	3 Mar. „
John Howell, w., & Mary Dove, w. ..	12 June „
Benjamin Howes & Elizabeth George ..	4 Aug. „

John Nudd & Judith Harby Willows ..	12 Jan.	1796
Thomas George & Jemima Smith	10 Oct.	„
William Buttifant [*signs* Butterfunt] & Eliza-		
beth Myhill	14 Oct.	„
John Oakley, w., & Mary Gray	12 Dec.	„
John Flaxman, p. Repps, & Margaret Smith	19 Dec.	„
John Mann & Sarah Mortar	23 Apr.	1798
Samuel Durrant & Mary Short	11 Oct.	„
Jonathan Norman, w., & Mary Breeze ..	8 Nov.	„
John Cannon & Mary Ward	21 Jan.	1799
James Spanton, p. Great Yarmouth, & Ann		
Dutchman	11 Feb.	„
John Sexton & Ann Barnard	26 Feb.	„
Thomas Mason & Mary Bollom	10 June	„
Stephen Wright & Charlotte Nudd ..	22 Aug.	„
Thomas George & Sarah Myhill	21 Jan.	1800
Henry Martins, p. Brunstead, & Charity		
Church	9 June	„
Thomas Bunn & Elizabeth Harby, *lic.* ..	2 Oct.	„
George Bell, p. Catfield, & Sarah Slopar ..	16 Dec.	„
William Slopar, p. Filby, & Ann Howard ..	26 Dec.	„
William Turner & Mary Theory	27 Apr.	1801
Daniel George & Diana Mason	1 June	„
Edward Gibbs & Phillis Wenn	15 July	„
James Moore & Lucy Gibbs	8 Sept.	„
William Mortar & Hannah Turner ..	23 Nov.	„
John Church & Esther Hows	28 Dec.	„
George Lee, w., & Elizabeth Plumb ..	25 May	1802
John Nudd & Ann Spanton	14 June	„
William Mills & Elizabeth Linwood ..	18 Oct.	„
John Bush & Mary Harmer	2 Dec.	„
Dionysius Frankling & Elizabeth Goose ..	29 Dec.	„
John Gibbs & Ann Crowe, *lic.*	13 Apr.	1803
John Chapman & Ann Bell	6 June	„
William George & Pamela Turnmore ..	15 Aug.	„
John Annison, w., p. Great Yarmouth, & Ann		
Harby, *lic.*	23 Feb.	1804
James Germany, p. South Walsham, & Ann		
Baker	24 Apr.	„
Samuel Burton, w., & Ann Knights ..	24 Dec.	„

William Howse & Sarah Taylor ..	25 Aug.	1805
Thomas Mason, w., & Elizabeth Church ..	27 Aug.	„
John Riches & Margaret Sloper	21 Oct.	„
Thomas Wright & Ann Money	18 Nov.	„
William Hodds, p. Blofield, & Sarah Mortar	24 Dec.	„
Francis Crane & Mary Gibbs	6 Jan.	1806
William Lingwood & Mary Wigg	13 Oct.	„
John Allen & Elizabeth Tungate ..	15 Dec.	„
William Roberts & Ann Priest [? Puart] ..	27 Jan.	1807
Joseph Pollard & Elizabeth Allon ..	19 Mar.	„
William Chapman & Juliet Moore	27 Oct.	„
James Bishop & Elizabeth Bacon	10 Dec.	„
Philip Gibbs & Hannah Gedge	29 Feb.	1808
Samuel Box, w., p. Great Yarmouth, & Tabitha Money, *lic.*	29 Mar.	„
George Lee, w., & Mary Grimmer, w. ..	5 Nov.	„
George Ransome & Hannah Bishop, *lic.* ..	9 Mar.	1809
John Durrant & Elizabeth Wilworth ..	8 May	„
Robert Morter & Sarah Ellis Gregory ..	11 Oct.	„
Thomas Howard & Kezia Kidman ..	23 Jan.	1810
Samuel Nave, w., & Mary Lees, w. ..	15 Oct.	„
Samuel Ford, w., & Elizabeth Fisher ..	20 Nov.	„
William Trory & Ann Kerrison	10 Dec.	„
John Mason & Frances Bell	25 Dec.	„
Samuel Burton, w., & Elizabeth Dyball ..	10 June	1811
John Sims & Mary Gedge	16 Sept.	„
John Crowe & Hannah Salmon, *lic.* ..	29 Sept.	„
Thomas Croxton & Elizabeth Austwick ..	12 Nov.	„
William Mason & Mary Cooper ..	17 Dec.	„
Joseph Fox & Sarah Dove	24 Dec.	„
Samuel Nockolds, w., & Mary Atkins, w., *lic.*	11 Jan.	1812
Thomas Dane & Mary Randles	10 Feb.	„
George Bacon & Sarah Croxton	16 June	„
John Raven & Hannah Wright, *lic.* ..	23 Aug.	„

Marriages at Bedingham,

1561 to 1812.

NOTE.—Volume I.—Bound in thin parchment, 7 in. by 12 in., parchment
leaves, in good preservation, 1561 to 1708.

Volume II.—Bound in thin parchment, 8 in. by 13½ in., parchment
leaves, 1709 to 1737.

Volume III.—Bound in stiff covers covered with parchment, 6¼ in.
by 14¾ in., parchment leaves, 1737 to 1753.

Volume IV.—An Act of Parliament Register, bound in stiff covers
covered with brown leather, 8½ in. by 10¼ in., 1754 to 1812.

Volume V.—Bound in stiff covers with brown leather, 9¾ in. by
13 in., parchment leaves, 1781 to 1800, a duplicate in part of
Volume IV.

Volume VI.—Bound in stiff covers covered with parchment, 9½ in.
by 12 in., parchment leaves, 1783 to 1786, a duplicate in part of
Volumes IV and V. Each entry in this Volume has a stamp
marked sixpence impressed in the margin against it.

These entries up to 1619 were copied by Rev. R. Fetzer Taylor,
Rector of Hedenham, and from 1620 to 1708 by Miss Fetzer Taylor,
by leave of Rev. L. Morgan, Vicar of Bedingham, who also copied
those from 1709 to 1812.

VOLUME I.

Robert Fletcher & Elizabeth Fordame	.. 12 Oct.	1561
John Gosling & Anne Weare ..	.. 1 June	1562
Thomas Woodyard & Margaret Davye	.. the same daye	
William Woodcocke & Agnes Starffe	.. 11 July	1562
Richard Pryor & Agnes Grene ..	.. 1 Oct.	,,
William Spilling & Margaret Skeet	.. the same daye	
William Sparham & Agnes Wilton	.. 3 Dec.	1562
James Spencer & Anne Benidicke ..	.. 18 Apr.	1563
John Spilling & Ales Goslinge ..	.. 13 June	,,
Robert Whall & Margaret Goslinge	.. 1 May	1564
Rychard Bristowe & Margaret Symons	.. 9 Oct.	,,
John Randoll & Ellen Woodcocke ..	.. 14 Jan.	,,
Rychard Gaselye & Mary Wauller	.. 1 Mar.	,,
Edward Spillinge & Alice Allen ..	.. 7 Oct.	1565
John Sadde & Julyan Bancraft ..	.. 23 Sept.	1566

Thomas Rychardson & Agnes Cole	.. 14 July 1567
William Thacker & Joane Smith ..	.. 19 June 1569
Robert Lynde & Joane Benedicke ..	.. 18 Sept. „
Mychaell Archer & Agnes Fisher ..	.. 9 Oct. 1571
John Whitinge & Joane Petingayle	.. 20 July 1572
Thomas Skeet & Philip Hullet	.. 19 Oct. „
Thomas Fenne & Joane Whall	.. 8 Nov. 1573
John Killiat & Alice Davye	.. 20 June 1575
John Crickmer & Margaret Carian	.. 17 July „
George Browne & Jane Blumfeild ..	.. 17 Sept. „
Thomas Thacker & Joane Singler ..	.. 6 Nov. „
Nycholas Thacker & Elizabeth Causeler	.. 2 June 1577
William Read [?] & Margaret Hayle	.. 1 Oct. „
William Mingaye & Agnes Gose ..	.. 13 Oct. „
Thomas Prior & Agnes Wright	.. 3 Oct. „
Francis Tuttall & Jane Penetent ..	.. 20 Oct. „
Rychard Whall & Anne Goslinge ..	.. 14 Apr. 1578
John Thacker & Christiana Burward	.. 13 Sept. 1579
Bartlemew Holder & Anne Crouch	.. 7 Apr. 1580
Rychard Seman & Anne Cole, w. ..	.. 9 Dec. 1584
John Fitton & Anne [———]	.. 12 Apr. „
Thomas Mylls & Alice Pyke	.. 17 June 1585
John Bodorne & Susanne Pitte	.. 8 Aug. „
William Baker & Agnes Huggard ..	.. 5 Sept. „
Arthur Wilton & Martha Goslinge	.. 10 Oct. 1588
Roger Fenninge & Alice Priest	.. 17 Sept. 1589
Thomas Rudde & Jane Huggard ..	.. 7 Dec. „
Thomas Game & Elizabeth Atkins ..	.. 8 Feb. „
John Smith & Jane Huggard	.. 24 Aug. 1590
Rychard Purser & Joane Harvye ..	.. 22 Apr. 1592
Edmund Hayles & Elizabeth Whall	.. 17 May „
Thomas Pook & Jane Gosse	.. 9 Nov. „
Rychard Whall & Margaret Goslinge	30 Nov. „
Rychard Killiat & Elizabeth Purser	.. 12 Aug. 1593
Matthew Brasen & Elizabeth Osbestone	.. 20 May 1594
John Gooch & Margerie Goslinge ..	.. 7 Oct. 1595
Thomas Stubbs & Alice Korbell [?] *alias* Fuller	4 Apr. 1597
John Gooch & Margaret Elson	.. 1 May „
Thomas Alborowe & Agnes Milburne	.. 24 Apr. 1598
William Thurton & Joane Alexander	.. 3 June „

Rycharde Smythe & Suzane Randoll	.. 30 July	1598
John Lone & Margaret Purser	.. .. 23 Aug.	,,
William Spilling & Alice Purser	.. .. 28 Nov.	,,
Marmaduke Browne & Margaret Goslinge	.. 8 Mar.	,,
Matthew Brasnet & Elizabeth Miller	8 May	1599
Jeffrey Hendrye [?] & Barbara Tuttall	.. 3 June	,,
John Andrews & Anne Purser	10 Jan.	1600
Peter Garthrope & Marye Mene	.. .. 3 Feb.	,,
John Holbrooke & Elizabeth Killiat	.. 20 July	1602
Eleazar Folgate & Elizabeth Seaman	.. 21 Mar.	,,
John Route & Alice Crickmere	.. .. 5 Dec.	1603
Rychard Seman & Elizabeth Lachilus	.. 6 Nov.	,,
Thomas Swanne & Susane Meriman	.. 15 Dec.	1604
John Neall & Margaret Boxforth	.. .. 23 Apr.	1605
William Weston & Elizabeth Smith	.. 20 Oct.	1606
George Fowler & Margaret Shall	.. .. 22 Apr.	1607
Robert Bennet & Anne Ward	.. 13 May	,,
George Elsye & Barbara Blithe	.. .. 27 Sept.	,,
Thomas Smith, gent., & Elizabeth Gosling, gentlewoman	.. .. .. 10 Feb.	,,
Edward Andrews & Susan Greene	.. 8 Nov.	1608
William Woolnoe & Elizabeth Plummer	.. 5 June	1609
Henrie Sadde & Johana Strongier	.. .. 24 Aug.	,,
William Sherringham & Anne Laccheler	.. 26 June	1610
William Purser & Dionise Davie	.. .. 16 Sept.	1611
John Aldrich & Ales Base	.. .. 28 June	1612
Lionn Ghasty & Mary Vesey	.. .. 11 July	1613
Robert Davy & Mary Wates, w.	.. .. 19 Oct.	,,
Henry Bunnett & Bridgett Blythe	.. .. 28 Oct.	1614
Willyam Smithe, clerke, & Mabell Lynsie, w.	9 Jan.	,,
William Blythe & Ann Wilton	.. .. 4 May	1615
John Plummer & Margaret Murton	.. 19 June	,,
Edmund Reeve & Mary Mayse	.. 25 Aug.	,,
Willyam Meeke [?] & Elizabeth Taylor	.. 25 Sept.	,,
Stephen Payne, of Topcroft Chappell, this p., & Bridgett Smith, of Fresingfeld	.. 6 Oct.	1616
Thomas Goldham & Ann Mingay	.. .. 28 Oct.	,,
Richard Boade & Alice Staff	.. .. 8 Sept.	1617
John Sawer & Judith Bemont	.. .. 19 Sept.	,,
William Andrewes & Elsabeth Sheldrake	.. 30 Oct.	,,

Willyam Turpen & Alice Fenninge	..	3 Feb.	1617
John Plumer & Prudence Twissellton	..	22 Sept.	1619
Robert Tyte & Mary Strowger	.. ..	7 Oct.	„
Thomas Ward & Ellen Mingay	.. ..	25 Apr.	1620
John Davye & Mary Killett	.. ..	— — —	
Peter Brooke & Lucye Cushian	.. ..	4 Oct.	1621
William Smithe & Mary Sherman, w.	..	5 Oct.	„
John Davy & Annice Harplie	..	8 Oct.	„
Richard Strowcher & Jane Strogar	..	22 Jan.	„
Peter Daynes & Alyce Sallowes	..	15 July	1622
Richard Whale & Mathew Rix	..	10 Oct.	„
Robert Blundell & Elizabeth Homes	..	24 Feb.	„
Robert Sparke & Ruth Locke	.. ..	3 Apr.	1623
Jeffery Mingay & Grace Hilliard	.. ..	3 Oct.	„
Robert Jermy & Jane Gay	..	19 Dec.	1624
Margaret Gosling & Richard Withe	..	3 Sept.	1629
Robert Bacon & Anne Racye	..	5 Nov.	„
Henry Wesgate & Mary Alboroughe	..	28 Oct.	1630
Daniel Palmer & Mary Greene, w. ..	..	9 Aug.	1631
John Wolnoughe & Alice Whall	..	2 Feb.	„
Thomas Carver & Prudence Goslinge	..	11 Dec.	1632
John Crickmer, w., & Anne Andrewes, w.	..	— —	1634
Ephraim Rudde & Mary Corbin	..	4 Nov.	„
Edward Calvert & Susan Payne	..	4 Jan.	1635
William Bacon & Winnifrede Ponsunbye	..	14 Feb.	1636
George Maries & Margaret Howard	..	20 June	„
Thomas Bacon & Frances Gosling ..	..	23 Aug.	„
William Spillinge & Anne Wattes ..	..	6 Aug.	„
Thomas Skeet & Susan Wilton	..	19 Dec.	1637
Thomas Stymer & Susan Sheldrake	..	26 June	1638
Thomas Greene & Susan Gosling ..	..	20 Aug.	„
Richard Shelford & Elizabeth Gosling	..	20 Oct.	1639
Christopher Jermyn & Elizabeth Fayrechild	5 Apr.	1640
Thomas Rodgers & Margery Chapman	..	27 July	„
Samuell Steed & Ann Ston	.. ..	7 Jan.	„
Linot Cooke & Honor Gowinge	..	16 May	1641
James Brassene & Elezabeth Cuningham	..	12 Jan.	„
Thomas Hollines & Anne Freman ..	..	17 Jan.	„
Thomas Fenn & Margaret Colman ..	..	2 May	1642
David Turner & Alice Read	.. ..	25 Oct.	1643

Robert Randall & Dorothey Smyth	1 Oct.	1644
Richard Shrew & Elizabeth Smith ..	16 Sept.	1645
William Spoon & [———] Woolmer	23 Sept.	„
John Pitcher & Margaret Buttols ..	9 Jan.	„
George Smith & Frances Goodwin	23 Sept.	1647
John Smith & Kathrine Man	5 Oct.	„
John Oberton & Mary Randall	14 Oct.	„
Richard Crickmer & Jane Pollard ..	17 —	1648
Richard Vineyard & Mary Snell ..	26 June	„
Edmund Gegge & Elizabeth Smith	5 July	„
John Jonas & Alice Read ..	26 Feb.	1649
Thomas Rud & Margaret Rouse ..	2 Nov.	1652
Gaudy Hacon, clerke, & Bridget Gosling	16 Apr.	1658
John Sewell, w., & Mathew Pingle, w.	21 July	1659
William Puncher & Mary Gurney ..	9 Oct.	1660
Robert Bunne & Mary Mayes	31 Oct.	1661
Samuel Fuller & Elizabeth Sutton, w.	21 Jan.	„
William Goate & Ann Watson	13 Oct.	1663
William Copping, clerk, & Elizabeth Stone ..	7 Dec.	„
John Singler & Elizabeth Dunt	28 Aug.	1664
Robert Jay & Lucy Wilton	3 Jan.	„
James Tilney, of Hedenham, w., & Sarah Kipping, of Denton	25 July	1665
Robert Killet & Mary Keble	26 Sept.	„
Edmund Eley & Mary Bays	3 Oct.	„
Arthur Smith & Martha King	5 Oct.	„
Robert Selling & Mary Smyth	3 July	1666
John Carion & Audrey Blundell ..	15 Apr.	1667
Richard Swan, of Bungay, w., & Dinah Linds, of Bedingham	1 Oct.	1668
Edmund Johnson & Sarah Bottred..	30 Sept.	1669
John Mallom, gent., & Mrs. Elizabeth Copping, w.	7 Apr.	1670
Thomas Woolmer & Elizabeth Borrowes, of Earsham ..	30 June	„
John Watson & Susanna Williams	21 May	1671
Robert Bardwell & Mary Mallorum	30 Sept.	„
Henry Reynolds & Margaret Boddom	16 Oct.	1673
William Townshend, of Norwich, w., & Bridgett King, of Woodton, w.	8 Oct.	1674

John Carver, of Hedenham, & Susan Becket	15 Apr. 1675
Daniel Randall & Elizabeth Todd	4 Feb. 1676
Jeremiah Howerd, of Fressingfield, co. Suffolk, & Mary Mingay	7 Oct. 1677
William Cole, of Burrow, & Susan Keable ..	13 Jan. ,,
John Brown, of Seething, & Esther Brown, of Fritton	9 Sept. 1678
John Noble, w., & Elizabeth Moore, both of Fressingfield, co. Suffolk	1 Dec. ,,
Thomas Chimney & Mary Rudd .. .	12 Apr. 1680
Thomas Stone, gent., w., & Catherine Jay, of Earsham, w.	9 June 1681
Edmund Spilling & Elizabeth Bolt, both of Earsham	22 Apr. 1683
Thomas Emmerson & Margaret Edwards ..	1 Oct ,,
John Stannard, of Bungay, & Hannah Ashford	12 Feb. ,,
Henry Rainolds, of Kirbie, & Sarah Becket ..	30 Sept. 1684
Edmund Jonson, w., & Elizabeth Bennet, w.	16 Nov. ,,
Robert Diggerne & Temperance Becket ..	27 Nov. ,,
Nathaniel Rivil, w., of Topcroft, & Temperance Becket, w.	1 Oct. 1685
James Randoll & Temperance Diggerne, w. ...	18 June 1686
Thomas Havers, clerk, of Intwood-cum-Keswick, & Anne Pipe, of Laxfield ..	7 July 1687
William Roper, w., & Marie Webster, w., both of Earsham	2 Feb. ,,
Richard Cottingham & Martha Jay, w. ..	1 Oct. 1688
Richard Floures & Agatha Simes	2 Oct. ,,
Henry Colman, of Harlston, & Rose Allen, of Metfield, co. Suffolk	15 Oct. 1689
Richard Rix & Mary Bencely	— — ,,
John Baldry & Sarah Catling	22 Apr. 1690
Edward Shirman, w., & Mary Briggs, w. ..	5 Oct. ,,
Henry Warnes & Mary Auger, of Seeding ..	13 Oct. ,,
Edmund Rudd, w., & Sisley Cantlin ..	1 Dec. ,,
Robert Churchman & Mary Ofield, w., both of Bungay, S. Mary's p. ..	25 June [?] 1691
Michael Briant & Elizabeth Harvie, both of Bungay	30 June [?] ,,
Francis Fairchild & Mary Trogmartin ..	9 June 1692 [?]

Robert Elliot, of Ditchingham, & Elizabeth
Browne .. .. 1 Dec. 1693
John Salman & Jane Gunns .. .. 5 Feb. ,,
Henry Chittleburge & Ann Thurston, w. .. 19 June 1695
John Jackley, of Kirstead, & Susan Brook .. 1 Oct. ,,
Phillip Faired & Mary Below .. .. 3 Oct. ,,
Edmund Jonson & Mary Sinckler .. .. 14 Oct. ,,
William Lake & Sarah Richmond, both of
Hedneham .. .. .. 9 May 1696
John Wade, w., & Elizabeth Lown, both of
Woodton . .. . 4 Oct. ,,
Thomas Smith, of Spexhall, & Sarah Gunns 6 Oct. ,,
Robert Livock, of Porland, & Elizabeth Smith 4 Oct. 1698
John Gunns, w., & Mary Bert .. .. 14 Nov. ,,
John Wales, w., & Bridgett Snell, both of
Denton .. .. 1 Dec. ,,
Henry Jay & Elizabeth Linnox .. .. 10 Feb. ,,
Edmund Simons, of Bungay, & Elizabeth
Loome, of Woodton .. .. 9 Jan. ,,
Richard Wisman & Mary Scrivener, both of
Shotsham .. .. 17 Sept. 1699
John Ferman & Jane Funton .. .. 1 Oct. ,,
Robert Bacon & Elizabeth Pinner, both of
Denton .. .. 16 Feb. ,,
Robert Downes, w., & Sarah Gray .. 16 June 1700
James Sherwood & Ann Plummer .. .. 22 Oct. ,,
John Sparrow & Anne Pitcher, both of
Woodton .. .. 4 Apr. 1701
Edward Golt, w., & Elizabeth Poll .. .. 8 June ,,
Thomas Fryar & Lucie Williams .. .. 30 Sept. ,,
Thomas Thorp & Magdaline Jay .. .. 12 Apr. 1704
William Palmer, w., & Ann Chittleburgh, w. 5 Feb. ,,
John Castleton & Ann Gary .. .. 8 Feb. ,,
Gregorie Johnson, of Topcroft, & Ann Tuttle,
of Pullam Market .. .. .. 4 Oct. 1705
Thomas Bellow, of Lacenham, & Mary Cariage 25 Nov. ,,
Edward Shermon & Ann Rudd .. .. 23 Sept. 1706
Thomas Baker, of Beccles, & Elizabeth Crisp,
of Worlingham .. .. .. 1 Oct. ,,
William Poll, of Topcroft, & Mary Germie .. 28 Sept. 1708

VOLUME II.

John Colman & Thomsin Wadsdale	.. 30 Nov. 1709
Giles Bladwell & Elizabeth Dove ..	.. 8 Sept. 1710
Nicholas Jones & Elizabeth Riches	.. 19 Sept. „
Charles Ward & Ann Smith ..	.. 27 Dec. „
John Fodder & Mary Randoll ..	.. 10 June 1711
James Hagas & Honour Brown ..	.. 1 Sept. „
John Shermon & Elizabeth Ward ..	.. 2 Oct. „
Edward Osborn & Mary Skeet ..	.. 30 Jan. „
Richard Fauset & Ann Bull ..	.. 16 June 1712
John Newby & Elizabeth Balls ..	.. 28 Oct. „
John Whal & Ann Williams ..	.. 30 Oct. „
Robert Patterson & Elizabeth Millington ..	8 Dec. „
William Lamb & Mary Maise ..	.. 23 Oct. 1713
George Park & Sarah Howes ..	.. 24 Jan. 1714
John Thurston & Anne Gostling ..	.. 21 Feb. „
Henry Edwards & Elizabeth Turner ..	12 June 1716
Thomas Simons & Mary Moutin ..	.. 9 July „
[———] [———] & [———] Randol	.. 24 Apr. 1717
John Pointer & Susan Loaseman ..	.. 8 Oct. „
John Willymoore & Susan Debage ..	2 Apr. 1718
Robert Westgate & Susanna Brows ..	6 May „
Robert Thorp & Mary Stanhaw ..	.. 14 May „
Thomas Agas & Thomasen Hill ..	.. 8 June „
Reuben Pitcher & Susanna Gates ..	.. 19 May 1719
William Fairehead & Elizabeth Rix ..	2 June „
Edward Reat & Bridget Dye ..	.. 7 June „
John Legget & Susan Killet ..	.. 9 Oct. „
Richard Lidiman & Mary Sallows ..	.. 5 Feb. „
John Mallet & Mary Gunns ..	.. 15 Sept. 1720
Charles Brown & Elizabeth Bury ..	.. 29 Sept. 1721
John Maior & Mary Gunns ..	.. 27 Mar. 1722
James Randol & Elizabeth Johnson ..	15 May „
Hillary Goldspink & Elizabeth Kendale ..	25 June „
Robert Lamb & Alice Colman ..	.. 11 Sept. „
William Fenn & Mary Copping ..	.. 2 Oct. „
Erasimus Stannow & Dorcas Weston ..	1 Oct. 1723
James Thorp & Martha [———] ..	.. 3 Dec. „
William Hunt & Mary Lann ..	.. 14 July 1724

John Gunns & Elizabeth Wright	.. ..	24 Oct. 1724
Robert Benham & Elizabeth Bird	.. ..	30 Sept. „
Samuel Moyal & Mary Blumfield	.. ..	7 Nov. „
William Chasteny & Lucy Frier	.. ..	4 Nov. 1725
Philip Palmer & Susannah Lynsey	..	12 Apr. 1726
James Randol & Briget Bird	.. ..	21 June „
John Brewer & Elizabeth Vincent	.. ..	21 May 1727
James Pooly & Anne Tilney	.. ..	26 Dec. „
William Holmes & Elizabeth Kimmin	..	3 Oct. 1728
Thomas Jessop & Susanna Everitt	..	9 Oct. „
Richard Palmer & Sarah Philpot	.. ..	16 Dec. „
Robert Brown & Sarah Read	.. ..	16 Jan. „
Thomas Bensly & Elizabeth Roberts	..	24 Sept. 1729
George Dye & Elizabeth Thacker	.. ..	13 Nov. „
William Aggas & Martha Fulcher	.. ..	9 Dec. „
John Legate & Susanna Lowly	.. ..	6 Jan. „
Nathaniel Liliston & Ann Bird	.. ..	23 Feb. 1730
Jonathan Bishop & Mary Gumming	..	24 Aug. „
Samuel Fhink & Elizabeth Tibnum	..	7 June 1731
Robert Fickling & Elizabeth Linze	..	5 Aug. „
Richard Faired & Susanna Killet	.. ..	23 Sept. „
John Gerard & Mary Shreeve	.. ..	12 Oct. „
Aaron Moor & Anne Sayer	.. ..	22 Oct. „
John Knott & Mary Norton	.. ..	29 Nov. „
Israel Hobman & Elizabeth Cottingham	..	10 Apr. 1732
William Cossey & Amey Dey	.. ..	10 Apr. „
Samuel Adley & Elizabeth Fryer	.. ..	15 Apr. „
Daniel Meer & Elizabeth Brierton	.. ..	30 May „
John Cooper & Sarah Skeyte	.. ..	31 May „
Gregory Stanley & Anne Thurston	..	29 Jan. „
John Hammond & Elizabeth Robson	..	5 Apr. 1733
John Palmer & Sarah Fickling	.. ..	1 Oct. „
Nathaniel Skeyte & Mary Fairweather	..	24 Oct. „
John Atkinson & Martha French	.. ..	30 Oct. „
Edward Scrivener & Mary Bishop	.. ..	31 Oct. „
Benjamin Thrower & Susanna Dunnett	..	7 Nov. „
Jacob Bennett & Mary Gerard	.. ..	24 Dec. „
Timothy Moor & Ann Baker	.. ..	25 Jan. „
George Liddimy & Mary Bullock	.. ..	23 Apr. 1734
Michael Roberts & Elizabeth Boyce	..	3 July „

John Fryar & Mary Lincoln	14 Aug. 1734
James Jacques & Rebecca Liddimy	27 Aug. „
Roger Roberts & Susanna Ebdom	16 Oct. „
William Claveland & Martha Neave	26 Dec. „
Robert Law & Elizabeth Goodings	6 Apr. 1735
Robert Plummer & Elizabeth Kiddle	18 Oct. „
Merchant Berry & Mary Mallom	1 Jan. „
Robert Johnson & Sarah Dibal	8 Mar. „
John Taylor & Margaret Chapman	22 June 1736
John Meadows & Susannah Sporle	26 July „
Daniel Dove & Elizabeth Berry	1 Nov. „
John Heslop & Rachel Pitt	10 Nov. „
Henry Meek & Elizabeth Mills	30 Dec. „
William Smith & Elizabeth Ives	31 May 1737
John Child & Dorothy Huby	7 Oct. „
John Fowle & Sarah Stannard	9 Oct. „
Abraham Bennett & Elizabeth Gates	18 Oct. „
John Walds & Mary Smith	7 Nov. „

VOLUME III.

John Roberts & Sarah Tooke	30 May 1738
John Ringer & Mary Cooper	13 Aug. „
Robert Johnson & Elizabeth Jarmyn	19 Oct. „
Aaron Townshend & Jemima Barns	17 Nov. „
John Knights & Amy Manser	23 Nov. „
Thomas Fryer & Mary Roberts	4 Mar. „
James Took and Mary Butcher	24 Apr. 1739
John Tuck & Tabitha Tibbenham	11 June „
Bosom Body & Ann Wilkinson	18 Sept. „
William Lawter & Ann Wurr	2 Oct. „
Mathew Woods & Elizabeth Poll	2 Oct. „
Thomas Brooksby & Sarah Rade	29 Feb. „
William Smith & Ann Jarmy	7 Oct. 1740
James Thorpe & Elizabeth Hacon	12 Oct. „
Samuel Crisp & Hannah Dogget	14 Oct. „
Thomas Read & Sarah Benham	15 Dec. „
Isaac King & Elizabeth Nash	31 Mar. 1741
John Mitchells & Elizabeth Whiting	8 Oct. „
John Thurston & Ann Martin	5 Nov. „
James Aldus & Sarah Tower	22 Nov. „

John Nash & Elizabeth Fosdike ..	18 Feb.	1741
Samuel Gates & Elizabeth Roberts	.. 29 June	1742
Thomas Townshend & Martha Garrode	.. 5 Oct.	„
William Buck & Susanna Mallom ..	.. 19 Oct.	„
John Lock & Sarah Raven ..	.. 5 Nov.	„
William Boore & Elizabeth Barnham	.. 1 Jan.	„
Thomas Bouton & Elizabeth Edwards	.. 11 Apr.	1743
Thomas Britiff & Elizabeth Rust ..	30 Sept.	„
Daniel Berry & Martha Norman ..	.. 17 Oct.	„
George Buckingham & Lydia Cushen	.. 24 Oct.	„
Henry Fuller & Martha Nobbs ..	.. 21 Nov.	„
Philip Sherman & Elizabeth Lockwood	.. 7 Dec.	„
Henry Sherman & Margaret Ellis ..	.. 2 Jan.	„
William Websdale & Rebecca Ingledow	.. 12 Jan.	„
Joseph Perfert & Mary Bush ..	.. 26 Mar.	1744
Francis Knights & Elizabeth Brierton	.. 15 June	„
Isaac Skelton & Ann Hamond ..	.. 26 June	„
Thomas Norman & Mary Legate ..	.. 1 Oct.	„
John Haddark & Ann Gates ..	.. 1 Oct.	„
Samuel Pearse & Mary Fenn ..	.. 1 Oct.	„
John Legood & Susanna Gowel ..	.. 29 Oct.	„
John Fain & Elizabeth King ..	.. 20 Nov.	„
Samuel Watson & Mary Bouton ..	.. 10 Dec.	„
Daniel Benham & Ann Soanes ..	.. 27 Dec.	„
Clement Boughton & Elizabeth Reeve	.. 25 Mar.	1745
Joseph Gowen & Sarah Durrent ..	.. 1 Oct.	„
Thomas Johnson & Elizabeth Blois	.. 3 Nov.	„
John Trappet & Elizabeth Reyner ..	.. 6 Nov.	„
John Lawn & Martha Bramble ..	.. 9 Dec.	„
James Buck & Elizabeth Crancher ..	.. 9 Dec.	„
John Sprat & Mary Tuck	.. 10 Feb.	„
Samuel Meadows & Mary Jarvise ..	.. 10 Feb.	„
Thomas Brandwell & Sarah Sayer ..	.. 21 Apr.	1746
Francis Skelton & Sarah Esto ..	.. 22 June	„
Nathaniel Howles & Sarah Baldry ..	.. 3 Oct.	„
Thomas Sharman & Sarah Tuck ..	.. 19 Oct.	„
William Man & Margaret Driver ..	.. 29 Oct.	„
John Flint & Sarah Bensley ..	.. 6 Nov.	„
Thomas Fryar & Elizabeth Roberts	.. 16 Apr.	1747
John Armsby & Mary Gands ..	.. 21 Apr.	„

William Faired & Frances Thurston	20 Oct.	1747
William Benham & Mary Mouldin ..	3 Nov.	„
Christopher Riches & Sarah Dunnet	16 Nov.	„
Thomas Roberts & Sarah Fared	10 Feb.	„
John Gosling & Mary Benham	25 July	1748
Robert Barber & Mary Palmer	30 Sept.	1749
Richard Bunn & Elizabeth Bensley	9 Oct.	1750
John Trower & Mary Scott	9 July	1751
Samuel Strutt & Bridget Stannard	18 Sept.	„
John Beets & Susan Willoughby	1 Oct.	„
John Alborow & Sarah Coppin	24 Apr.	1753
John Gates & Mary Willoughby	12 Oct.	„
John Legood & Sarah Sherman	19 Oct.	„
James Banham & Elizabeth Kemp ..	22 Oct.	„
William Betts & Sarah Frost	5 July	1754
Alexander Revell & Susanna Banham	28 Oct.	„
Thomas Seager & Frances Edwards	10 Dec.	„
Robert Revell & Martha Carsey	13 Jan.	1755
John Banham & Diana Banham	4 Mar.	„
Robert Fuller & Mary Whyitt	20 May	„
Richard Palmer & Ann Roberts	27 Apr.	1756
Thomas Morris & Rachel Woolstone	3 May	„
Robert Lord & Margaret Howles	21 Sept.	„
John Woolston & Sarah Frestone ..	27 Dec.	„
Joseph Wright & Mary Stanly	31 May	1757
John Baldwin & Sarah Diver	21 Sept.	1758
Isaac Le Strainge & Susanna Carr ..	25 June	1759
Henry Legood & Mary Andrews	13 Nov.	„
Benjamin Hunt & Sarah Betts	29 Jan.	1760
William Duncher & Mary Wright ..	10 Oct.	„
Thomas Danford & Elizabeth Willoughby	2 Nov.	1761
Robert Carver & Amey Fairhead	3 Nov.	„
Philip Palmer & Susan Johnson	8 Feb.	1762
Thomas Chipperfield & Elizabeth Woolstone	8 Nov.	„
John Cunningham & Mary Palmer ..	31 May	1763
Samuel Read & Elizabeth Frost	15 Nov.	„
Richard Lyddiman & Mary Gates ..	22 Nov.	„
Robert Dains & Sarah Palmer	7 Jan.	1764
John Nobbs & Elizabeth King	15 Sept.	1765
Charles Crowe & Mary Willoughby	14 Oct.	1766

William Larke & Elizabeth Fenn ..	.. 18 Oct.	1766
John Gervase & Mary Thirston ..	.. 25 Mar.	1767
Thomas Downing & Elizabeth Parsons	.. 25 Apr.	1768
Samuel Rix & Sarah Andrews ..	.. 26 Apr.	„
John Rendelsom & Mary Meadows	.. 24 Sept.	„
John Button & Mary Armsby	.. 28 Mar.	1769
John Lacey & Tabitha Rix	.. 17 July	„
John Youngman & Mary Armsby ..	.. 27 July	„
Amos Rackham & Susan Palmer ..	.. 7 Nov.	„
Robert Lord & Sarah Bullen ..	.. 27 Nov.	„
James Bullen & Elizabeth Page ..	.. 16 July	1770
Albert Thrower & Elizabeth Salmon	.. 18 Dec.	„
William Day & Elizabeth Palmer ..	.. 5 Apr.	1774
Robert Larter & Susan Cook ..	.. 17 Nov.	„
Edward Reeve & Susan Bullen ..	.. 21 Feb.	1775
John Roberts & Elizabeth Sayer ..	.. 23 May	„
Joseph Foulger & Mary Barber ..	.. 7 Oct.	„
John Quantrum & Elizabeth Pease	.. 26 Aug.	1776
Benjamin Blomfield & Elizabeth Walker	.. 29 Oct.	„
William Williams & Elizabeth Brown	.. 7 Oct.	1777
Philip Girling & Sarah Thorpe ..	.. 9 June	1778
Francis Folgate & Sarah Burcham ..	.. 27 Sept.	„
George Borrett & Elizabeth Button	.. 3 Aug.	1779
Richard Fairhead & Martha Lacy ..	.. 17 Jan.	1780
John Ellis & Ann Williamson ..	.. 16 May	„
Robert Hanner & Rose Brown ..	.. 9 Aug.	„
Edward Webster & Ann Gray ..	.. 3 June	1781
Samuel Shaw & Elizabeth Bird ..	.. 11 Oct.	„
Charles Crowfoot & Elizabeth Barber	.. 11 Oct.	„
Joseph Baldry & Mary Legwood ..	.. 9 Apr.	1782
Jacob Button & Elizabeth Wright ..	.. 7 Oct.	1783
John Youngs & Mary Sharman ..	.. 14 Oct.	„
Joseph Wright & Rose Musket ..	.. 30 Nov.	„
Edmond Daines & Susanna Palmer	.. 14 Mar.	1784
Daniel Balls & Sarah Scales ..	.. 25 May	„
Francis Evelyn & Susanna Hunt ..	.. 10 Oct.	1785
William Dann & Charlotte Spratt ..	.. 13 Jan.	1786
James Fairhead & Susanna Warnes	.. 13 Feb.	1787
William Yarrington & Catharine Kirkby Bacon	.. 1 May	„

James Legood & Mary Bullen	.. ..	5 June 1787
Thomas Read & Sarah Howse	.. ..	2 Oct. „
Peter Tuck & Hannah Chipperfield	..	6 Jan. 1788
Thomas Bullen & Mary Smith	.. ..	3 June „
Ephraim Spratt & Martha Wright	.. ..	17 Nov. „
Thomas Russells & Sarah Mudd	.. ..	14 July 1789
John Barber & Sarah Legood	.. ..	8 Oct. „
William Fairhead & Mary Crowe	.. ..	7 Dec. 1790
William Punchard & Susanna Crowe	..	11 Oct. 1791
Gostling Stanley & Sarah Bloom	.. ..	2 Nov. „
Abraham Legood & Susanna Lord	..	21 Feb. 1792
Robert Legood & Ann Cunningham	..	18 Sept. „
David Todd & Ann Wright	.. ..	29 Nov. „
John Cunningham & Elizabeth Clippen	..	6 Mar. 1793
Edward Legood & Elizabeth Palmer	..	22 Apr. „
Robert Palmer & Hannah Brock	.. ..	6 Nov. 1794
George Baldwin & Susannah Symonds	..	5 Apr. 1796
Thomas Everett & Ann Cann	.. ..	7 July „
John Nobbs & Susannah Smith	.. ..	9 Oct. „
Thomas Falgate & Susannah Steward	..	20 Nov. „
John Punchard & Susannah Symonds	..	11 Dec. „
Edward Yallop & Mary Storer	.. ..	6 Nov. 1797
John Quantrell & Elizabeth Marshall	..	18 Dec. 1798
Thomas Wiskins & Sarah Martin	.. ..	26 Feb. 1799
Edward Watkins & Mary Bedwell	.. ..	16 Apr. „
Robert Foulger & Elizabeth Yallop	..	30 May „
William Jeffries & Susannah Hunt	..	25 June „
John Summons & Mary Boughton	..	11 Oct. „
Amos Fisher & Mary Wright	.. ..	9 July 1800
William Housago & Susanna Gillens	..	9 Oct. „
William Andrews & Elizabeth Chipperfield	..	17 May 1802
John Keet & Lydia Butcher	.. ..	23 June „
Edward Reeve & Jane Riches	.. ..	14 Oct. „
James Fairhead & Elizabeth Barber	..	25 Dec. „
Samuel Holland & Ann Mayhew	. ..	19 Apr. 1803
Thomas Brown & Elizabeth Williamson	..	10 Oct. „
Isaac Yallop & Mary Folkard	.. ..	15 Nov. „
James Yallop & Mary Lighton	.. ..	26 June 1804
William Balls & Elizabeth Cooper	.. ..	28 Jan. 1805
James Booty & Mary Brown	.. ..	29 Sept. „

William Patrick & Sarah Crickmore	..	17 May 1807
James Folkard & Mary Fairhead ..	..	24 Nov. „
William Brown & Hannah Smith ..	..	20 Mar. 1809
John Johnson & Phœbe Fairhead ..	..	29 Mar. 1810
Samuel Clarke & Phœbe Cunningham	..	1 Nov. „
Edward Quantrum & Hannah Shawl	..	9 July 1811
Thomas Brown & Elizabeth Rix ..	..	22 Oct. „
John Wilson & Mary Elvin ..	..	16 Nov. 1812

Marriages at Gresham,

1690 to 1812.

NOTE.—These Registers begin in 1637, but the writing is too faint to decipher till 1690, and are contained in three volumes.

Volume I.—Bound in a parchment page of an old service book, and contains entries of Burials, Baptisms, and Marriages, following each other promiscuously in order of date.

Volume II.—Marriages from 1733 to 1774. In the body of the book is a statement that "The Registers between 1713-1734 are in the Register books of the parish of Bessingham".

Volume III contains the usual forms of Marriages.

These extracts have been made by the Rev. E. C. Jervis, Vicar of Beckham, and are now printed under his supervision.

VOLUME I.

Nicholas Caston & Elizabeth Christian	.. 14 Jan.	1690
William Harrison & Hannah Goos ..	.. 24 Jan.	1695
John Caston & Mary Richardson ..	.. 24 Feb.	,,
John Arnold & Mary Jordan	.. 25 Feb.	1700
Peter Fellows & Jane Cowliel	.. 6 Nov.	1702
Robert Sharpin & Elizabeth Buckenham	.. 21 Jan.	1703
Christopher Fuller & Mary Dybal ..	.. — July	1704
John Christmas & Margaret Lound	.. 23 Oct.	1705
John Mory & Martha Dybal	.. 26 Sept.	,,
John Brown & Mary Stains	.. 1 May	1707
John Howes & Dorcas Gay	.. 2 Aug.	1709
John Nobbs & Mary Throrey	.. 10 Oct.	,,
Francis Massingham & Mary Pegtal	23 Dec. 713 [sic]	

VOLUME II.

John Adcock, p. Sconiston, w., & Mary Caston, w.	29 Oct.	1733
Thomas Riches, p. North Repps, & Martha Cook	29 Oct.	,,
William Riches, p. Cromer, w., & Elizabeth Clarke	24 Mar.	,,
Robert Sutton & Elizabeth Wix ..	.. 10 May	1734

James Bowing & Mary Gotts	1 July	1734
Samuel Wix, w., & Hannah Gotts	27 Sept.	,,
Thomas Dorr, p. Hindringham, w., & Mary		
Secker, of W. Beckham, w.	29 July	1735
Edmund Lake, p. Holt, & Elizabeth Lines ..	6 Oct.	,,
Samuel Adcock, p. Langham Regis, & Alice		
Causton	10 Oct.	,,
Robert Downing, p. Kelling, & Anne Winn ..	10 Feb.	1736
John Reynolds, senr., w., & Anne Pells ..	5 Oct.	1737
Thomas Nicholds & Mary Smith, both p.		
Beeston-near-the-Sea	30 Sept.	1739
Robert Rainer, p. Wickmere, & Elizabeth		
Starling, *lic.*	28 July	1740
John Pendleton, of S. Gregories, Norwich, &		
Sarah Tower, of Ber Street, Norwich	13 Apr.	1741
Robert Starling & Martha Press, p. Thurgarton	19 Jan.	1742
Francis Mills, p. Aylmerton, & Mary Bacon ..	2 Feb.	,,
John Gay, p. Alborough, & Frances Copeman	25 Mar.	,,
John Wegg, w., & Sarah Frost	18 Apr.	,,
Thomas Carver, p. Holt, & Sarah England ..	31 July	,,
John Burton & Margarett Burton	14 Dec.	,,
[*No Marriages* 1743.]		
Nicholas Fox, p. Bassingham, & Amy Lubbock	5 Nov.	1744
John Burton, w., & Mary Jolley	29 Sept.	1745
John Woodhouse & Anne Browne	26 Mar.	1747
Philip Lambert, p. Burgh, near Aylesham, &		
Anne Smithson, p. Bassingham, w. ..	16 Apr.	,,
John Page, p. Barningham Town, & Sary		
Blackburne, w.	21 Sept.	,,
Thomas Lashing & Margaret Dye	1 Jan.	1748
Samuel Gotts & Anne Lines	1 Nov.	1749
John Lake & Matthew [*sic*] Garrett ..	1 Nov.	,,
James Lubbock & Mary Sturges	31 May	1750
William Balderstone, p. Bodham, & Sarah		
Everard	7 Oct.	1751
William Ram, w., & Elizabeth Bastard ..	5 Nov.	1754
William Golt & Sarah Burton, w.	14 Dec.	1756
William Cooke, p. Corpusty, & Mary Bush, *lic.*	1 Dec.	1758
John Wilkeson & Mary Thaxter	30 Oct.	1759
John Critoph & Elizabeth Wilkerson ..	21 June	1760

Young Wilkerson & Margaret Turrell, *lic.* [*sic*]   22 July   1760
James Wilkerson & Margaret Turell, *lic.* [*sic*]   22 July   „
John Fox & Ann Gotts, p. Matlask   ..   29 Sept.   „
John Abbs & Mary Wright   ..   ..   5 Jan.   1761
Richard Dobson, p. Letheringsett, & Mary
   Eglington, *lic.*   ..   ..   ..   24 Dec.   „
      [*On fly-leaf at beginning of book :—*]
Robert Thurston, p. Thurgarton, & Margaret
   Cooper   ..   ..   13 Aug.   1771
Charles England, p. Bassingham, & Mary
   Nutt, *lic.* ..   ..   16 Apr.   1772
James Frost, p. Bodham, w., & Mary Overton   20 Apr.   „
John Youngman, p. Town Barningham, &
   Elizabeth Fills   ..   ..   ..   17 July   „
William Cooper, p. Wiverton, & Sarah Emery,
   lic.   ..   ..   29 Sept.   „
John Oliver, w., & Mary Herring   ..   ..   17 Nov.   1773
John Fuller, p. Itteringham, & Susanna Bell,
   of Bassingham   ..   ..   ..   26 Nov.   „
William Youngman & Mary Newark   ..   7 Oct.   1774
Thomas Gotts & Sarah Wegg   ..   ..   10 Oct.   „
[*Eight out of the above nine entries also entered in Vol. III.*]

VOLUME III.
Robert Sonman & Susannah Everet   ..   12 Oct.   1762
Nicholas Thaxter, of Alby, & Mary Mack   ..   26 Jan.   1763
John Mason, of Trunch, & Elizabeth Rounce, *lic.*   27 June   „
Richard Stevenson & Elizabeth Fuller, w., *lic.*   19 Aug.   „
John Rounce & Elizabeth Fox, *lic.* ..   ..   7 Dec.   „
Nicholas Love & Jane Cooke   ..   ..   15 Oct.   1764
John Harmer & Ann Forbey   ..   ..   19 Nov.   „
James Pain & Elizabeth Brumbal   ..   ..   17 Dec.   „
Joseph Ward, of Beeston, & Elizabeth Legg   6 Apr.   1765
John Wegg, w., & Rose Wilkins   ..   ..   29 May   „
Charles King, of Aylmerton, & Winefred
   Everet   ..   ..   22 Aug.   „
Joseph Leak & Sarah Rounce, *lic.* ..   ..   22 Sept.   1766
James Clark & Mary Gotts   ..   ..   13 July   1767
Abraham Leman, of Baconsthorpe, & Mary
   Lake, *lic.* ..   ..   6 Dec.   1768

Francis Chaplain & Anne Caston	18 July 1769
William Knights, of Edgefield, & Mary Hammond, *lic.*	7 Sept. 1770
William Stibbard & Mary Smyth	2 Nov. „
Robert Thurston, of Thurgarton, & Margaret Cooper	13 Aug. 1771
Charles England, of Bassingham, & Mary Nutt	6 Apr. 1772
James Frost, of Bodham, & Mary Overton ..	20 Apr. „
John Youngman, of Town Barningham, & Elizabeth Fills	17 July „
William Cooper, of Wiverton, & Sarah Emery, *lic.*	29 Sept. „
John Oliver, w., & Mary Herring	17 Nov. 1773
William Youngman & Mary Newark ..	7 Oct. 1774
Thomas Gotts & Sarah Wegg	10 Oct. „
Clarke Miller, of Sheringham, & Esther Nutt, *lic.*	12 Dec. „
Joseph Page, of Hanworth, & Hannah Joy ..	9 Oct. 1775
William Jordan & Margaret Black	3 June 1776
Brightmeer Shore & Martha Vial	22 Oct. „
Edward Cooper & Susanna Shore	27 Dec. „
Matthew Andrews & Anne Bennett, *lic.* ..	23 Mar. 1777
John Smith, w., & Anne Paul	— — „
Robert Critoph, w., & Mary England, w., *lic.*	18 Dec. „
Henry Monument, of Felbrigg, & Mary Gipson	23 July 1778
Joseph Thurston, of Hanworth, & Judith Trollope	19 Oct. „
William Gower, of Thornage, & Elizabeth Lubbock	12 Mar. 1779
John Crasp, of Sheringham, & Honoria Shore	27 May „
John Cooper & Elizabeth Coe	23 June „
James Shore & Mary Dyball	27 Sept. „
Charles Loynes, p. Briston, & Jane Mann ..	3 Oct. 1780
James Downing Black, p. Thurgarton, & Elizabeth Salmon, *lic.*	24 Sept. 1781
Fuller Fox & Anne Ward	19 Mar. 1782
John Ward & Edna Bird	11 Dec. „
John Shore & Sarah Woodhouse	7 Jan. 1783
Robert Cubitt & Mary Pellent	3 June „
Robert Nichols, w., & Mary Powditch, w. ..	12 Apr. 1784
John Burtton & Elizabeth Beckerson ..	2 Nov. „

John Attle, p. Barningham, Norwood, &
  Frances Bennett .. .. .. 24 May 1785
Thomas Burtten & Martha Robinson .. 27 Sept. „
William Temple, w., & Martha Leak, both p.
  East Beckham, their church being
  dilapidated .. .. .. 14 Nov. 1786
Samuel Gotts & Martha Woodhouse .. 16 Oct. 1787
John Dyball & Elizabeth Ward .. .. 22 Jan. 1788
Samuel Flogen & Elizabeth Field .. .. 18 Nov. „
William Jordan & Sarah Lubbock .. .. 23 May 1791
Henery Ransom & Mary Powditch .. 1 Nov. „
John Beevor, p. St. Martin's-in-the-Oak, Nor-
  wich, & Susanna Wire, w. .. .. 16 Oct. 1792
John Fox & Elizabeth Drury .. .. 29 Oct. „
William Youngman, w., & Sarah King . 17 Nov. 1793
Benjamin Comer & Ann Hardingham .. 13 Sept. 1794
William Critoph & Mary Youngman, *lic.* .. 9 Oct. „
John Paul, p. Aylmerton, & Ann Carter, w. .. 25 Oct. 1796
Richard Fuller & Elizabeth Johnson .. 11 Apr. 1797
Joseph Temple, p. East Beckham, & Frances
  Fills, w., *lic.* .. .. .. 24 July „
John Field & Susanna Newstead .. .. 15 May 1798
Robert Sunman & Ann Cooper .. .. 22 May „
John Doughty & Susanna Sunman .. 6 Sept. „
William Thurtle, p. East Beckham, & Lidyah
  Bell .. .. 11 Oct. „
Noah Twidney & Sarah Miller .. .. 23 Oct. „
George England, p. Frettingham, & Ann
  Critoph, *lic.* .. .. .. 10 Jan. 1799
Joseph Page & Martha Seckor .. .. 16 July „
Barnabas Lemon & Celia Critoph, *lic.* .. 22 Jan. 1801
Charles Loines, p. Edgefield, & Mary Shore,*lic.* 26 Jan. „
John Smith & Charlotte Lubbock .. .. 14 Apr. „
Isaac Orsband, p. Stow Bardolph, & Ann
  Hard, p. East Beckham, *lic.* .. .. 30 Jan. „
Henery Chamberlin, w., & Sarah Campling,
  St. James, Norwich, *lic.* .. .. 2 July „
Michael Ramsdle, w., & Ann Fox .. .. 26 Oct. „
John Black & Ann Frostic, w. .. .. 3 Feb. 1802
Thomas Platten & Ann Goots .. .. 23 Nov. „

Henry Crowe & Sarah Jordan, *lic.* ..   ..   28 Dec. 1802
William Lynes, w., & Mary Ann Funnell   ..   18 July 1803
William Catten, p. Runton, & Hannah
     Thompson   ..   ..   ..   2 Apr. 1804
William Neal & Hannah Burton   ..   ..   2 Aug. „
James Funnell & Ellen Starling   ..   ..   7 Dec. „
Robert Greenaker & Elizabeth Youngman ..   12 Feb. 1805
Samuel Ducker & Mary Temple   ..   ..   20 Feb. „
Robert Jackson & Mary Larke   ..   ..   13 Mar. 1806
Samuel Wright & Martha Youngman   ..   7 Apr. 1807
William Burcham & Martha Cooper   ..   2 June „
Edward Cooper & Mary Canham   ..   ..   25 Apr. 1809
Robert Dade, p. Hempstead, & Mary Critoph, w.   12 Dec. „
James Willmeson, p. East Beckham, & Frances
     Temple   ..   ..   6 Aug. 1810
James Massingham & Sarah Barstard   ..   22 Jan. 1811
William Field & Mary Curl   ..   ..   31 Jan. „
Henry Wrench & Ann Yarham, p. East
     Beckham, *lic.*   ..   ..   ..   29 May „
Robert Corbyn & Phœbe Shore   ..   ..   10 July „
Nicholas Hayhow & Mary Cooper ..   ..   4 Jan. 1812
Joseph Page, w., & Elizabeth Attle   ..   18 Feb. „
Jonathan Shore & Susanna Bayfield, *lic.*   ..   24 Oct. „
John Hardingham & Elizabeth Leak   ..   8 Nov. „

801

www.ingramcontent.com/pod-product-compliance
Lightning Source LLC
Chambersburg PA
CBHW020541270326
41927CB00006B/678